I0810414

IMAGES
of America

NORTH CASTLE

On the Cover: A moment in the life of Charles H. Ferris is captured in this early 1900s photograph. Ferris has hitched his horse and open buggy for a ride into town. A large maple tree shades the front yard and house. The Ferrises are representative of the families who farmed in North Castle at the beginning of the 20th century. The family farm of 32 acres was on Bedford Road, today's New York State Route 22, near Middle Patent Road north of Armonk. Charles and his wife, Cornelia E. Carson Ferris, had four sons, Howard, Ralph, Nathan, and Clinton; Howard and Ralph served in World War I. Cornelia Ferris was an elections inspector and was president of her parent-teacher association; according to a report in the December 19, 1929, *North Castle Sun*, she served with "her usual vim and vivacity." Charles was a founding member of the Banksville Junior Order of United American Mechanics, served on the North Castle Board of Assessors, was a justice of the peace, and in later years was a watchman for a quarry. (Courtesy of the North Castle Historical Society.)

IMAGES
of America

NORTH CASTLE

Sharon Tomback and
the North Castle Historical Society

ARCADIA
PUBLISHING

Copyright © 2017 by Sharon Tomback and the North Castle Historical Society
ISBN 978-1-4671-2467-6

Published by Arcadia Publishing
Charleston, South Carolina

Printed in the United States of America

Library of Congress Control Number: 2016945416

For all general information, please contact Arcadia Publishing:
Telephone 843-853-2070
Fax 843-853-0044
E-mail sales@arcadiapublishing.com
For customer service and orders:
Toll-Free 1-888-313-2665

Visit us on the Internet at www.arcadiapublishing.com

This book is dedicated to all who have come before us and helped evolve our present exceptional North Castle community.

Contents

Acknowledgments

From the time the North Castle Historical Society was incorporated in 1971, hundreds of volunteers have contributed thousands of hours of work, artifacts, oral histories, and financial donations to help preserve the history of North Castle. It is impossible to thank each of these volunteers individually, but without their commitment and support, this book would have been impossible to assemble. Members who support the historical society and IBM Corporation deserve special mention. The North Castle Historical Society's collections of photographs, publications, archives, and Historic Smith's Tavern Educational Complex of protected and preserved buildings and furnishings are priceless. Unless otherwise noted, all images in this book are from the collections of the North Castle Historical Society.

Incorporating founders Ronald R. Atkins, R. Eugene Curry, Dorothy T. Hubbell, Sally Spencer Hurwitz, Hon. James D. Hopkins, Richard N. Lander, and Doris Finch Watson provided vision, energy, leadership, and guidance for the society.

Thank you to the current board of trustees of the society for your support and encouragement and especially to board president Anna Maria Marrone.

Thank you to my editor at Arcadia Publishing, Caitrin Cunningham.

Introduction

The eagle depicted on North Castle's town seal, with his wings spread and eyes ever watchful, is perched atop the shield symbolizing protection. Our struggle for independence is portrayed through a cannon and a flag. Early settlers are represented by corn, wheat, and potatoes, agricultural staples that helped to sustain life. The shoe on the last and the shoemaker's hammer and thread are reminders that North Castle was the birthplace of custom-made shoes, a prosperous home industry during the latter part of the 1800s.

The town of North Castle borders Greenwich, Connecticut; Bedford, New York; and White Plains, New York. North Castle has three distinct divisions: North White Plains in the southwest, Armonk in the middle, and the Eastern District including Banksville in the east. Town government is in Armonk.

There are three major river systems: the Mianus River in the Eastern District, the Byram and Wampus Rivers in the center of town, and the Bronx River and Kensico Reservoir in the western and southern sections of town. Early settlements grew around North Castle's streams and lakes.

The earliest inhabitants were Indians. Of the several tribes belonging to the Wappinger Confederacy, the Siwanoys inhabited the North Castle area. They were part of the eastern division of the great Algonkian-speaking group, once the most widely distributed linguistic family in North America. Each tribe had a *sachem* (chief) at the head. Many place names today are derived from these early people, such as Armonk, Wampus, Mianus, and Kensico (Cokenseko).

Town meeting records date to 1736, although New York governor William Burnet issued "Ye Pattent of North Cassell or otherwise called California Pattent" in 1721 in response to a petition from Lancaster Symes, Peter Fauconnier, Robert Walters, and Cornelius Depeyster. The petition reiterated the dates and descriptions of the East, Middle, and West Patents and asked that they be combined. No explanation for the choice of names is known. The town of New Castle was created out of North Castle in 1791, and borders changed, resulting in an irregularly shaped North Castle.

In early November 1776, atop Miller Hill in today's North White Plains, Patriot forces retreating northward from New York City stopped and stood their ground, and British troops turned back toward New York City. Great decisions affecting the Revolution were made in the Elijah Miller House and at Reuben Wright's Mills (both locations in today's North White Plains). In 1780, British major and spy John Andre was held overnight at Thomas Wright's Mill in today's Armonk.

A list of North Castle freeholders in 1763 was printed by the New York Historical Society in 1951 in an article by E. Marie Becker entitled "The 801 Westchester County Freeholders of 1763." Of the 101 occupations listed, 69 were yeomen (farmers); others cited their occupations as hatter, millwright, cordwainer (shoemaker), weaver, carpenter, blacksmith, currier, cooper, merchant, miller, doctor, and smith.

During the 1800s, farmers in North Castle supplied apples, potatoes, dairy products, and chickens to the New York City market and supplemented their incomes by making shoes. At the beginning of the Civil War, 75 percent of the soldiers from the area were shoemakers. North Castle was the birthplace of custom-made shoes.

At the beginning of the 20th century, wealthy men from New York began building large summer estates here. Among them were banker Cornelius R. Agnew, who created his great Wenga Farm, headquarters for IBM Corporation today. Accountant Elijah Sells's North Castle Farm became part of today's Windmill Farm. Bankers Samuel Fuller, Samuel McRoberts, John McHugh, and John McGee; brokers John H. Watkins, George M. Sidenberg, and Eugene Meyer (also owner of the *Washington Post*); manufacturer States D. Tompkins; writer Richard Harding Davis; and medical researcher Dr. Rufus Cole all created large estates in North Castle.

In 1908, the first Westchester auto race and the first international stock car race in America sped through North Castle. The 32-mile route through Westchester County over local roads, many of which were unpaved, was traversed eight times. North Castle's Wampus Lake (today's Wampus Pond), Armonk, and Kensico were on the route. Special trains brought hundreds of visitors.

Beginning in 1909, more than 4,000 acres were acquired by New York City to build the great Kensico Reservoir and Dam, including the entire village of Kensico, which was inundated. Hundreds of skilled workers were required to quarry stone in today's Quarry Heights, operate rail trains to ferry materials, and to construct the dam. Housing, schools, and churches were needed. The workers and their families required food and clothing. Today, descendants of many of these workers live in North Castle.

Reportedly, Prohibition was not actively enforced in Armonk. Dimly lit dance halls and restaurants evolved. Some estate owners forbid their workers to go to Armonk. By the early 1930s and until the early 1940s, the magic of national radio broadcasts from Armonk attracted big-name jazz bands and a New York City crowd.

In 1957, the North Castle Players, a community theatrical group, performed a musical satire. The theme song chorus was "We've got three banks, four churches and seventeen bars so life will never be risky. With three banks, four churches and seventeen bars we got money, salvation and whiskey."

Armonk had an active airport from 1925 until the 1960s. Parachute jumping, stunt flying, barnstorming, wing walking, air shows, and rides for a fee were weekly entertainments. Charles Lindbergh visited overnight in 1928; the Goodyear blimp landed in 1938. Neighbors complained of dust, noise, and traffic, and some sued the airport operators.

Many of the large estates of the early 1900s have given way to residential subdivisions, business parks, and corporate headquarters. The United Nations proposed to headquarter in North Castle, but residents were vehemently opposed. Interstate 684 was built through the center of North Castle; New York's Route 22 was rerouted.

The more than 200 photographs in this book capture moments in time. They reflect rural life on family farms; they also reflect a few lavish gentlemen farmers' summer estates. These images reflect the schools and churches, the farm stands, and night clubs. This small farming community with open fields and rock walls during the horse and buggy days was discovered during the era of fast racing cars and faster flying airplanes.

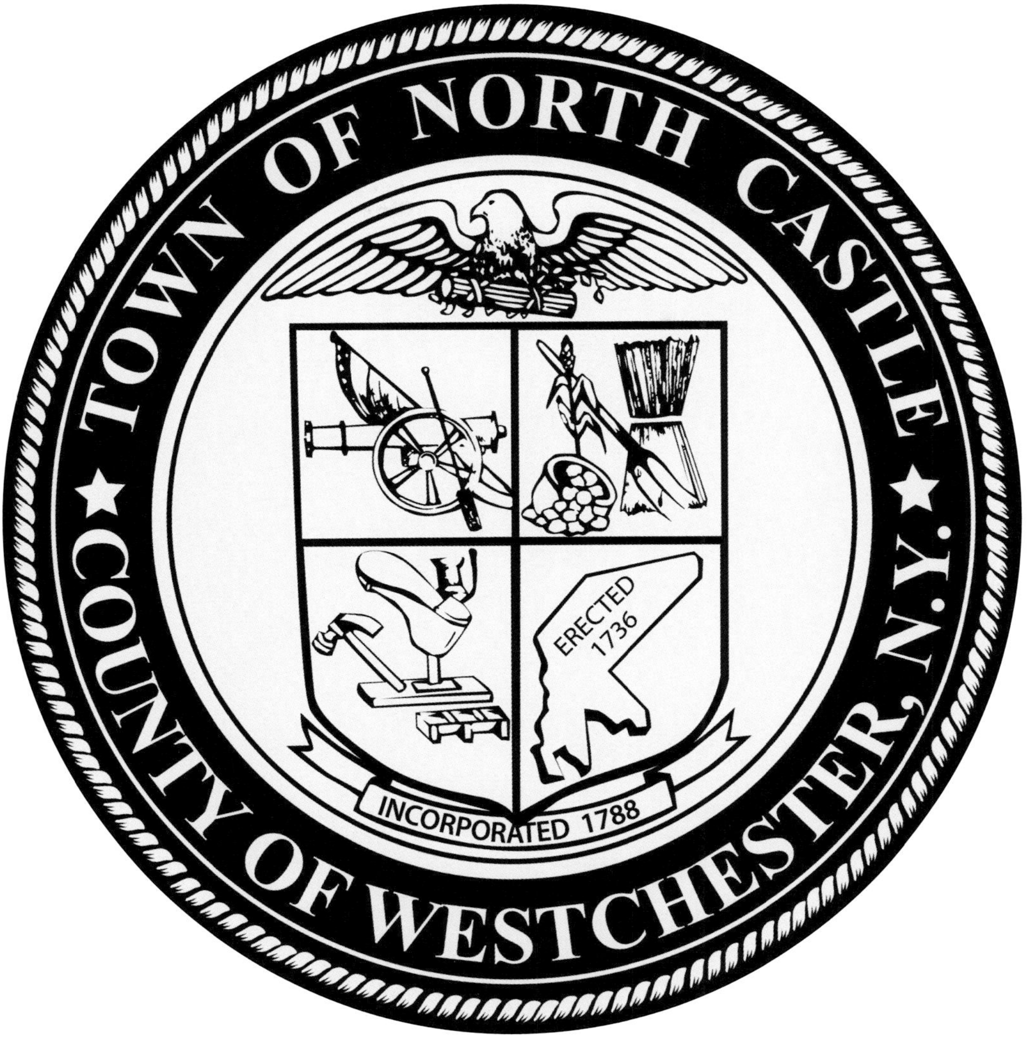

Town Seal of North Castle. Four important periods in North Castle's past are depicted: protection, independence, early settlers, and shoemaking. The first recorded town meeting, in 1736, is represented across stylized boundaries of the town. Incorporated in 1788, when the New York legislature divided Westchester into towns, North Castle is one of Westchester County's 20 original towns. (Courtesy of Adam Kaufman, director of planning, Town of North Castle.)

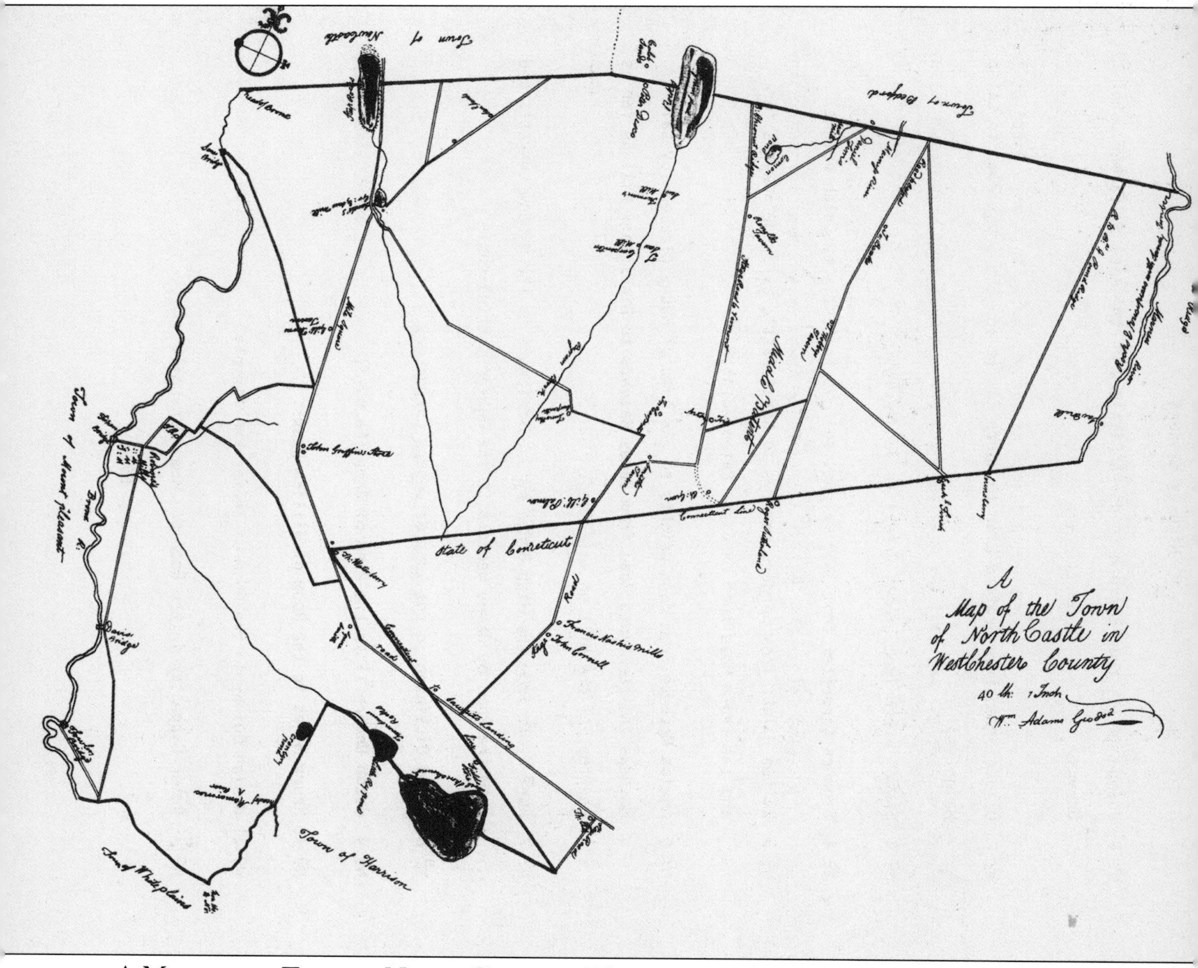

A Map of the Town of North Castle in Westchester County, 1797, by William Adams. This early map shows the boundaries of North Castle along with neighboring entities: the towns of Pound Ridge, Bedford, Mount Pleasant, White Plains, and Harrison, and the state of Connecticut. Ponds and streams, pathways and roads, and some residences, bridges, mills, and stores are noted.

One

Indians, Caves, and Rock Shelters

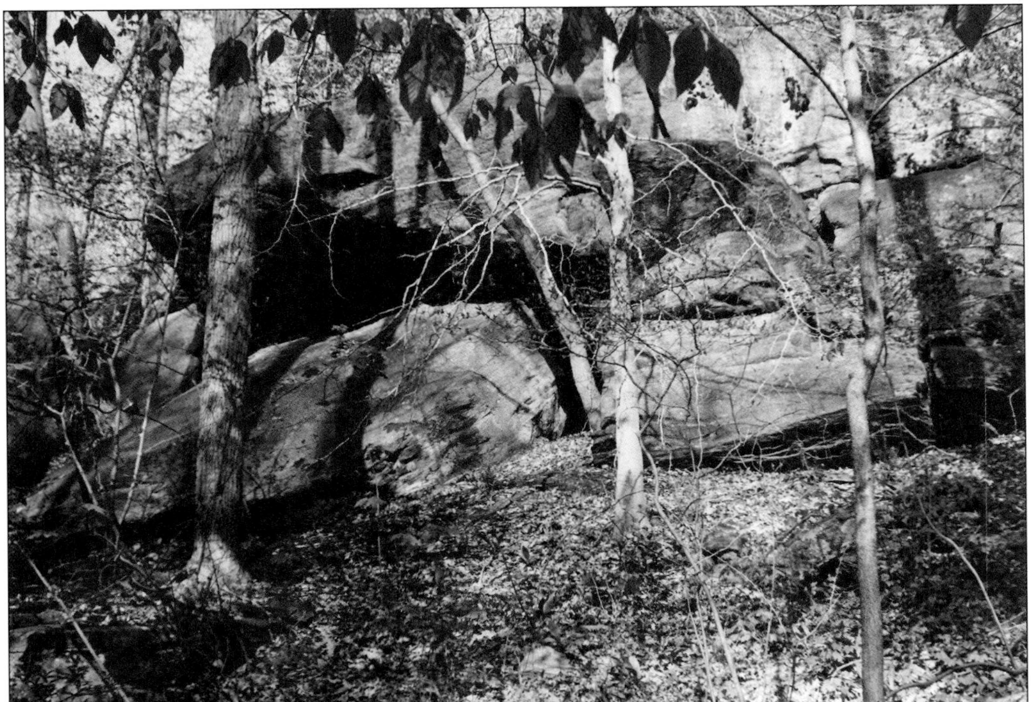

Entrance to Finch's Rock House. In 1900–1901, M.R. Harrington of New York's American Museum of Natural History determined that this cave/rock house in today's Windmill Farm, Armonk, served as Indian housing in two distinct periods: Early Woodland and Historic. The inside measured 23 feet long, almost 10 feet wide, and 11 feet high. It offered two entrances, fresh drinking water nearby, and a location hidden from passersby. The western branch of the Mianus River is near here.

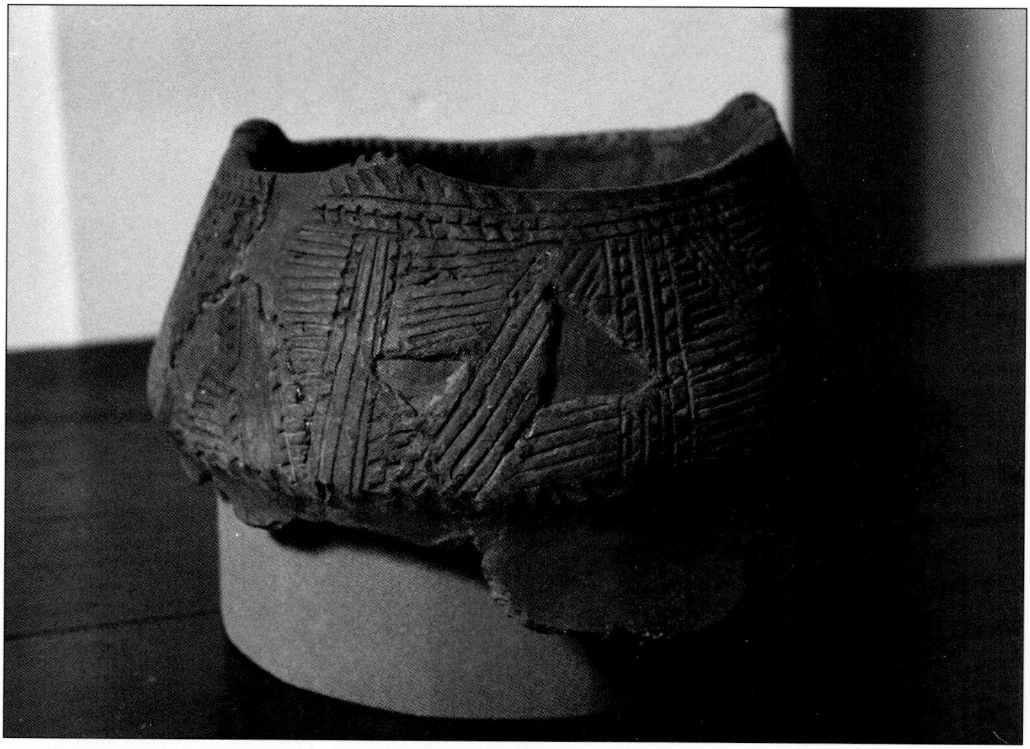

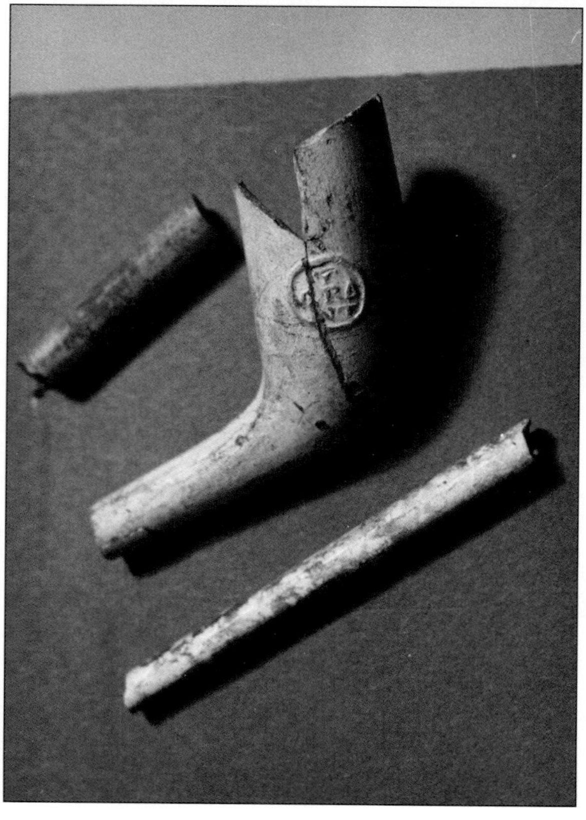

INDIAN POT RIM FROM FINCH'S ROCK HOUSE. Part of a larger collection from North Castle held by the American Museum of Natural History, this decorative pot rim was reconstructed from fragments found about 20 feet from Finch's Rock House. Other caves used as Indian shelters include Nebo Rock west of Armonk, Helicker's and Little Helicker's Caves near today's Kaysal Court in Armonk, and Quartz Quarry Rock Shelter north of Banksville.

BROKEN PIPE FROM FINCH'S ROCK HOUSE. Pieces of an English white clay trade pipe showing the hallmark of T. Grant on the bowl were found in 1900–1901 in the upper layer of earth at Finch's Rock House. This find proved the arrival of Europeans and Indian contact with them.

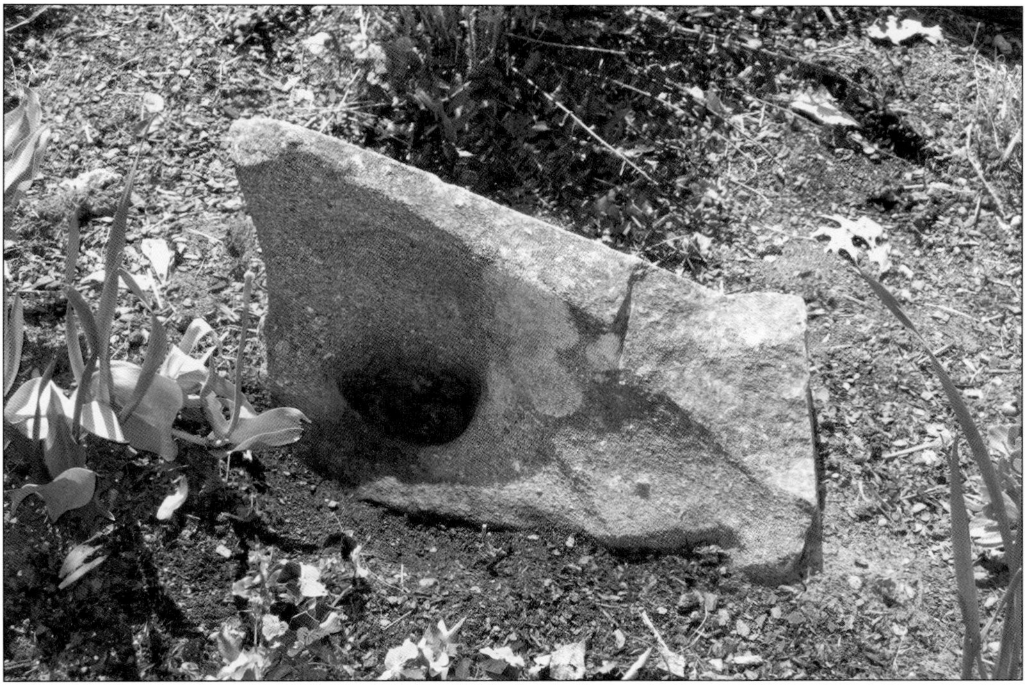

INDIAN GRINDING STONES. Shown are two examples of grinding stones used by the Indians of North Castle. Both grinding stones were found on Armonk farms and donated to the North Castle Historical Society. The pestles are missing. For many years, the larger stone was used for watering cattle. A third grinding stone stands in front of town hall in Armonk. It was found at the site of a legendary Indian cornfield near Creemer Road, Armonk, in 1920 and gifted to the town in 1960 by Mr. and Mrs. Clark Boughton. (Below, courtesy of Stephen Tomback.)

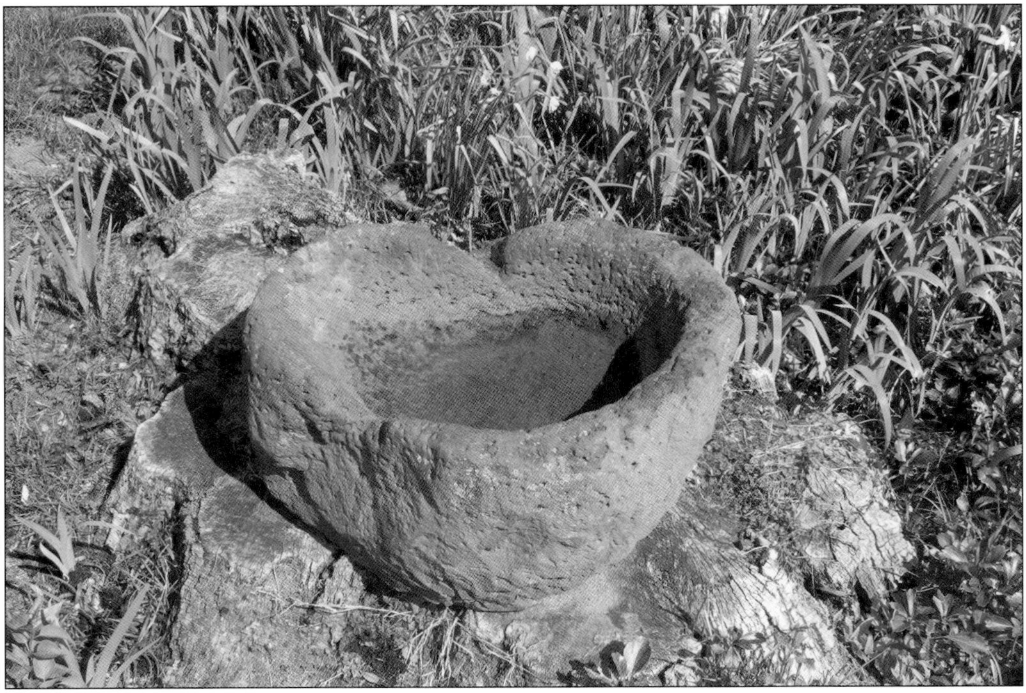

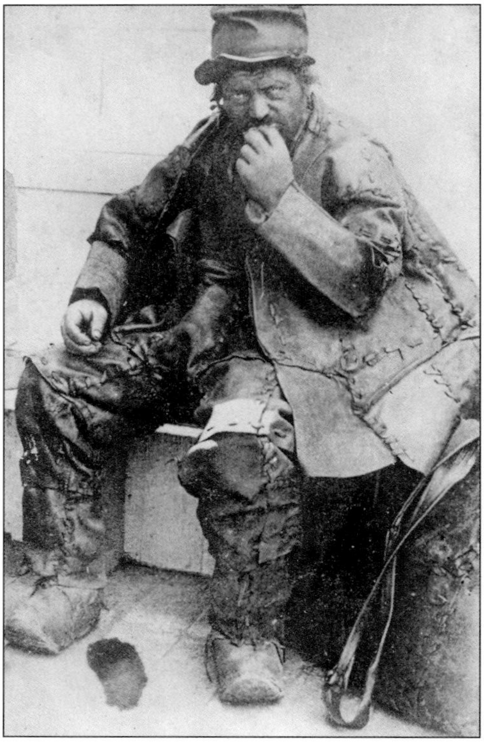

The Leatherman, Died 1889. The mystery of his name and family has never been solved. He dressed in leather patches held together with thongs and roamed a set circuit, including North Castle, every month or so beginning in the late 1850s. He slept in rough shelters and caves, including Bet Helicker's near Kaysal Court, Armonk, and possibly Finch's Rock House in today's Windmill Farm, Armonk.

Jimmy-under-the-Rock, Mid-1800s. Jimmy Johnson died about 1875. This unusual rock shelter was in North White Plains near today's Hillandale Avenue. An eccentric, he built his house and barns of rock and lived with his goats, pigs, chickens, and cow. He kept a horse for plowing and pulling his wagon. His bed was a wagon bolted to the ceiling and accessed with a 10-foot ladder.

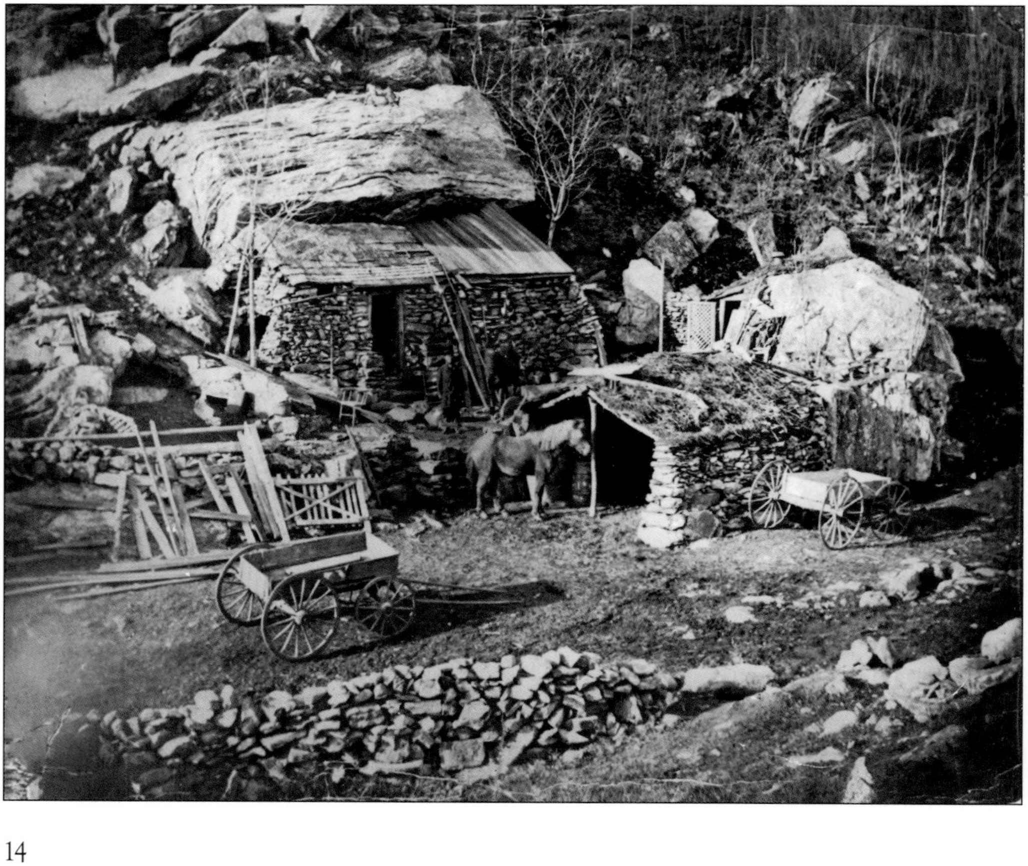

Two

WATER, MILLS, AND BLACKSMITHS

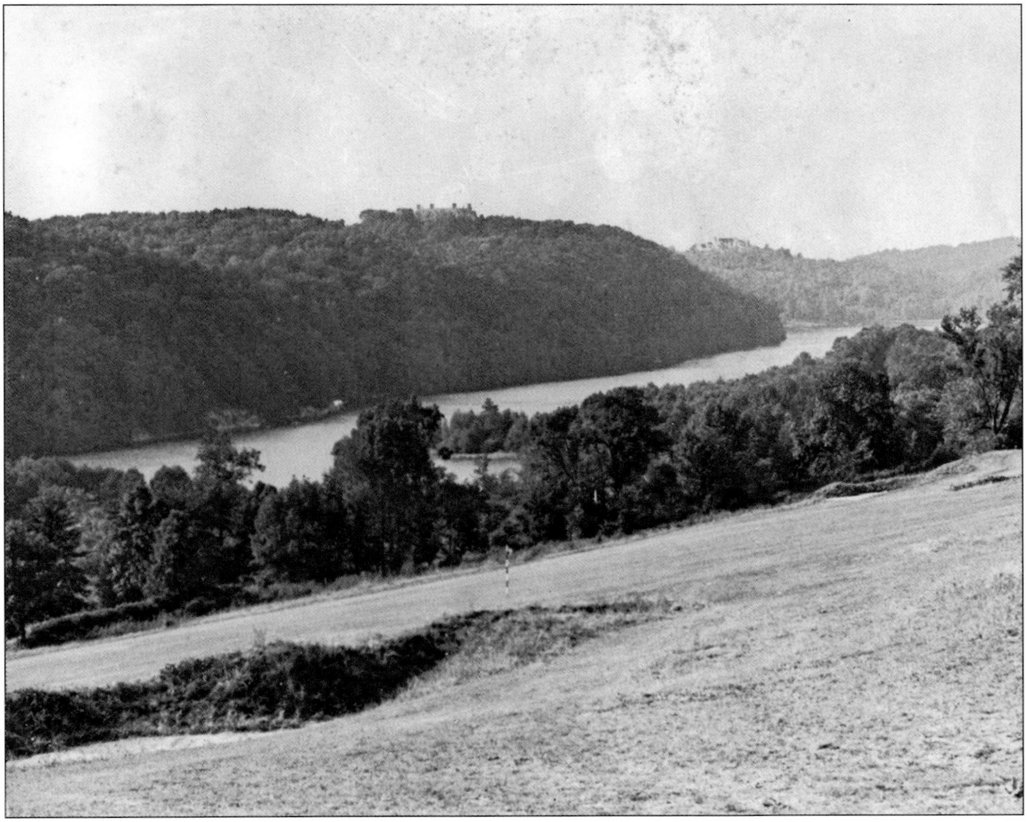

BYRAM LAKE AND TWO MANSIONS, C. 1940. Eugene Meyer's mansion, Seven Springs, appears on the hilltop at center. Meyer, a Federal Reserve chairman and publisher of the *Washington Post*, built the mansion in 1919. Today, businessman Donald Trump owns the 200-plus-acre estate, located partially in North Castle. The French Norman–style castle High Winds, built in 1937 for *Reader's Digest* owners Lila and DeWitt Wallace, appears on the right hilltop in the distance.

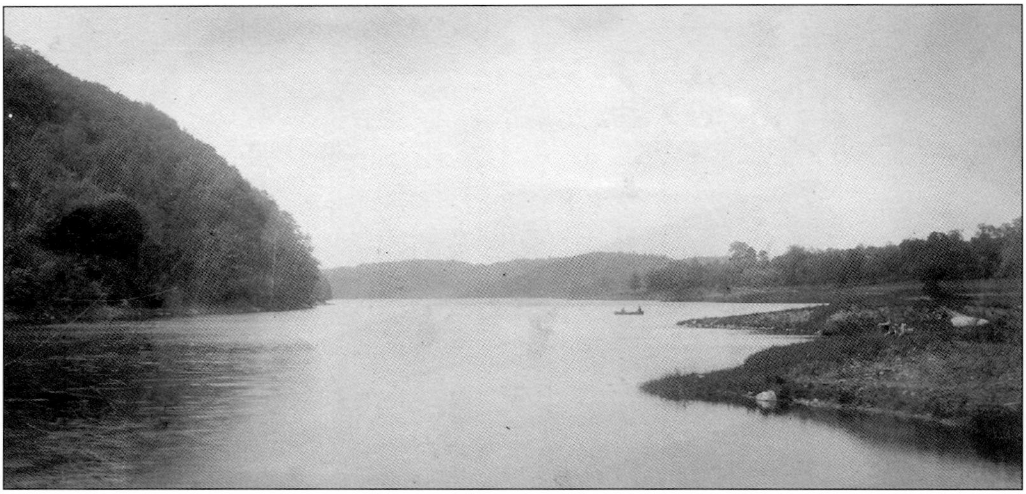

Boating on Byram Lake, Early 1900s. Illustrating the size of the lake, two people are boating (right of center) on the lake that provides water for today's Mount Kisco in the town of New Castle. In 1901, M.R. Harrington of the American Museum of Natural History verified that an Indian campsite had been at the south end of the lake.

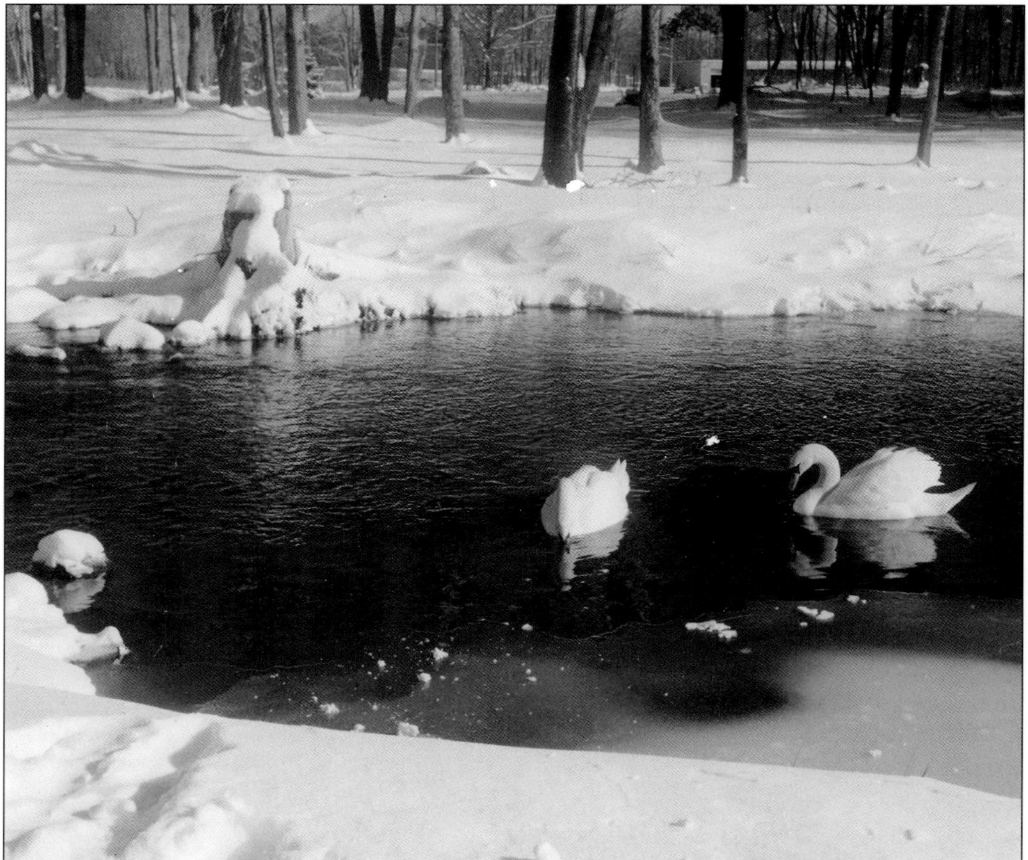

Swans at Wampus Brook Park, Mid-1900s. Swans once nested in Armonk hamlet across from St. Stephen's Episcopal Church and Cemetery.

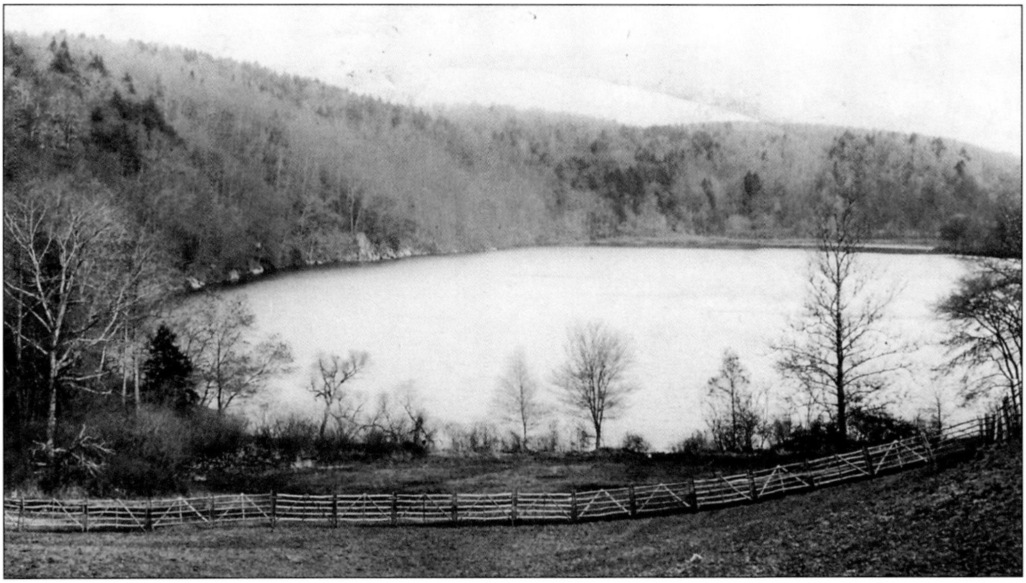

WAMPUS POND, ROUTE 128, ARMONK. Reportedly meaning "opossum," this pond is named for the Indian sachem Wampus, who sold the land to white men in the late 1690s. A very early Quimby (Quinby) family cemetery lies at the south end of the pond, deeded about 1802 to Chappaqua Friends Meeting, then taken by the City of New York for water supply and later sold to Westchester County in 1963.

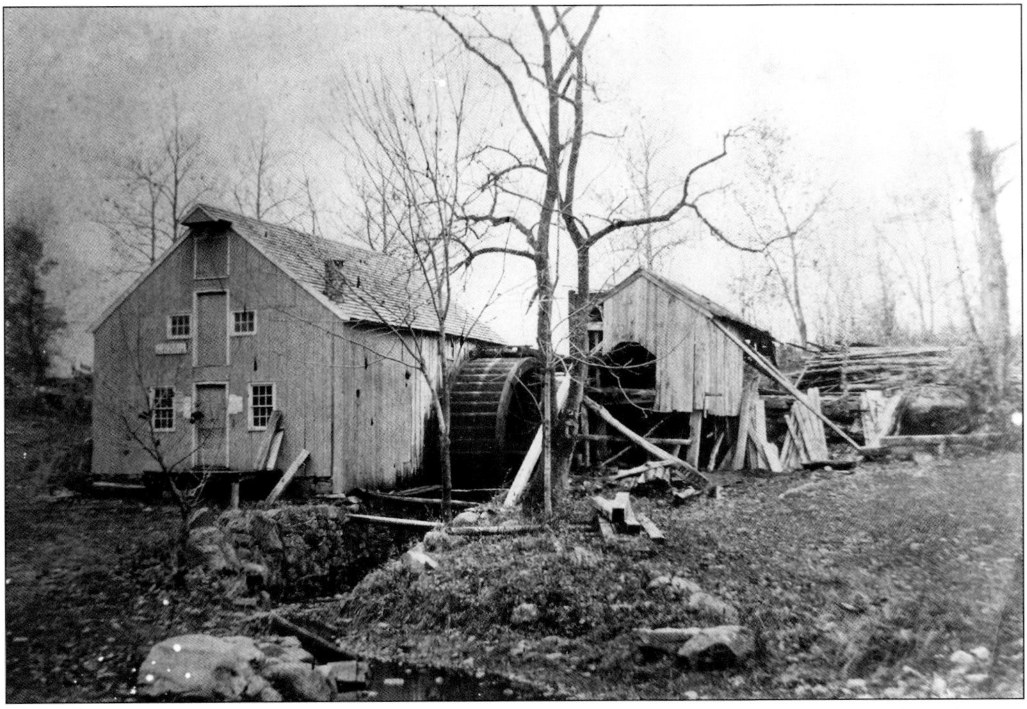

CARPENTER'S (SANDS) MILLS, 1860, BOYCE PHOTOGRAPHERS. John Hallock built a mill on this site in Mile Square as early as 1737. The mills were owned by Thomas Wright during the Revolution and by members of the Sands family from 1790 until 1859. They were sold to Jacob Bowron Carpenter in 1860. Today, the site is a park on Cox Avenue/High Street at Greenway Road, Armonk.

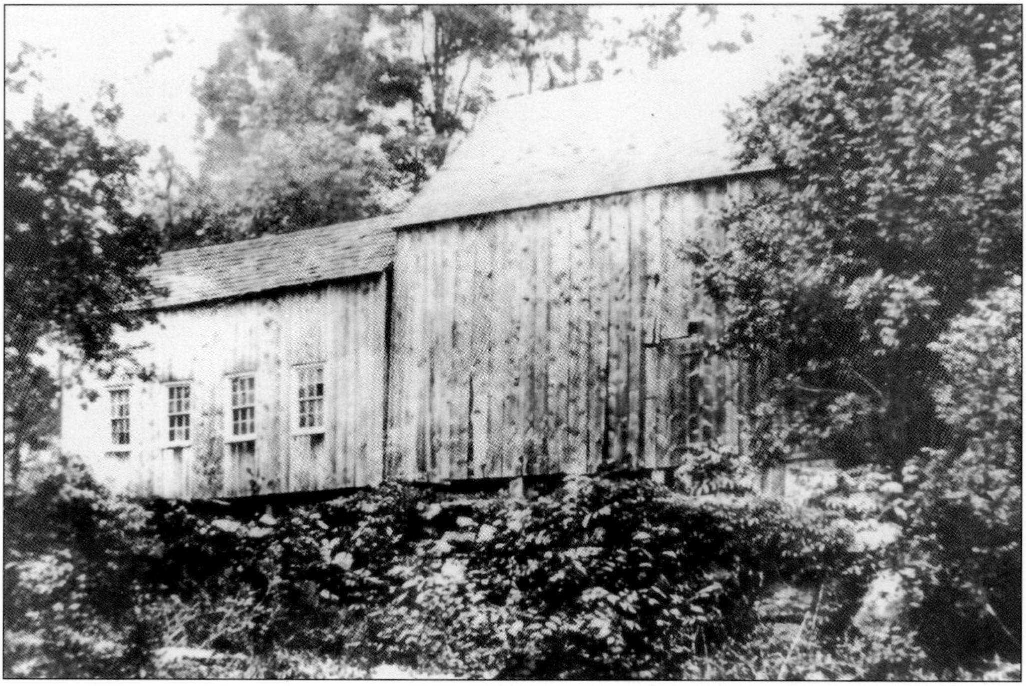

HISTORIC BARN AT WAMPUS MILLS, C. 1900. This barn, re-sided and re-roofed over the years, was the site where British spy Maj. John Andre was contained overnight after capture in Tarrytown, New York, on September 23, 1780. The mills were owned by Thomas Wright at that time. Lt. Col. John Jameson of the Continental Army headquartered here. Maj. Benjamin Tallmadge is credited with preventing Andre's return to traitor Benedict Arnold.

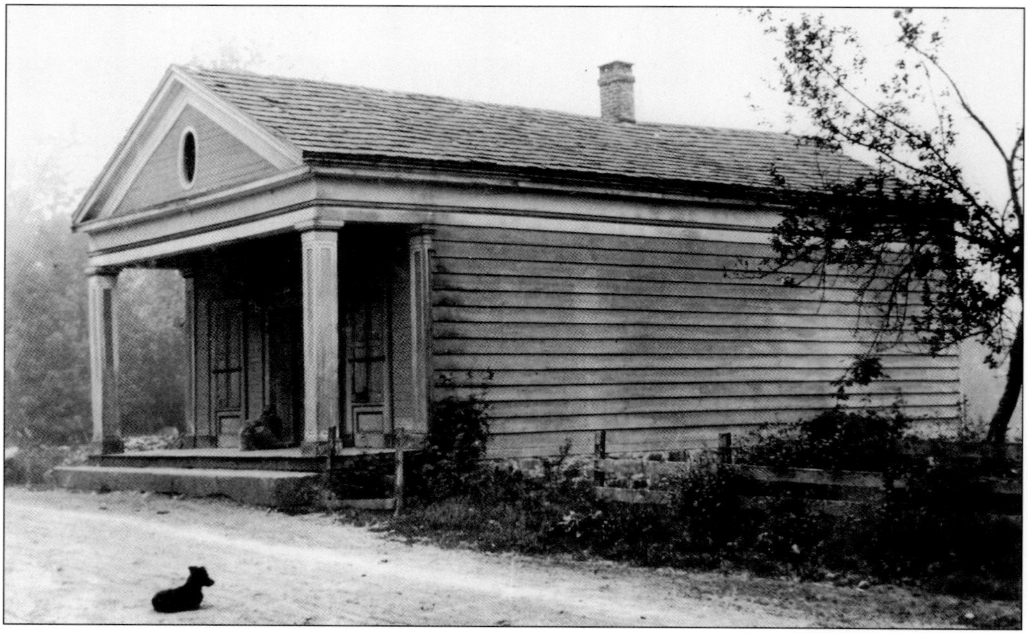

CARPENTER'S STORE, WAMPUS MILLS, 1903. According to the April 26, 1903, *New-York Tribune*, this building was a church years before, abandoned, and later used for a store. The area was then called the hamlet of Wampus Mills or the Mills. John Hallock built the first mill here about 1737.

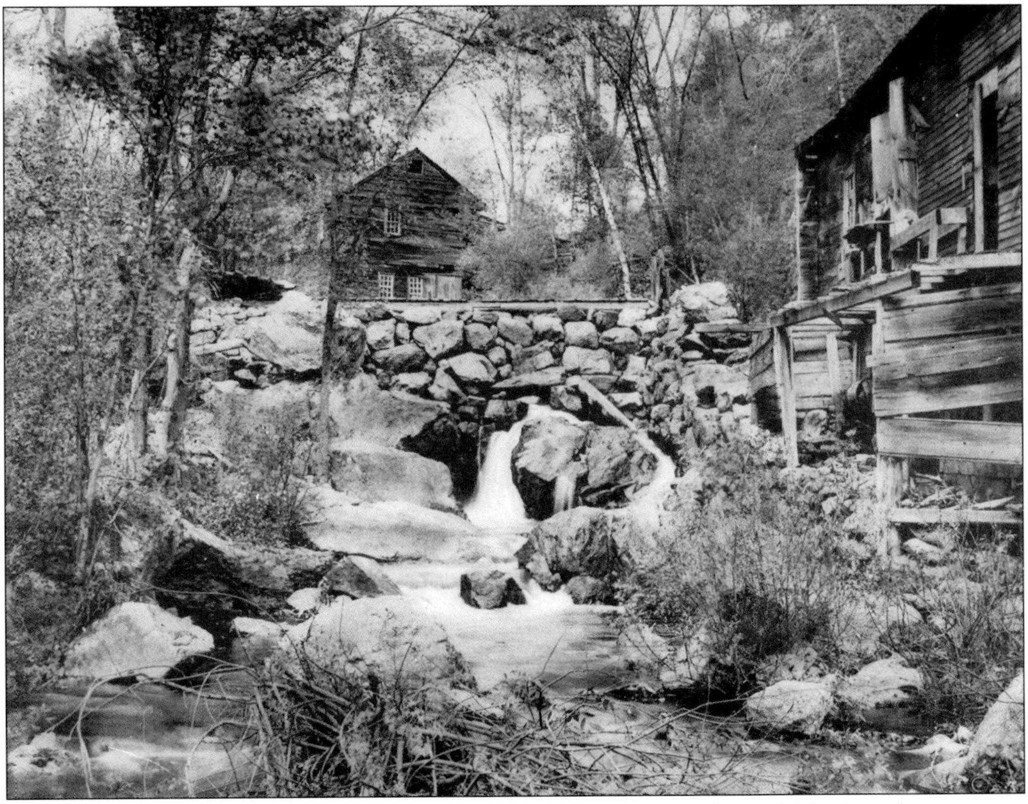

KNOWLTON'S MILL (AKA CARPENTER'S, SANDS, AND WAMPUS MILLS), C. 1900. A settlement grew around the pre–Revolutionary War mill called Hallock's, then Wright's, Latting's, Sands, Carpenter's, and Knowlton's, until destroyed by the City of New York in 1904 and 1905 for the water supply.

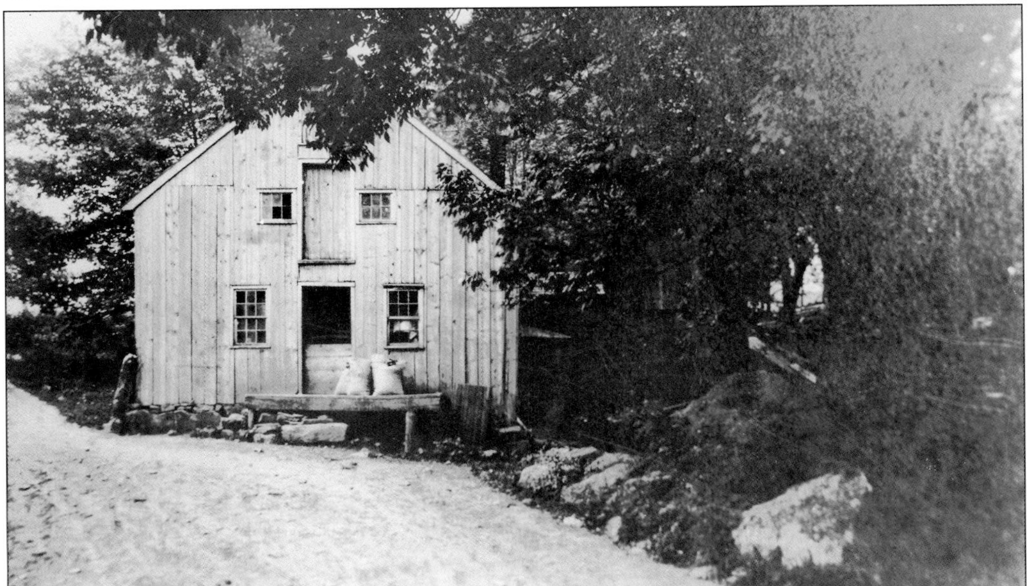

OUTBUILDING AT WAMPUS MILLS, C. 1900. This building was destroyed by the City of New York in 1904 for the water supply.

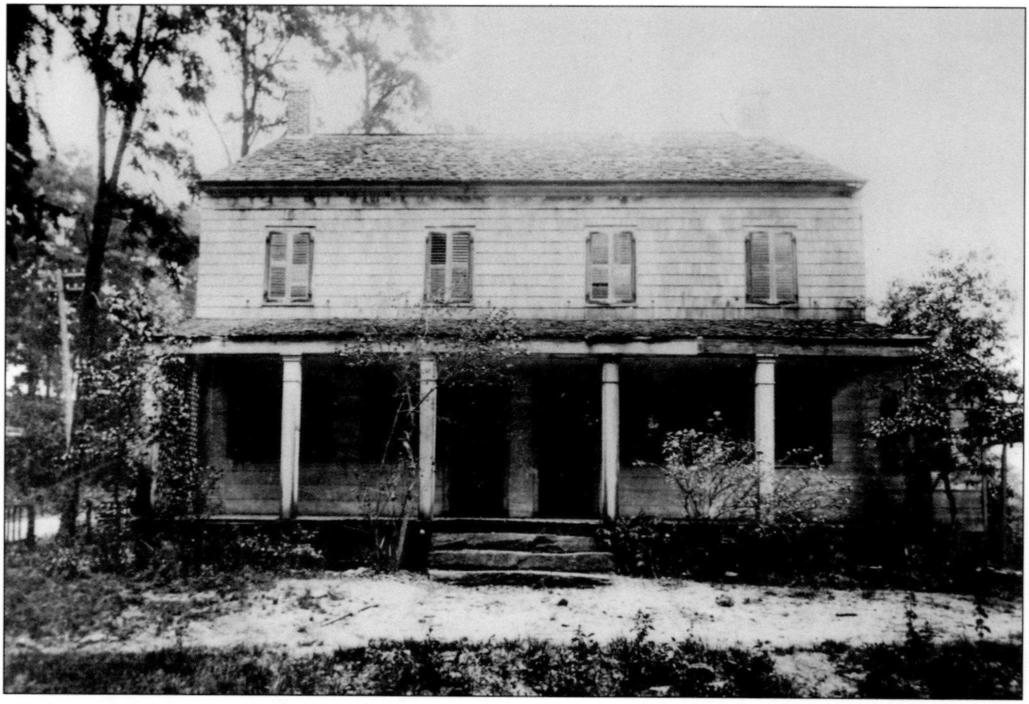

Home of John Sands, Built c. 1812. This house stood facing today's Greenway Road at Cox Avenue/High Street, Armonk. It was destroyed by the City of New York in 1904 for the water supply. John Sands purchased the mills from his older brother, Thomas, in 1794. According to an account book found beneath the flooring of the mill at the time of its demolition in 1904, he was a blacksmith when he bought the mills. A stone with the initials J.S. and the date 1812 survives and is believed to have been a gate stone at this home. The house had two front doors.

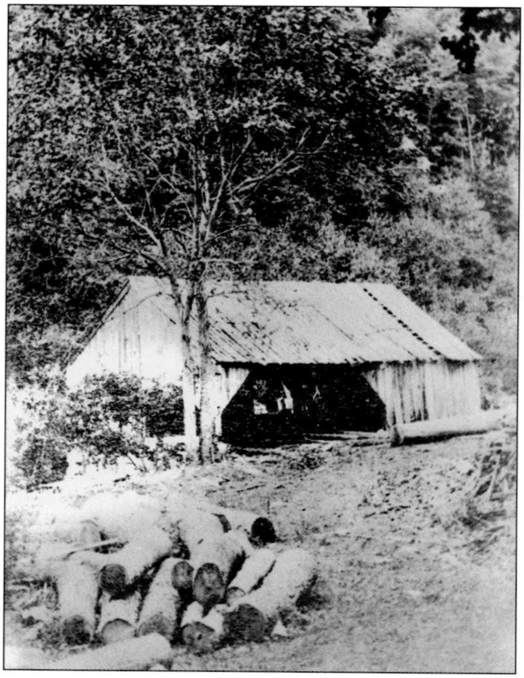

Forman-Tripp Sawmill. This photograph taken about 1900 shows John P. Tripp's sawmill, which stood below Byram Lake Dam, Armonk. Aaron Forman, town supervisor in 1757–1758, owned the sawmill. His daughter Susannah Forman married Jotham Carpenter, who took over in 1804. Isaac Tripp bought the mill in 1825 and added chair making. Son John P. Tripp continued the business until New York City demolished the mill about 1904 for water supply.

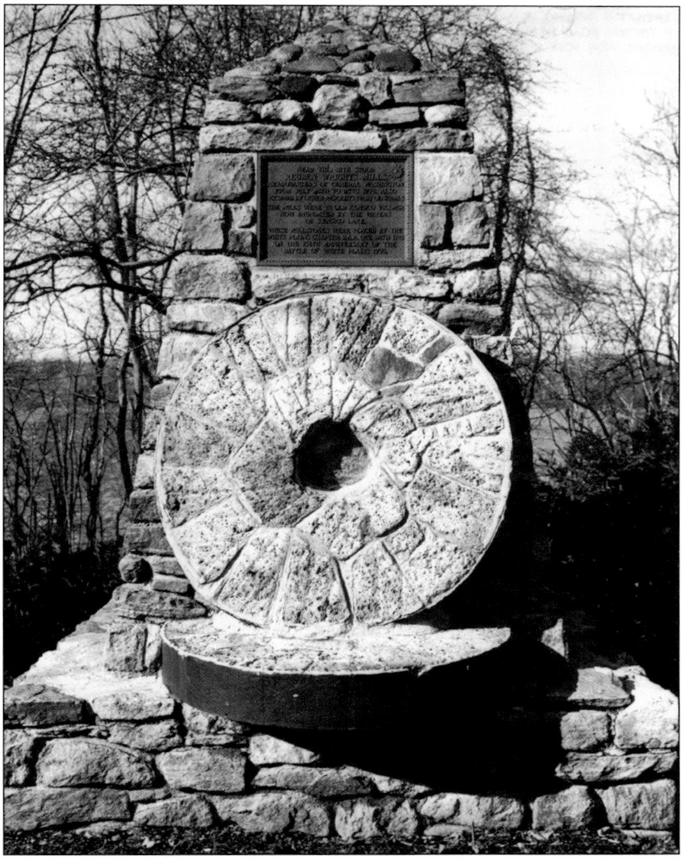

Monument to Reuben Wright's Mill, North White Plains. In 1932, the White Plains Chapter of the National Society Daughters of the American Revolution dedicated this monument just south of today's Rye Lake Bridge on Route 22. Still John Purdy owned the mill in 1753, and Wright owned it as early as 1763. The area, later known as Fisher's, Cox's, and Robbins' Mill, and then Kensico, is under the waters of Kensico Dam Reservoir.

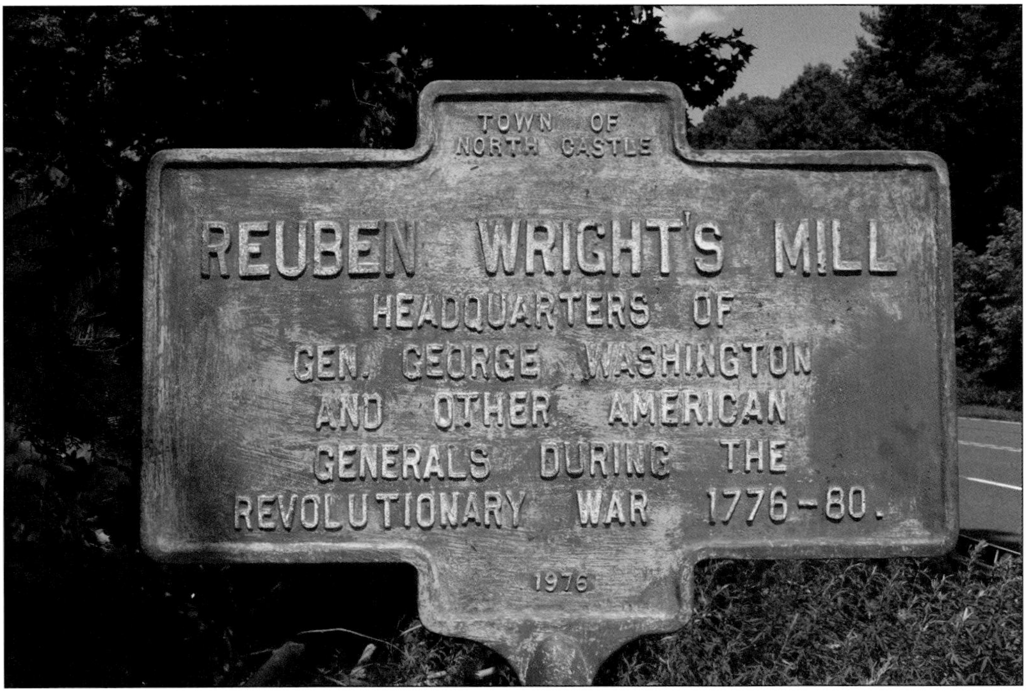

New York State Historic Marker Memorializing Reuben Wright's Mill. This marker reads: "Reuben Wright's Mill—Headquarters of Gen. George Washington and other American generals during the Revolutionary War 1776–1780."

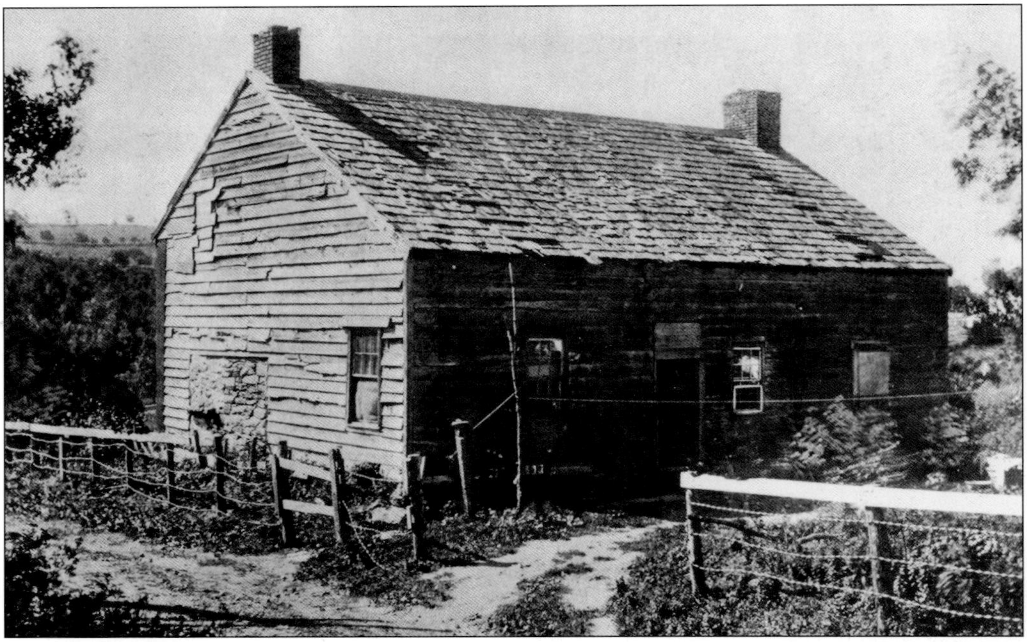

Wright-Robbins House, Village of Kensico. This photograph shows an old house of the mill owners just before it was taken down and the valley flooded by Kensico Dam in the early 1900s. Reuben Wright was a Quaker miller on Bear Gutter Creek from at least 1763 until 1784. The area was named Kensico in 1848.

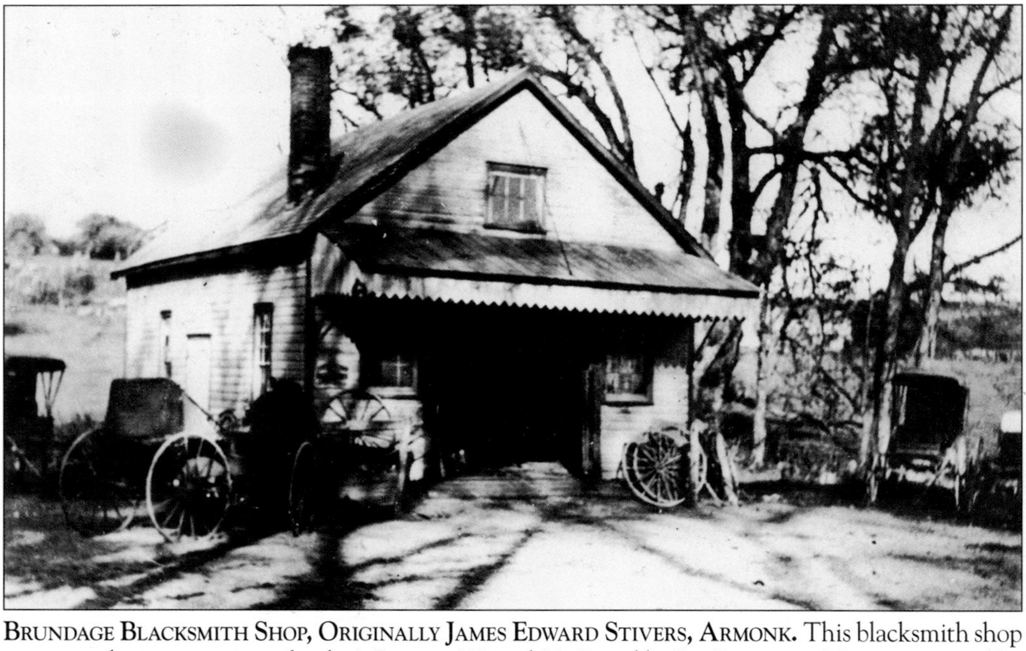

Brundage Blacksmith Shop, Originally James Edward Stivers, Armonk. This blacksmith shop was near the intersection of today's Routes 433 and 22. Saved by Dr. Benjamin Marx, preserved by the Cerak brothers in East White Plains, and assisted by the Armonk Lions Club, it became part of the North Castle Historical Society's educational complex. Other North Castle blacksmiths included Henry Sension, Benjamin F. Carpenter, Benjamin Creemer, Hiram Remington, William Paine, and Edward Deal.

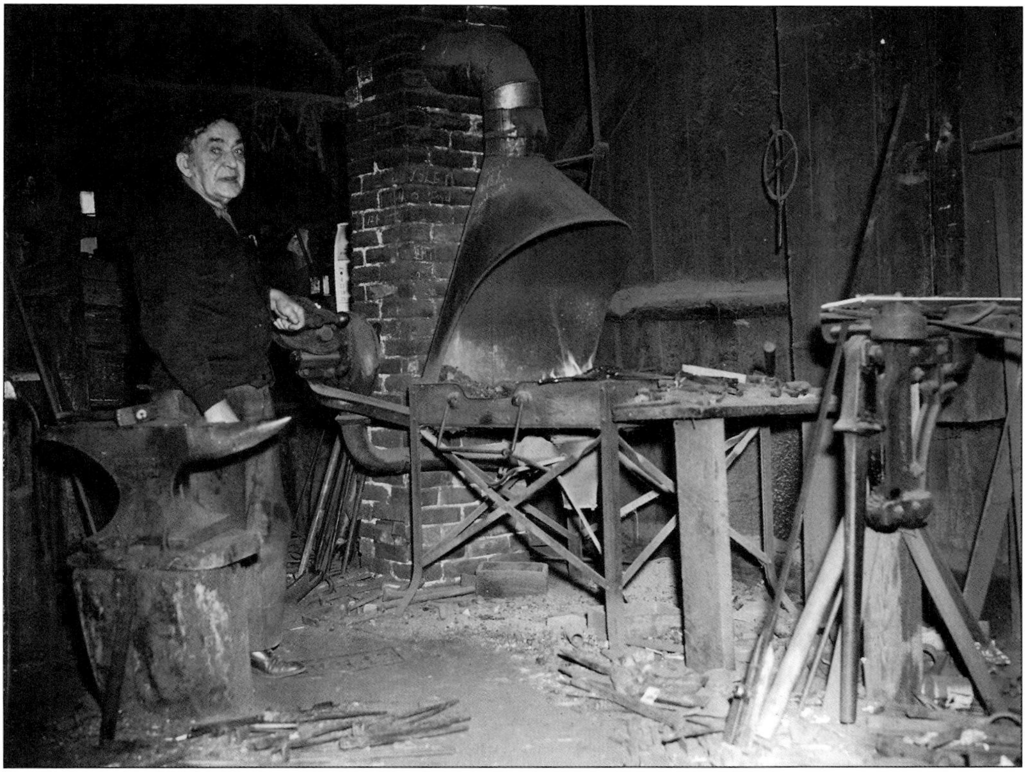

Harry Brundage at the Forge, the Last North Castle Blacksmith, Mid-1900s. Harry took over from his father, Maurice W. Brundage, and for 60 years worked in the blacksmith shop. He was a gentle friend to all. Many stories were swapped near his forge. He died on November 29, 1954, at age 75.

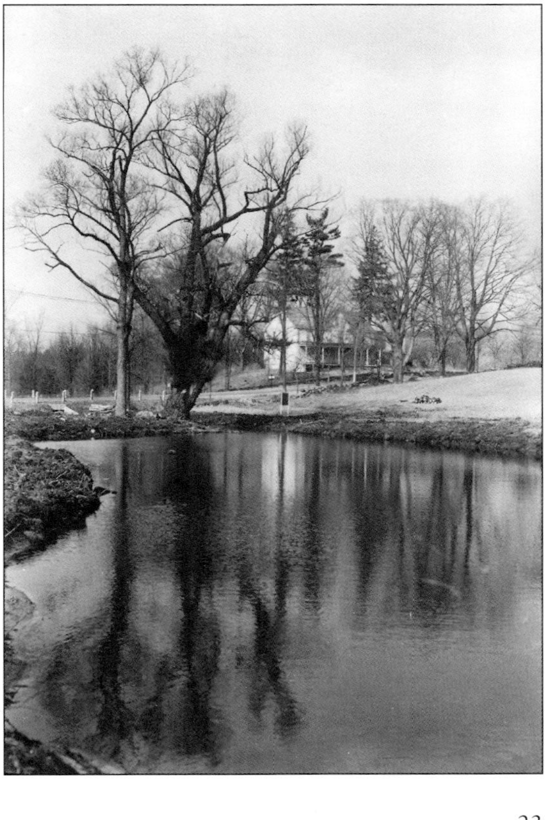

Pond at Brundage Blacksmith Shop, c. 1920. This photograph, taken at the intersection of today's Cox Avenue and Route 22 (Bedford Road) in Armonk, shows a large pond on Smith's Brook and historic Smith's Tavern in the background.

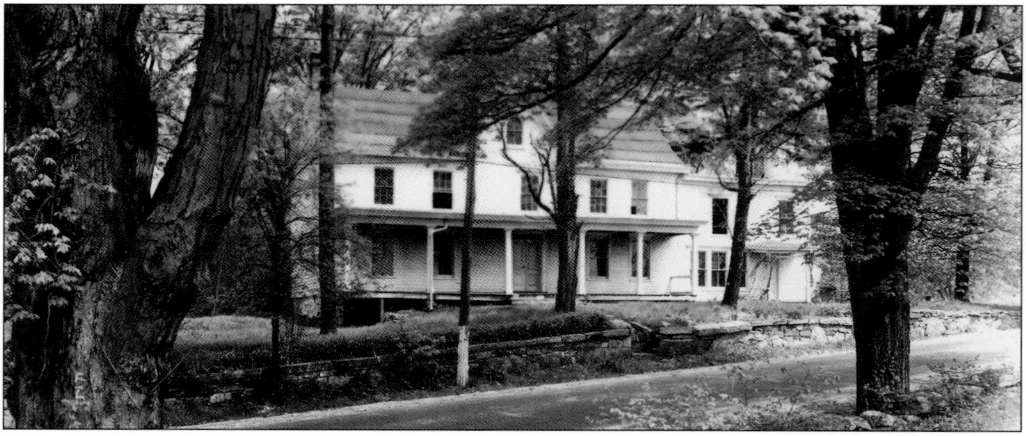

Smith's Tavern, c. 1920. The right portion of this house predates the American Revolution, and the left portion was built in the early 1800s. This view shows a front porch and window in the roof line above the front door. Capt. John Smith purchased this pre–Revolutionary War tavern in 1797. For generations, it served as an early stagecoach stop, tavern, post office, town hall, and center of community life. It stands today at 440 Bedford Road, Armonk.

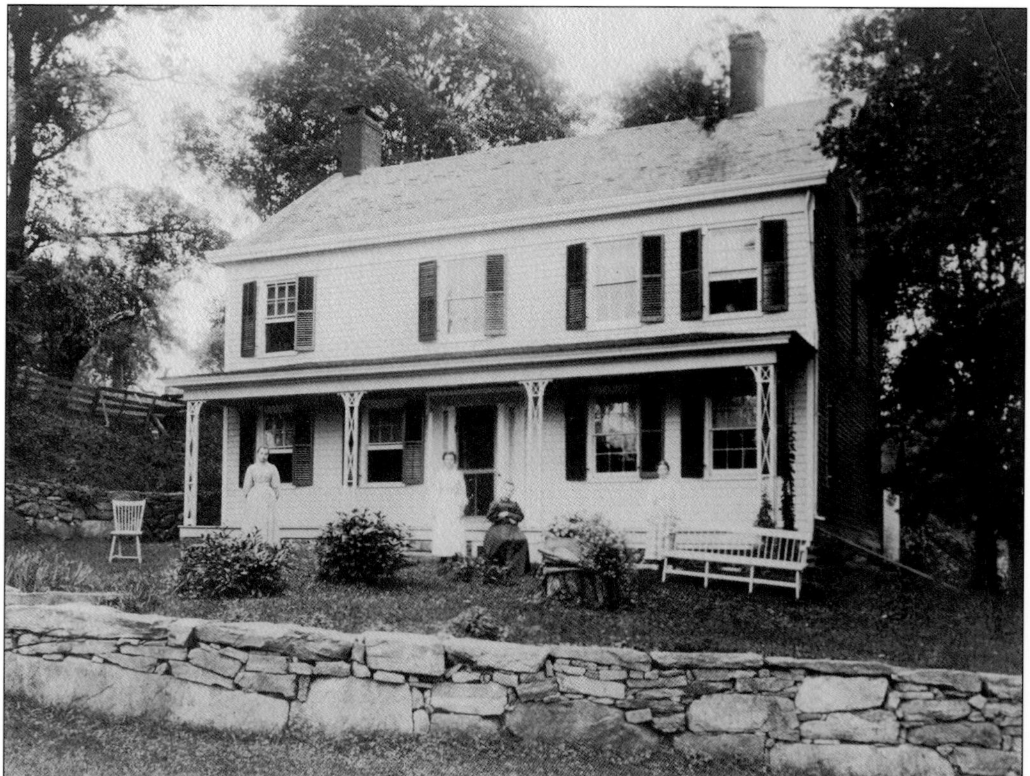

Thomas Hopkins–David Brundage House, 1900. From left to right are Mamie Tompkins Husted, Cora Tompkins, Evelina Brundage Tompkins (seated), and Mary Augusta Brundage Tripp. Mamie and Cora were daughters of Evelina. Mary Augusta was a daughter of Thomas Purdy Brundage. The house at today's 441 Bedford Road in Armonk, dating to about 1760, has been extensively remodeled. Thomas Hopkins's heirs sold to David Brundage in 1812. Four Brundage generations then lived and farmed here. British soldiers set fire to the house in 1779; American militiamen saved it.

Three

FARMS

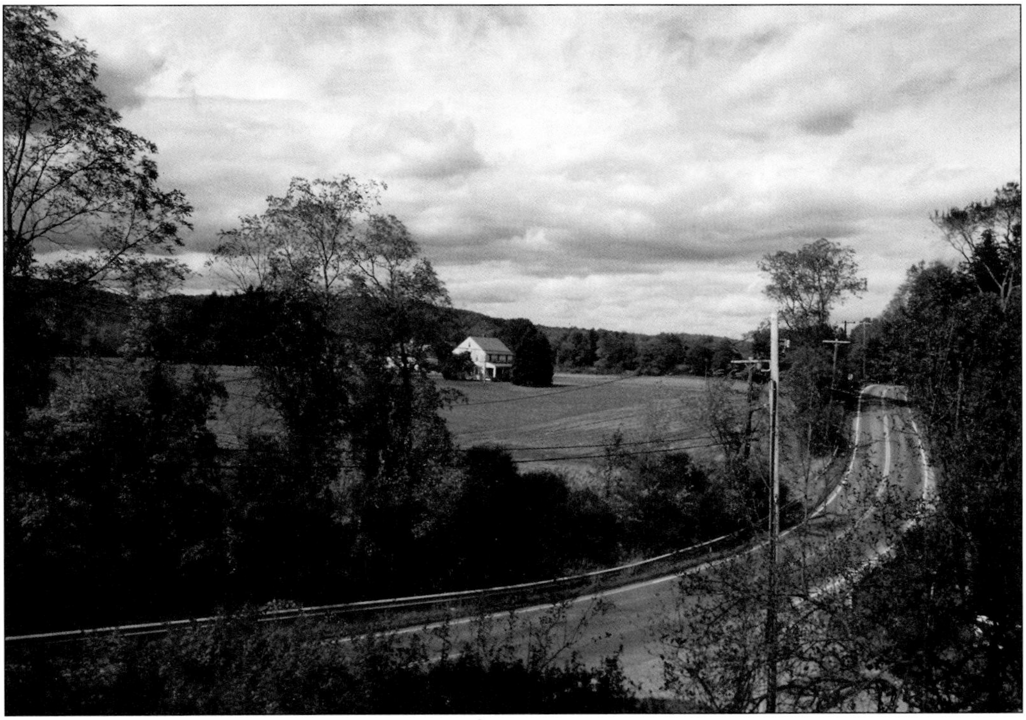

HENKER FARM, BEDFORD-BANKSVILLE ROAD, BEDFORD. The expanse of farmland surrounding the Henker farmhouse was planted in corn, tomatoes, and other vegetables. Going to the Henker farm for early corn and summer tomatoes was eagerly awaited every year from the late 1930s until the mid-1980s. Patrons came from all over Westchester County as well as Connecticut not only to buy but also to visit.

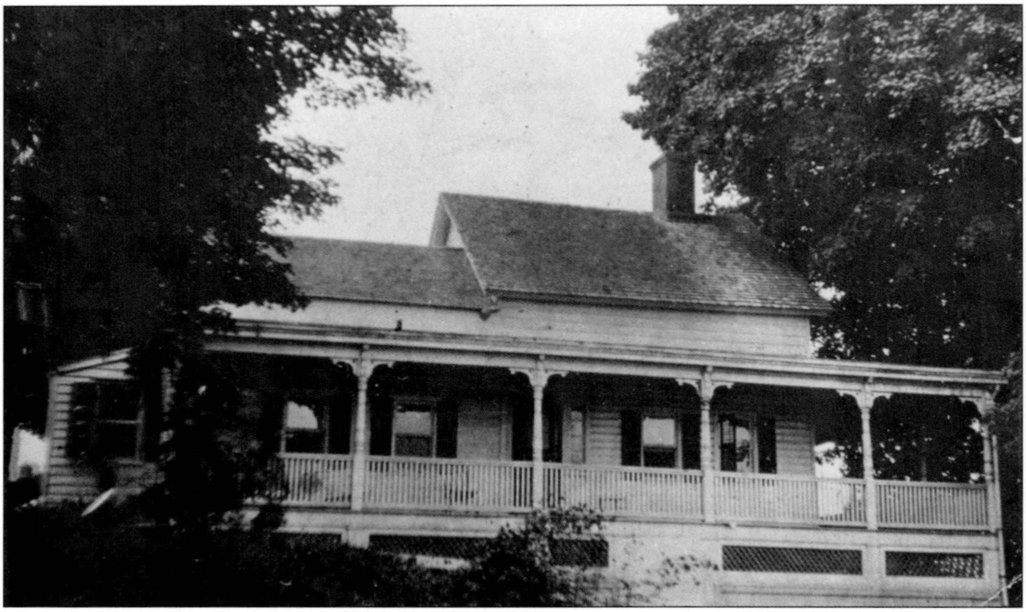

Charles Kaiser House, c. 1930. North Castle chicken farmer Kaiser made national news when he sued neighbor Walter S. Gifford, president of AT&T, claiming Gifford's dog killed many of his chickens. Barns and chicken coops surrounded the farmhouse on Round Hill Road, Armonk, before it was torn down. Earlier in the 20th century it was part of the 20-acre Enoch Sniffin farm.

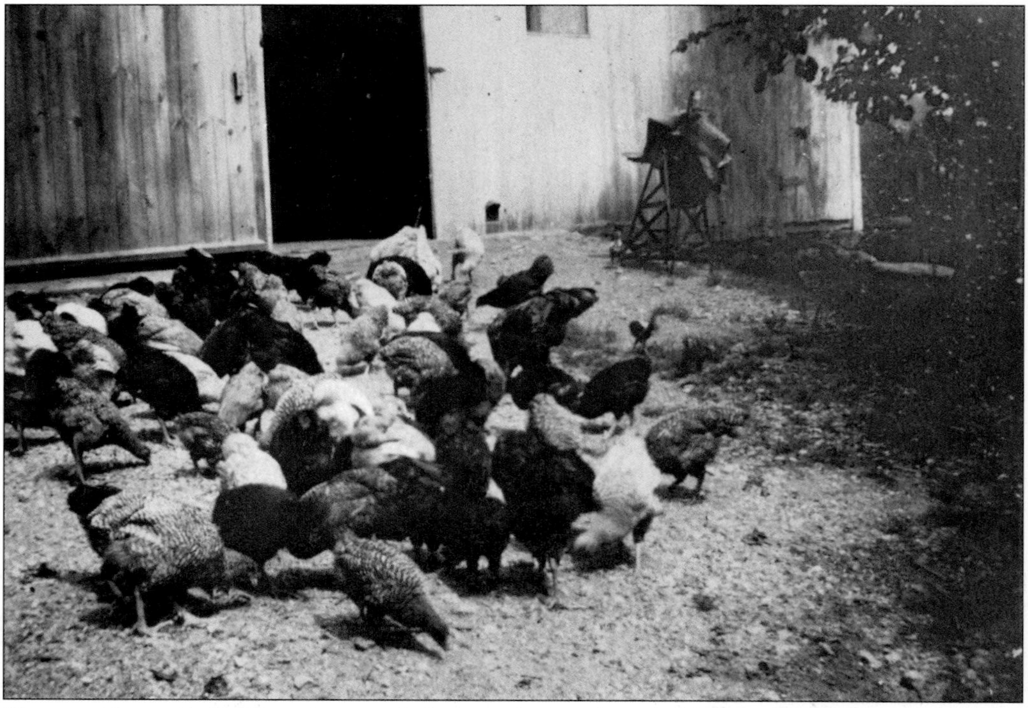

Chicken Farm, 1912. This photograph shows a chicken farm on Hickory Kingdom Road, Bedford. In addition to supplying eggs and food, chickens were bred to be shown competitively in local and regional poultry shows.

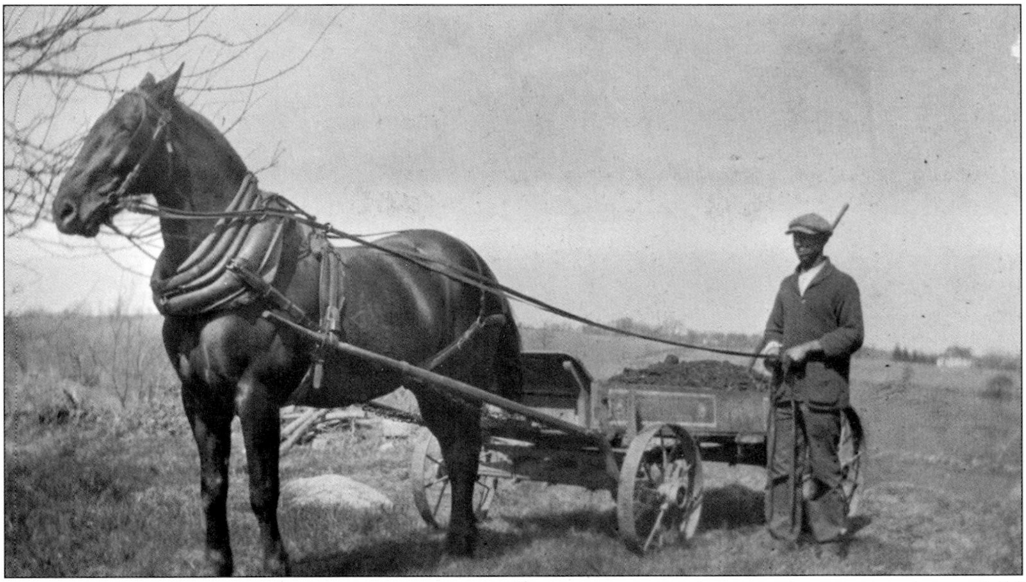

A BANKSVILLE FARMER, 1915. This wagonload of manure was being taken to fertilize a field or garden.

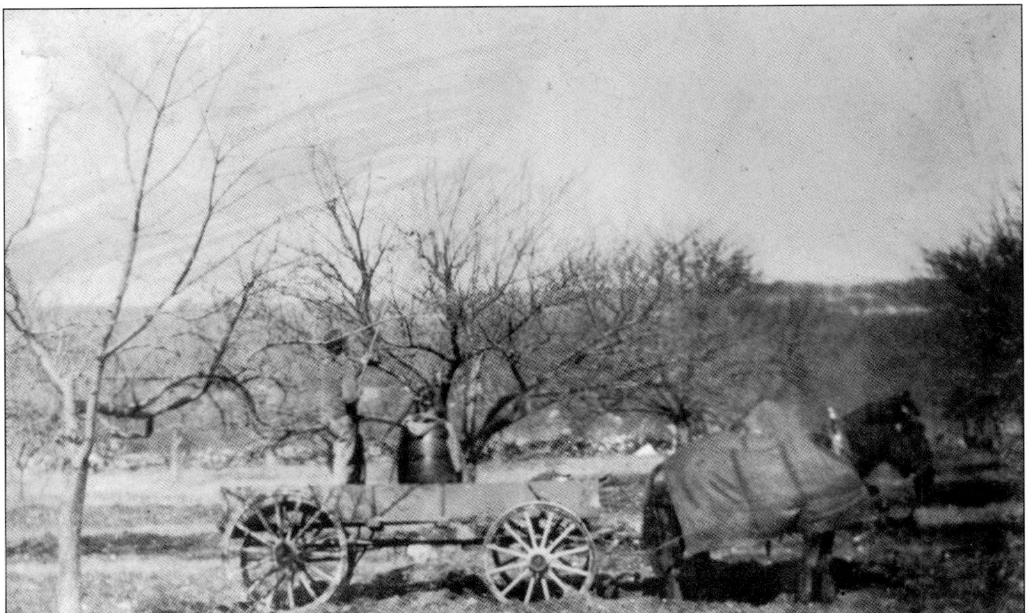

APPLE HARVESTING IN BANKSVILLE, 1915. The high apples were picked with a basket on a long pole. Apples were packed in barrels and sent to markets including Greenwich, Connecticut, and New York City.

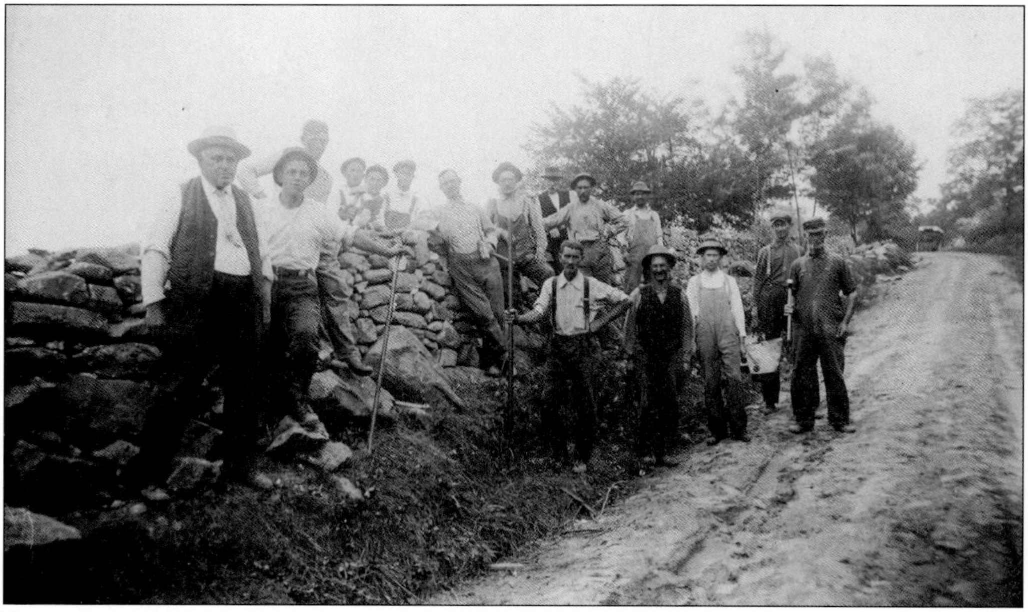

Rebuilding a Stone Wall, Early 1900s. Unfortunately, the location of this muddy, unpaved road and the names of the men working to rebuild the stone wall are not recorded. For many years, road maintenance was assigned to local farmers, who were in charge of keeping the roads in good repair and getting their own work crews.

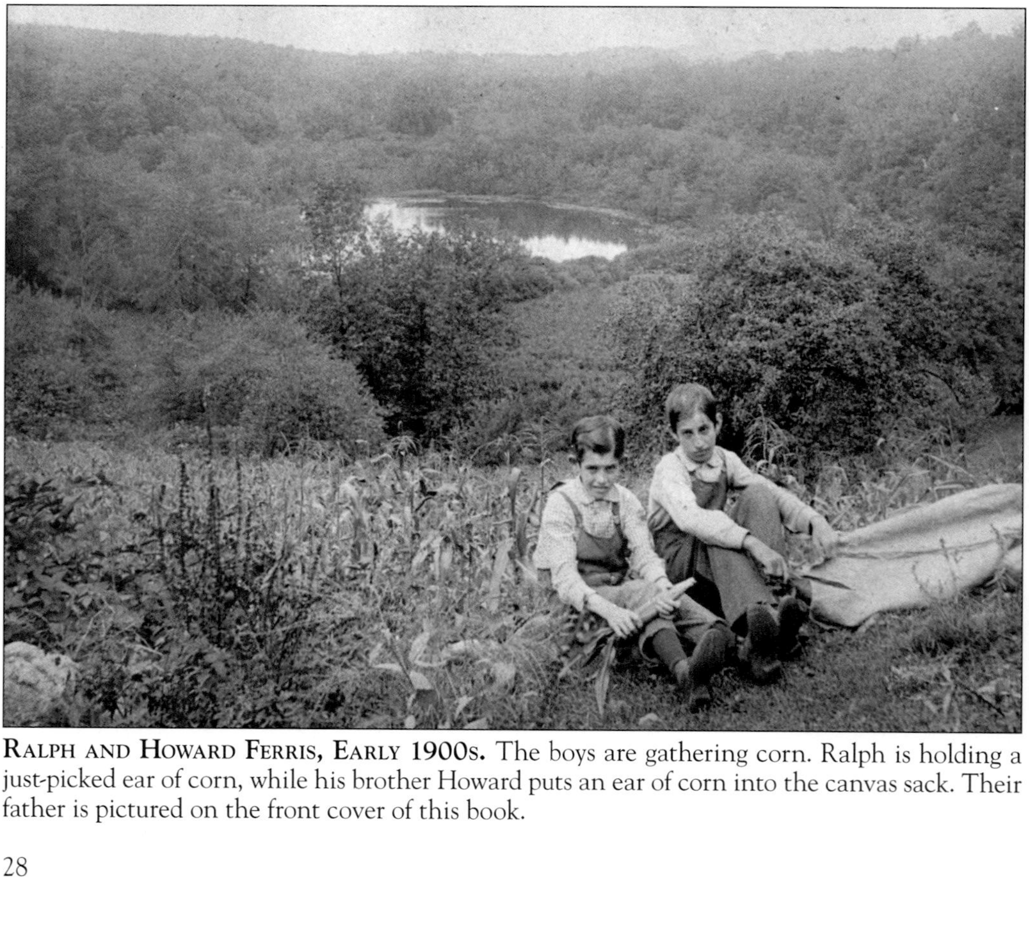

Ralph and Howard Ferris, Early 1900s. The boys are gathering corn. Ralph is holding a just-picked ear of corn, while his brother Howard puts an ear of corn into the canvas sack. Their father is pictured on the front cover of this book.

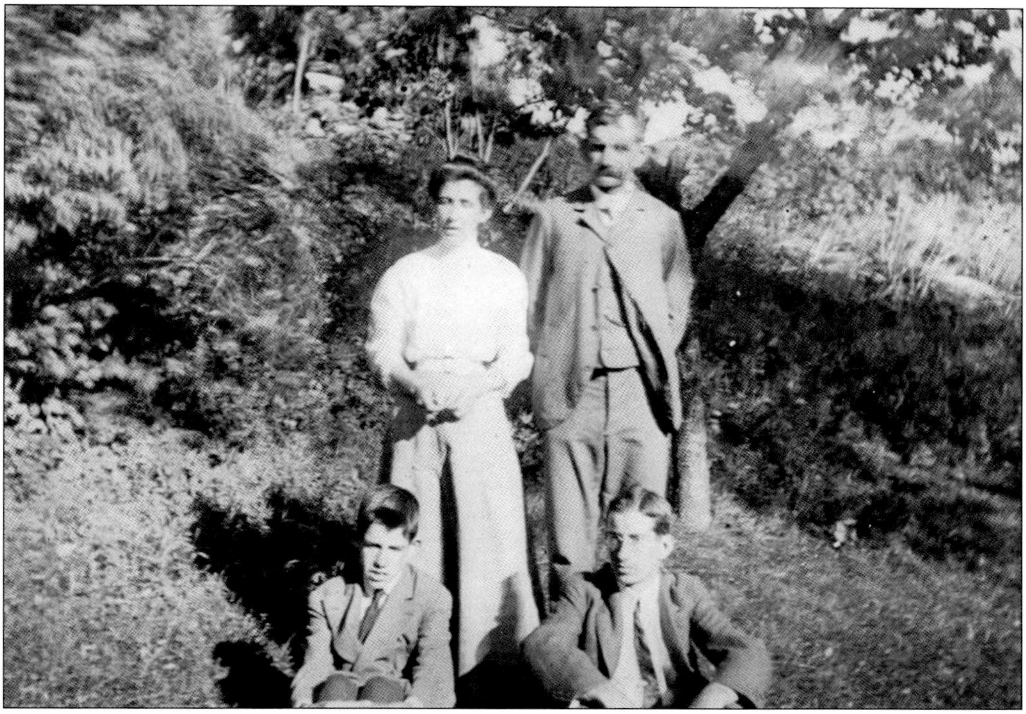

The Charles Ferris Family, Early 1900s. Charles and his wife, Cornelia E. Carson Ferris, and two of their four sons, Ralph (seated left), born 1894, and Howard, born 1892, are pictured in the yard of their farm on Bedford Road (today's New York Route 22). Another picture of Charles Ferris appears on the front cover of this book.

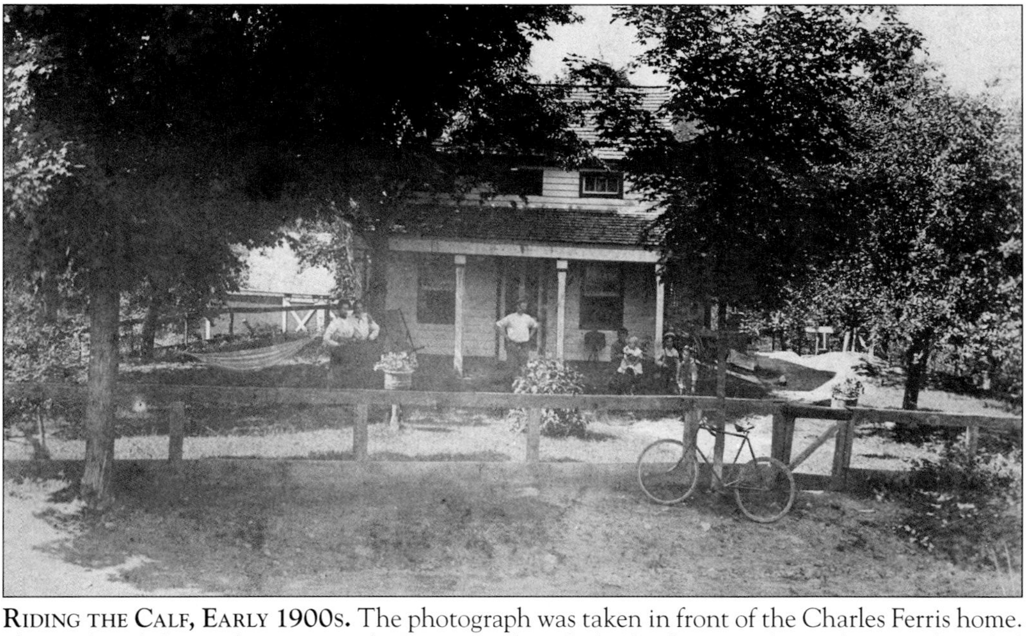

Riding the Calf, Early 1900s. The photograph was taken in front of the Charles Ferris home. Shown from left to right are Cornelia Ferris, unidentified, Charles Ferris (center), an unidentified woman and child, Howard Ferris, and Ralph Ferris. The unidentified child is being given a ride on a calf.

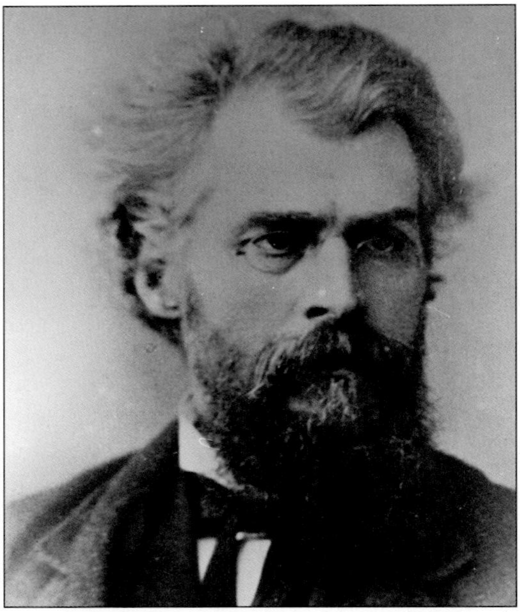

WILLIAM H. CREEMER, TOWN CLERK, 1876–1880, 1883–1884, 1885–1886. From 1885 to 1888, William Creemer copied by hand the old deteriorating town minute book, covering 1736 through 1848, thus preserving the records of that period. He also kept a daily journal for many years detailing his farm life: sowing, reaping, repairing machinery, cutting wood, and raising and trading live stock. He married Phebe Jane, a daughter of Reuben Green.

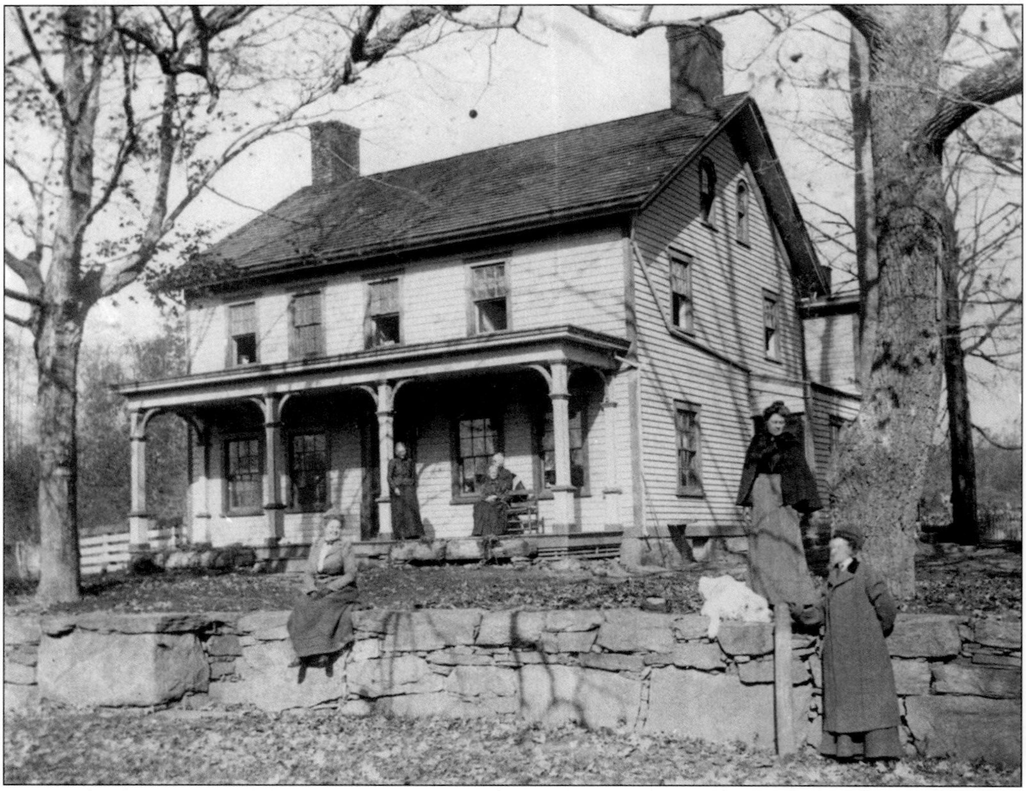

GREEN-CREEMER HOUSE, GREEN VALLEY, C. 1900. The women pictured are identified only as the Green-Creemer ladies. Prosperous North Castle farmer Reuben Green built this house in 1812. He was a founder and first vestryman of St. Stephen's Episcopal Church, Armonk, and served as assessor for North Castle during the 1830s. Daughter Phebe Jane married William H. Creemer in 1856. They supplemented farm income by accepting select summer boarders.

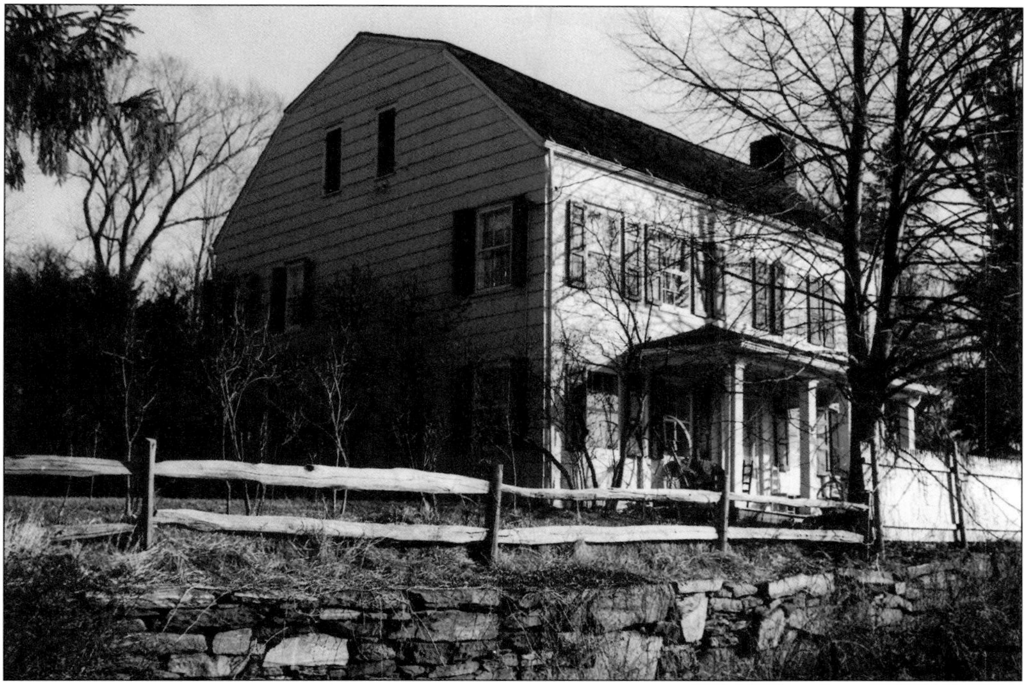

Banks-Guion House, Dating to the Late 1700s–Early 1800s. Research by owner George Pouder indicates that James and Tabitha Guion purchased this house in 1804 from Samuel and Charity Lyon Banks. James Guion served the town as assessor, commissioner of highways, commissioner of schools, and justice of the peace, as well as New York assemblyman between 1819 and 1821. The farm encompassed about 300 acres. This house is on today's Bedford-Banksville Road in Bedford.

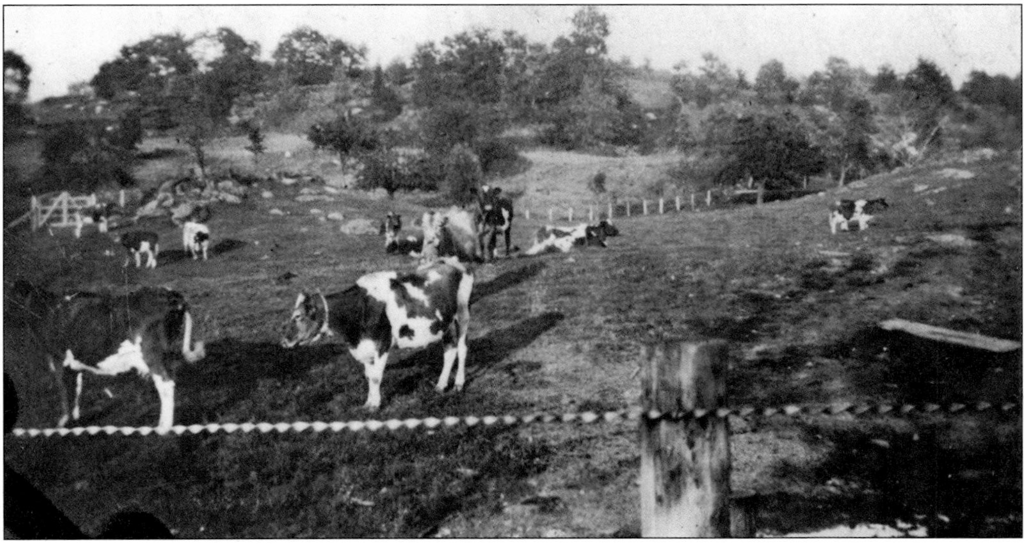

Cows on the Elroy Smith Farm, 1915. The sixth child of Richard Smith and Mary Peck Smith, Elroy grew up on and continued the family farm of about 300 acres belonging to the historic Banks-Guion House. Elroy married Mary Bush Hobby. Elroy was born in 1868 and died in 1931. He was a great benefactor of the Middle Patent Rural Cemetery, where a monument stands in his honor.

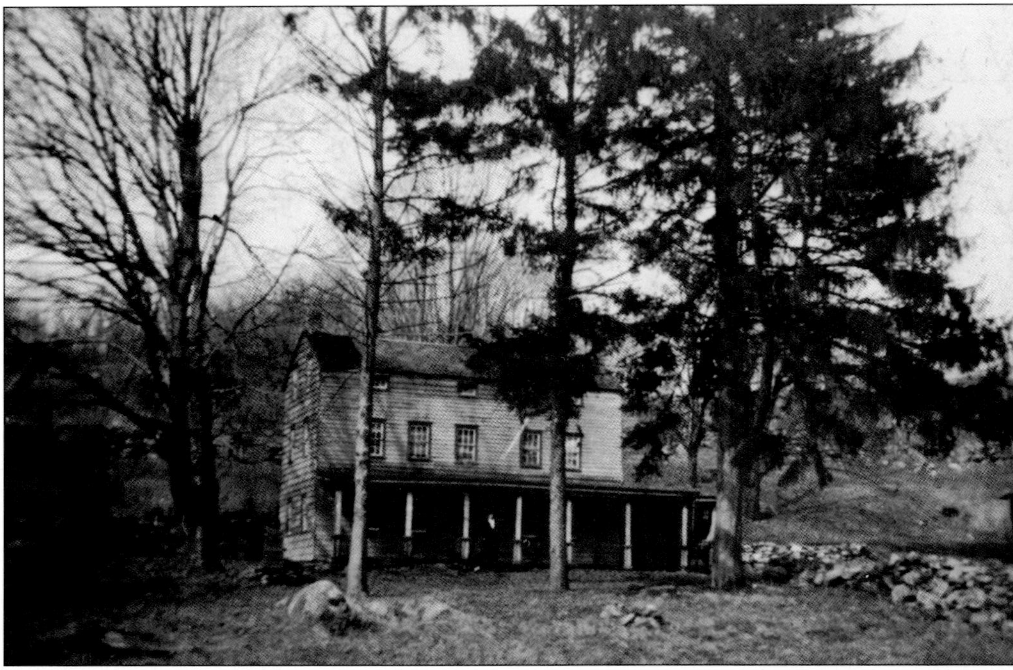

David H. Reynolds Farm, Dating to the Late 1700s. This early home on Hickory Kingdom Road in Bedford was torn down in the late 1970s. From the late 1700s until about 1870, the Reynolds family farmed here. Next it was the farm of Abel Miller until about 1915, when it was taken over by Miller's son-in-law Robert Ingersoll.

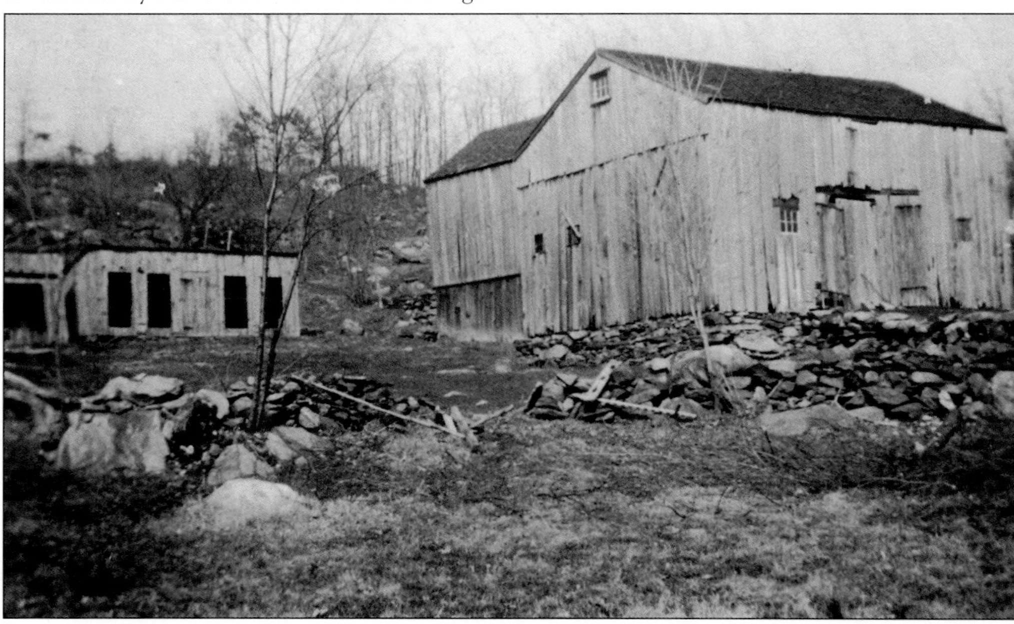

Abel Miller's Barns, Early 1900s. These barns and outbuildings are representative of those belonging to a prosperous North Castle farmer of the early 1900s. Abel Miller's farm was the old David H. Reynolds farm. For some years, Miller had a brick and mason building business in Brooklyn and commuted to New York, driving his horse and buggy to the Greenwich, Connecticut, railroad station.

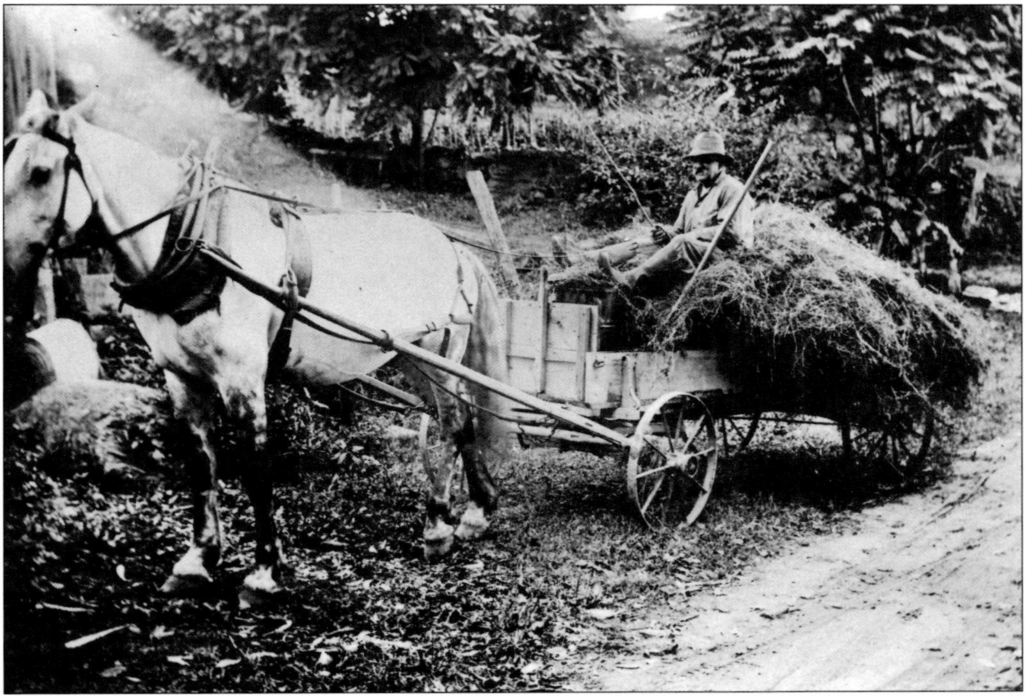

SNIFFIN FARM, HAULING HAY, EARLY 1900S. As early as 1914, George W. Sniffin owned a small North Castle farm that he called the Rock House Farm. He is shown here hauling hay to feed his farm animals.

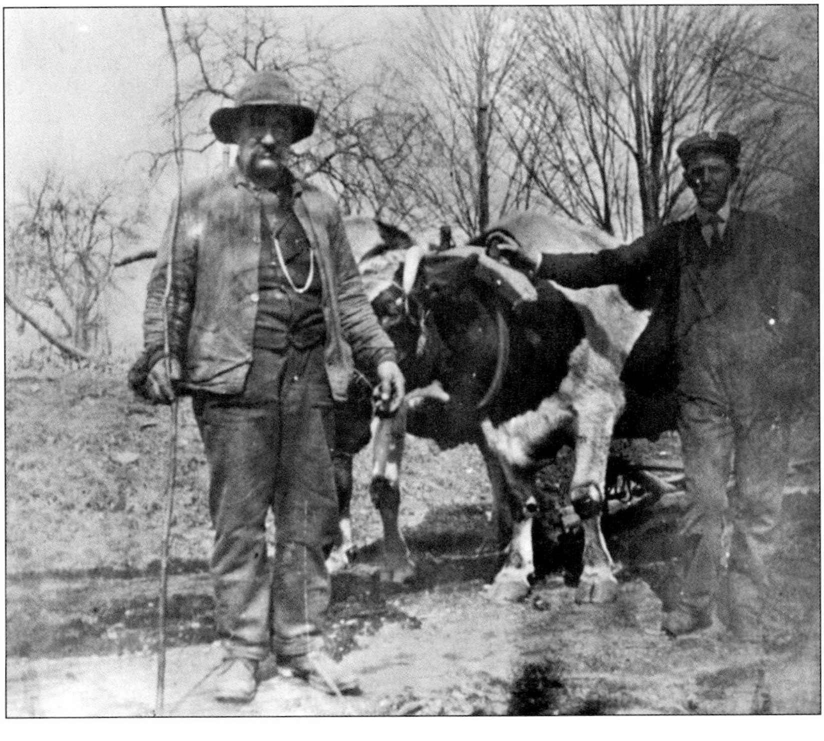

SNIFFIN FARM, A TEAM OF OXEN, EARLY 1900S. George W. and Stanley Sniffin (right) are shown with their team of oxen used to plow the fields on the farm.

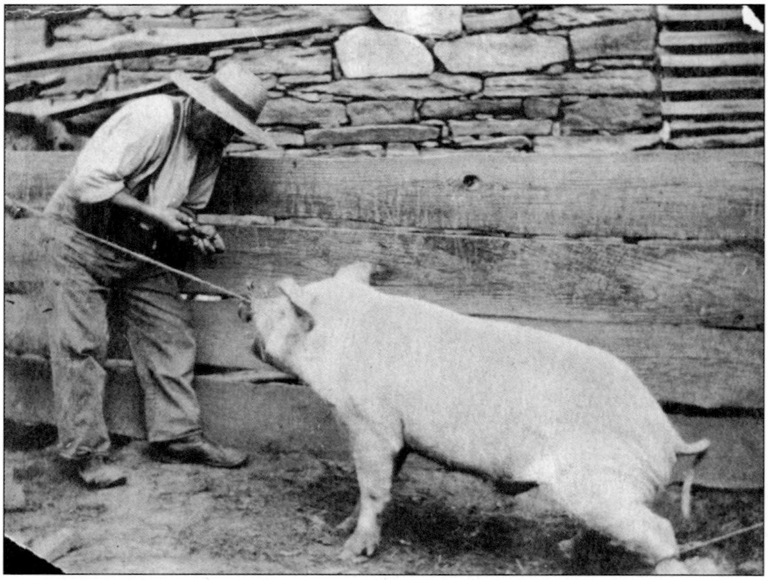

Sniffin Farm, Ringing a Hog, Early 1900s. George W. Sniffin is shown putting a nose ring in a hog. Nose rings were used to prevent hogs from rooting (digging with their snouts), which destroyed gardens and crops.

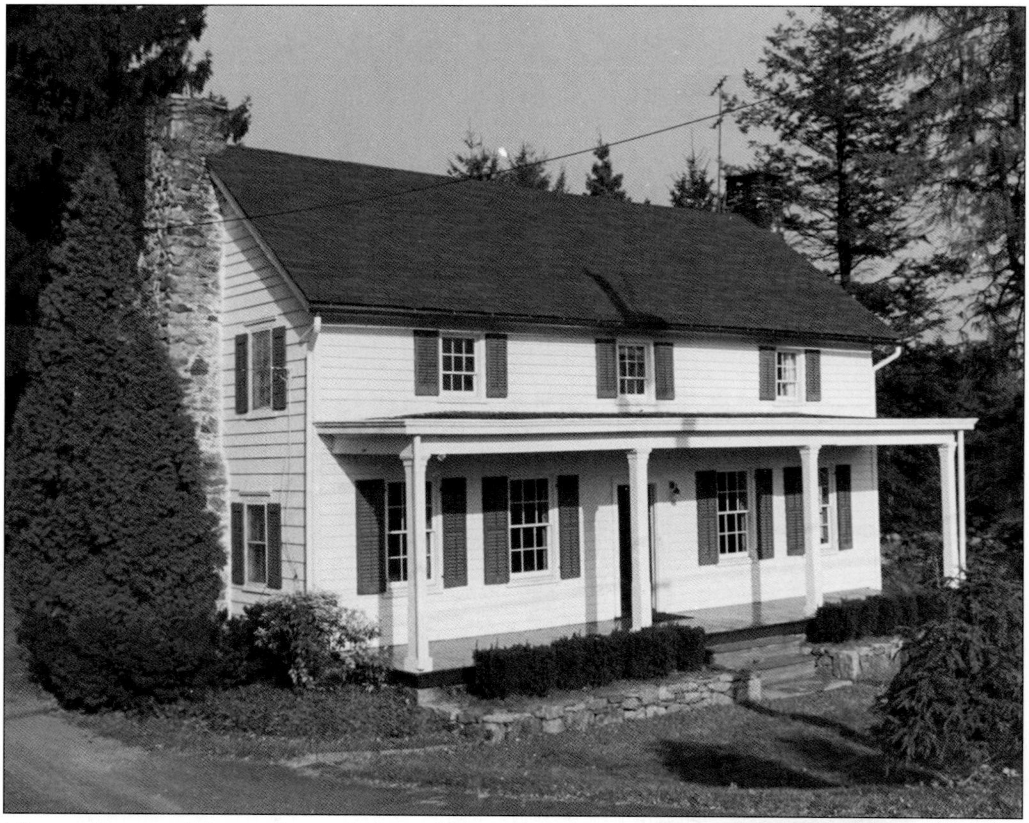

Mosses Quimby (Moses Quinby) Farm, Built before 1776. Mosses (as he signed his name) was North Castle's first recorded town clerk, serving from 1736 until 1741. A farm of about 160 acres during the American Revolution, some of the land at today's 82 Cox Avenue in Armonk was lost when Interstate 684 was constructed during the 1960s–1970s. Sold in 1797, the farm came back into the Quinby family in the mid-1850s.

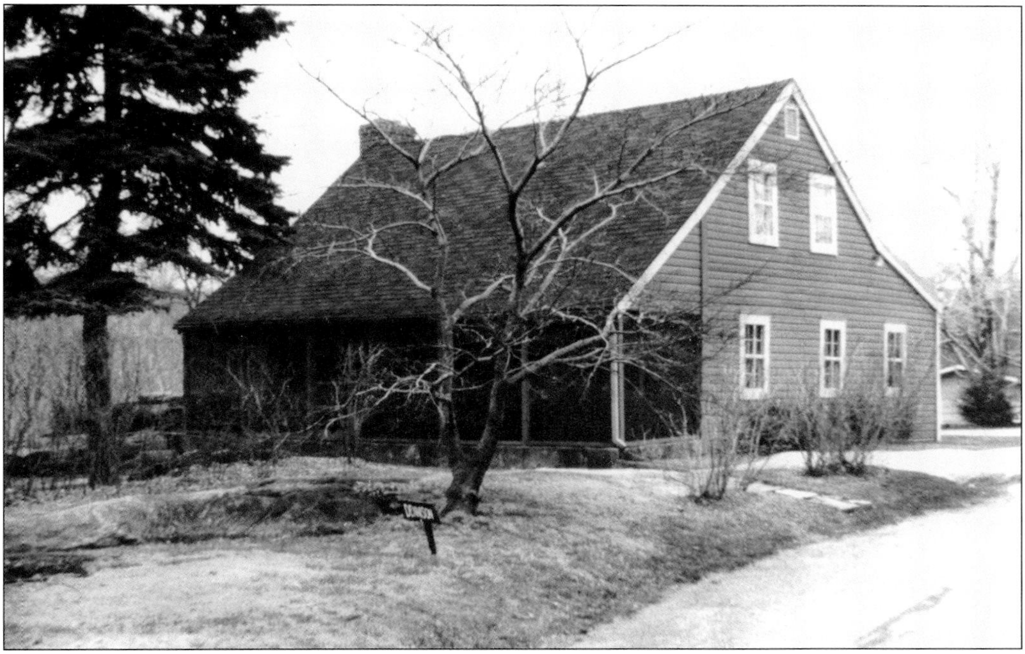

CHRISTOPHER ELIAS–DANIEL FEEKS FARM, BUILT IN THE LATE 1700S–EARLY 1800S. Elias, believed to be a deserter from the Hessian army during the Revolution, built a small two-room house on today's Banksville Road, Armonk. He farmed, prospered, and purchased land in small parcels. In 1815, he became a naturalized citizen. His daughter Ann married Daniel Feeks; their daughter Mary Feeks married Adam Shutts; their daughter Annie Shutts married John Bennett. All farmed here. The Bennetts' daughter Marjorie Dennison resided here.

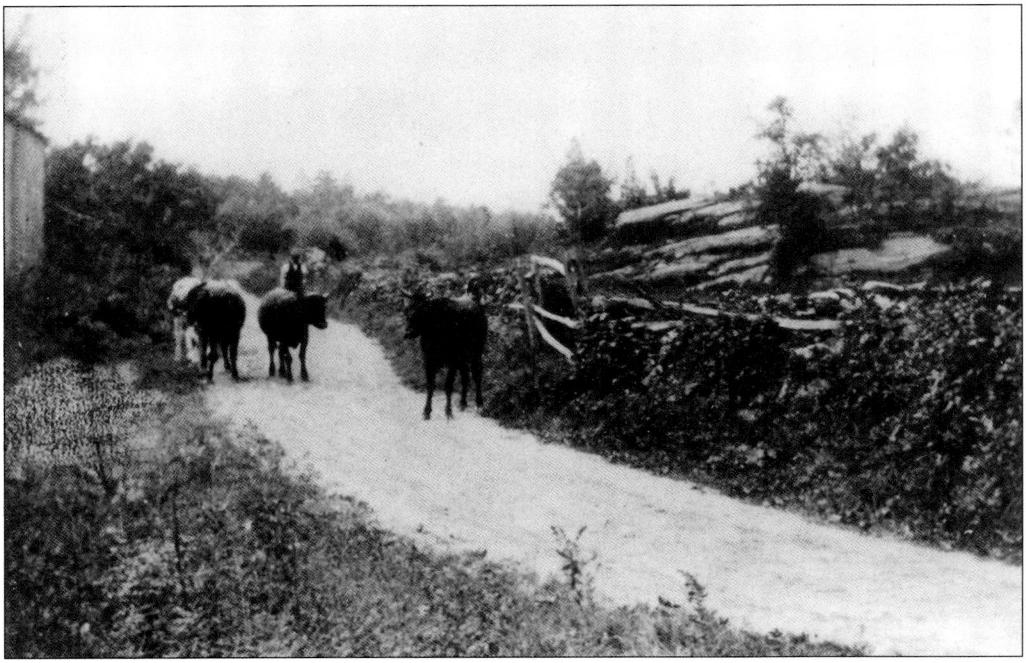

FARMER JOHN BENNETT, C. 1929. Bennett is shown driving his cows down an unpaved Banksville Road. He married Annie Shutts, a descendant of Christopher Elias and Daniel Feeks.

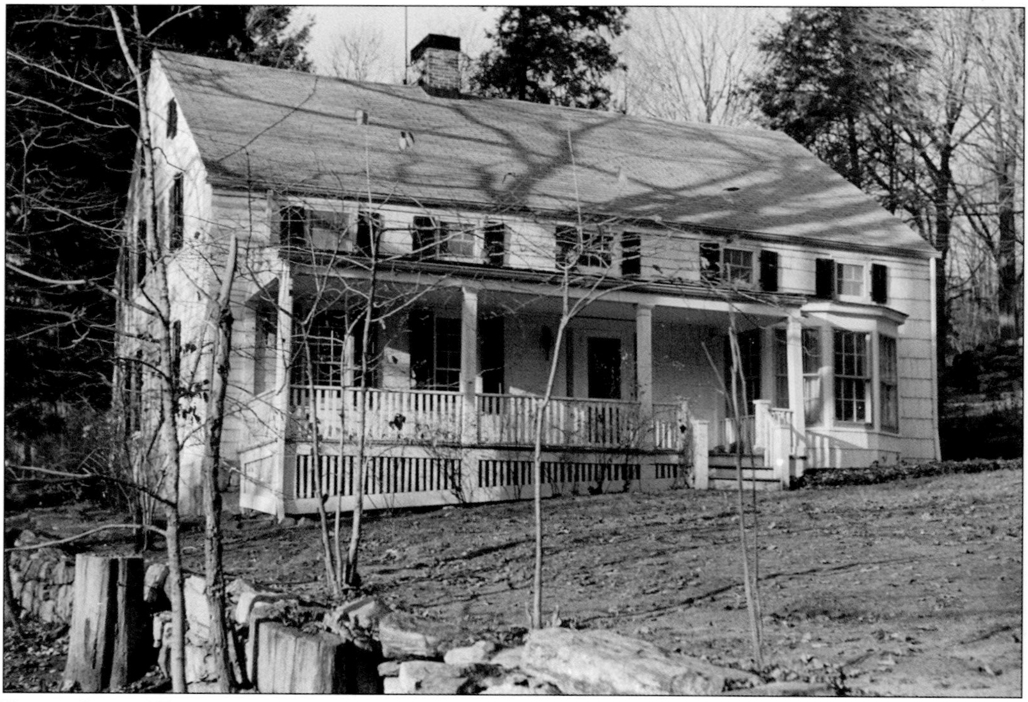

David Lane House, Dating to the Mid-1700s. David Lane served as town assessor as early as 1738. A 1762 surveyor's map shows 237 acres, "the road being deducted," and a 1779 tax list indicates the holdings of a prosperous farmer. The farm consisted of this main house, barns, stables, orchards, and meadows. On today's King Street, Armonk, the land was part of the original West Patent granted by King William III.

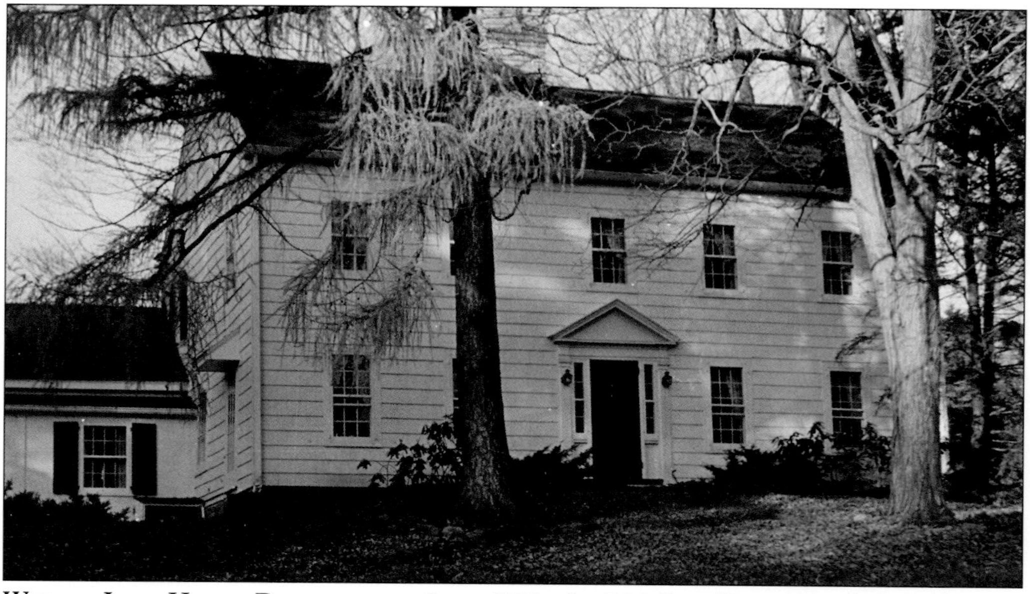

William Lane House, Dating to the Late 1700s. In 1826, David Lane gave the house and 90 acres to his son William for $5, reserving the right to store apples and use the cider mill. Later, this property on today's The Crossing in Armonk was owned by Charles Purdy and then his son Stephen, who was living here during his term as town supervisor from 1855 to 1860.

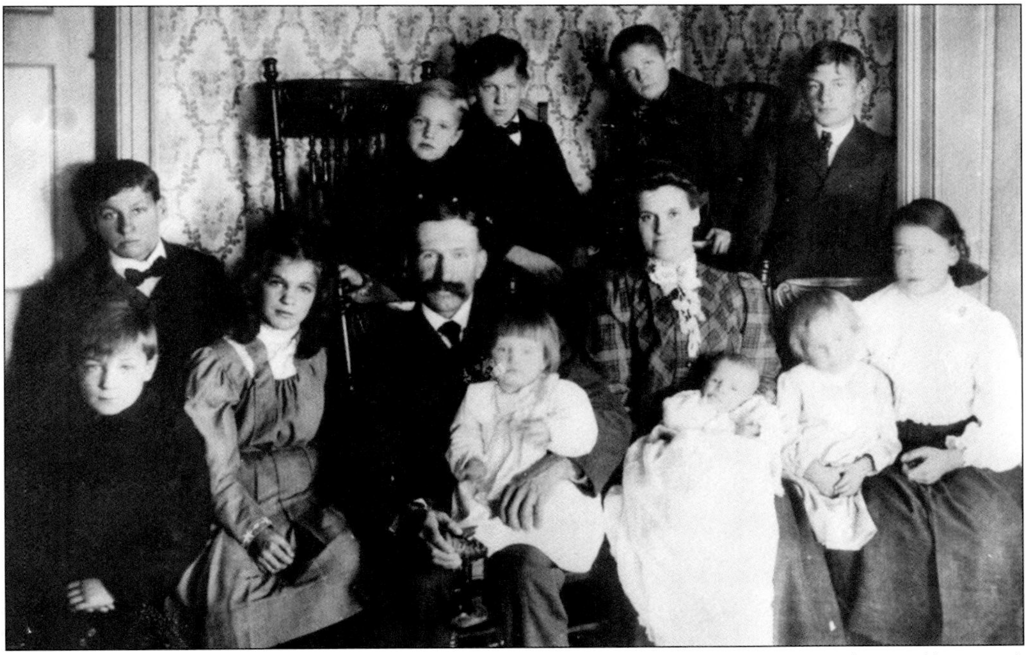

Albert H. and Nellie Husted Waterbury Family, c. 1907. From left to right are (first row) Nathan, Harry, Matilda, Albert (father), Frank, Nellie (mother), George, Elizabeth, and Helen; (second row) William, Abram, Albert Jr., and Horace. Albert's High View Dairy Farm encompassed about 188 acres on the west side of today's Whippoorwill Road near Half Mile Road in Armonk. He sold in 1916, and shortly thereafter, the home burned and the outbuildings fell into disrepair.

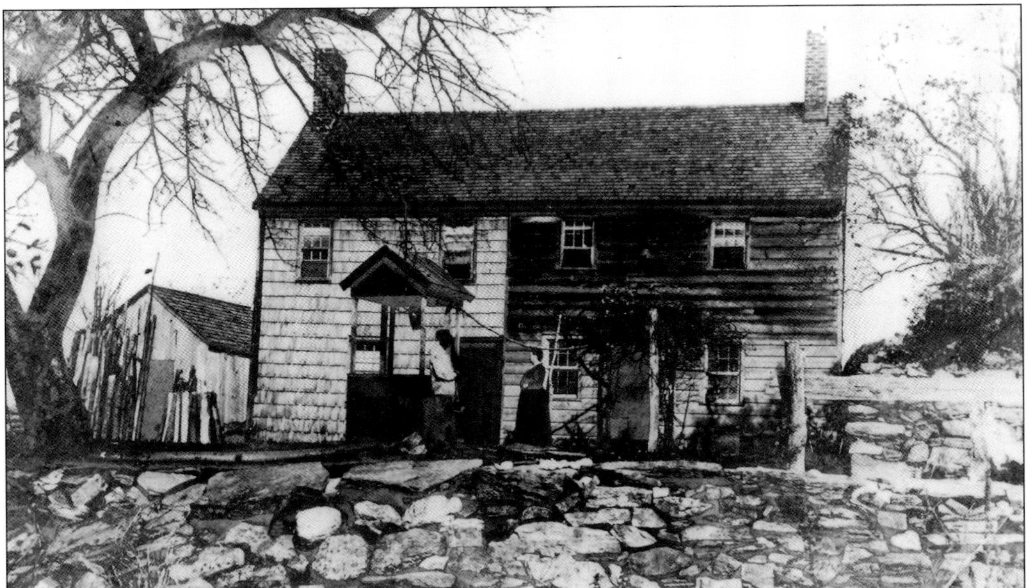

Martin Remsen Farm, Early 1900s. This farmhouse, with two front doors, doubled in size with the addition on the left. Note the water well in the front yard, the barn to the left, and an unidentified man and woman to the right of the well. Rachel Remsen died about 1951, her husband Martin Remsen in 1956. With another addition, this house stands on today's Devoe Road in Armonk.

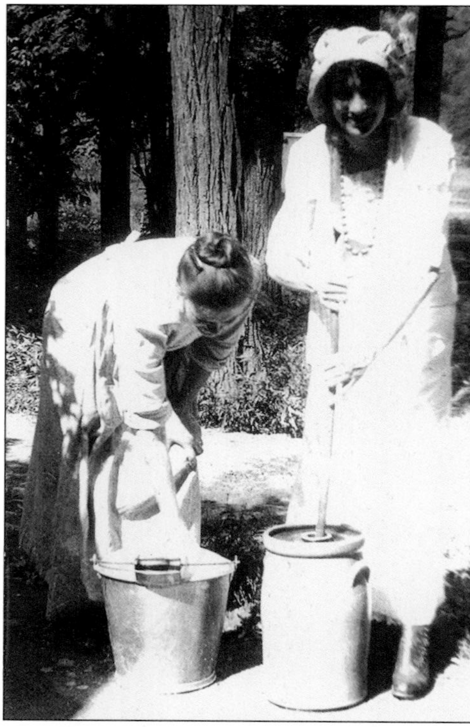

Churning Butter, Edith and Matilda Johnson, Early 1900s. First the cows were milked. After the milk was cooled and stored overnight, the cream was skimmed off the top. By agitating the cream in the churn, Edith and Matilda made fresh butter, and buttermilk remained in the churn.

Widow Banks House, Dating to the Mid-1700s. This house goes back to one of the earliest families in the Middle Patent: the family of Samuel Banks, who was buried in 1743. Deborah, the widow of Samuel Jr., who died in 1773, lived in this house during the Revolution, hence its name. Built as a "half house," the upstairs ceilings of the second half have adjusted heights in order to make the roof line even. The stone wall, built with the help of oxen, remains noteworthy today. The house stands today at 1 Banks Farm Road in Bedford.

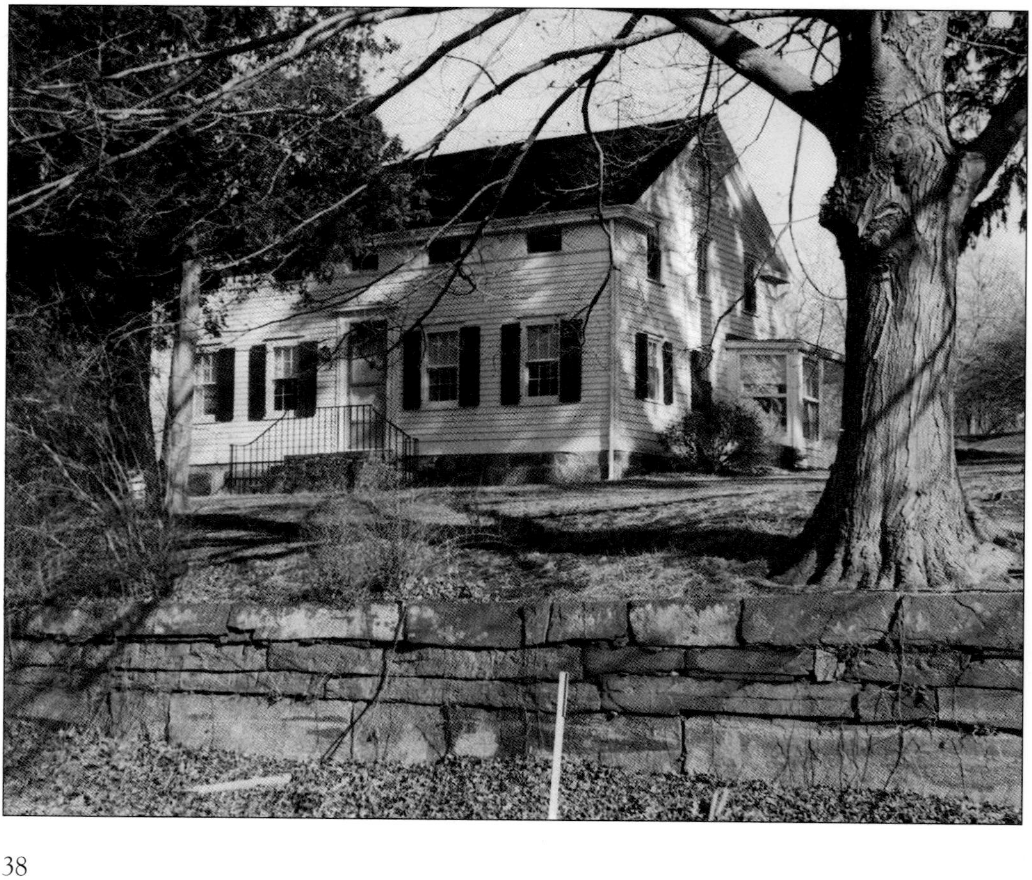

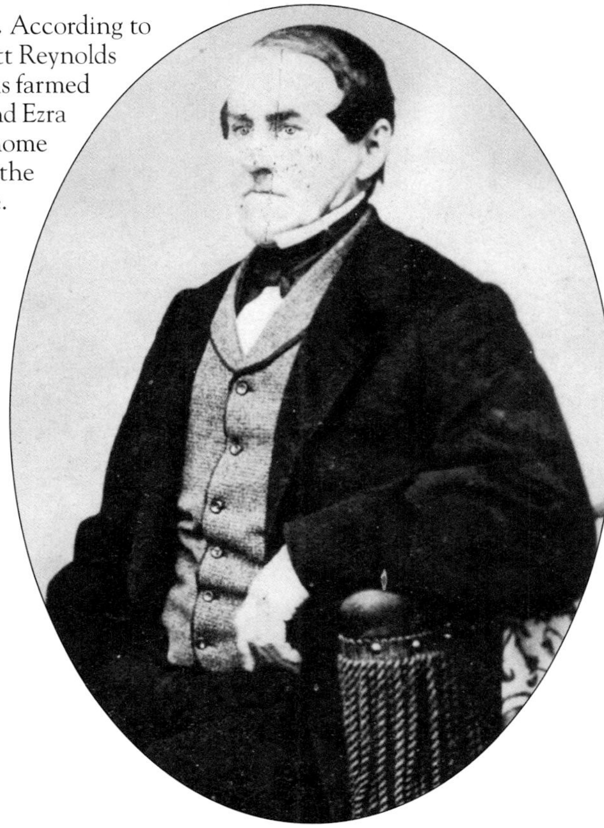

EZRA FOUNTAIN BANKS (1807–1880). According to a genealogical report written by Everett Reynolds Close Jr. in 1975, Ezra and Hester Banks farmed on today's Bedford-Banksville Road, and Ezra built an impressive stone wall at his home from rocks chiseled out of a ledge in the woods and brought by oxen to the site.

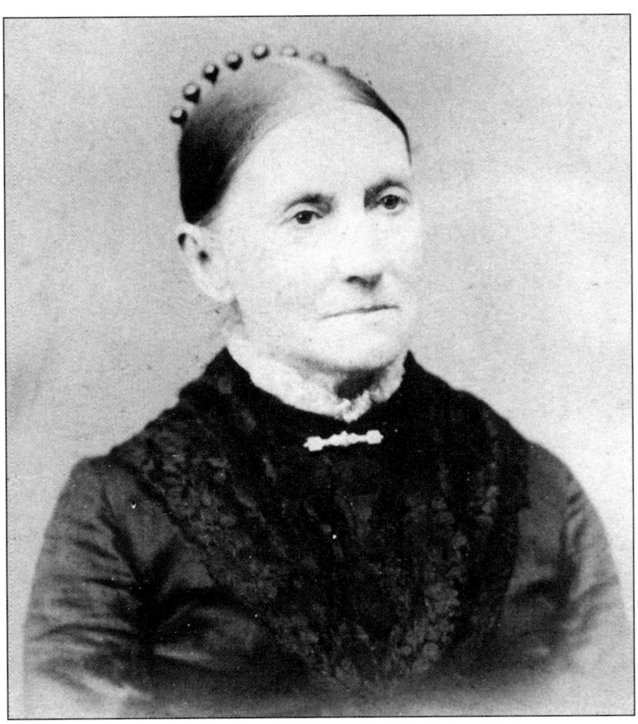

HESTER BRUNDAGE BANKS (1809–1889). Hester was a daughter of David and Elizabeth Lockwood Brundage and the wife of Ezra Banks. Granddaughter Jane Smith Close, who died in 1957, wrote that as a girl Hester did not eat tomatoes, as she thought they were poison.

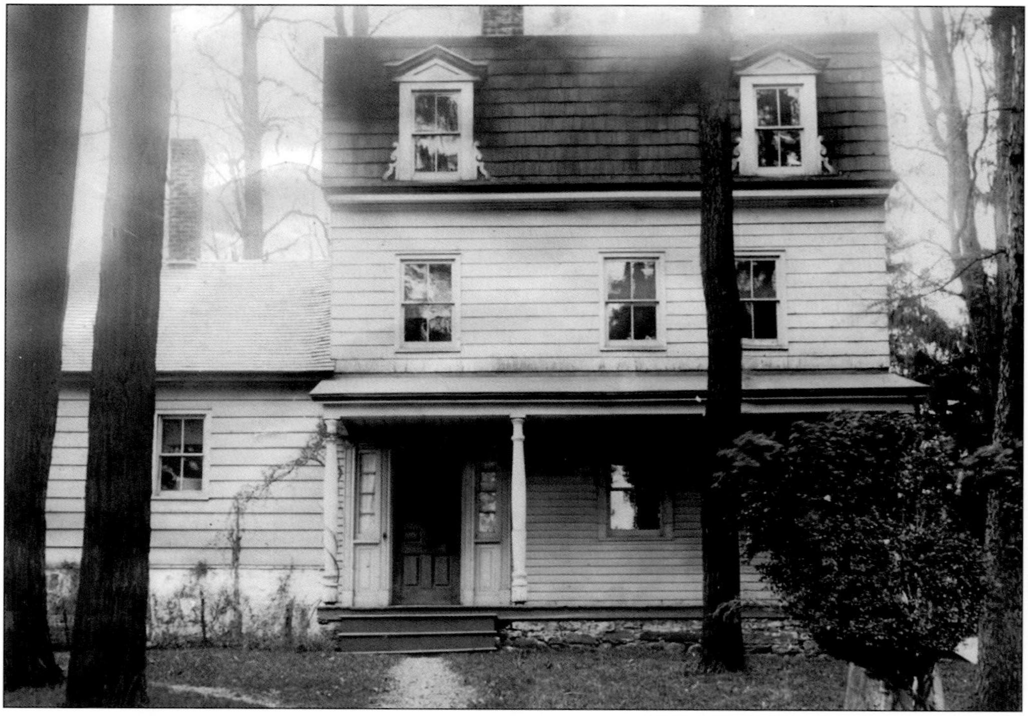

Eden Hunt Farm, Dating to the Early 1800s. The Hunt farm, on today's Old Mount Kisco Road, Armonk, was next to the Townsend holdings. Eden Hunt was the village grocer. He married Sarah A. Haight. Their daughter Elisabeth K. Hunt married Samuel O. Townsend (1821–1891), who consolidated the Hunt and Townsend farms when Eden died in 1843. Joseph Wago lived here in 1944. Joseph and Elizabeth Wago Sr. moved here in the 1920s.

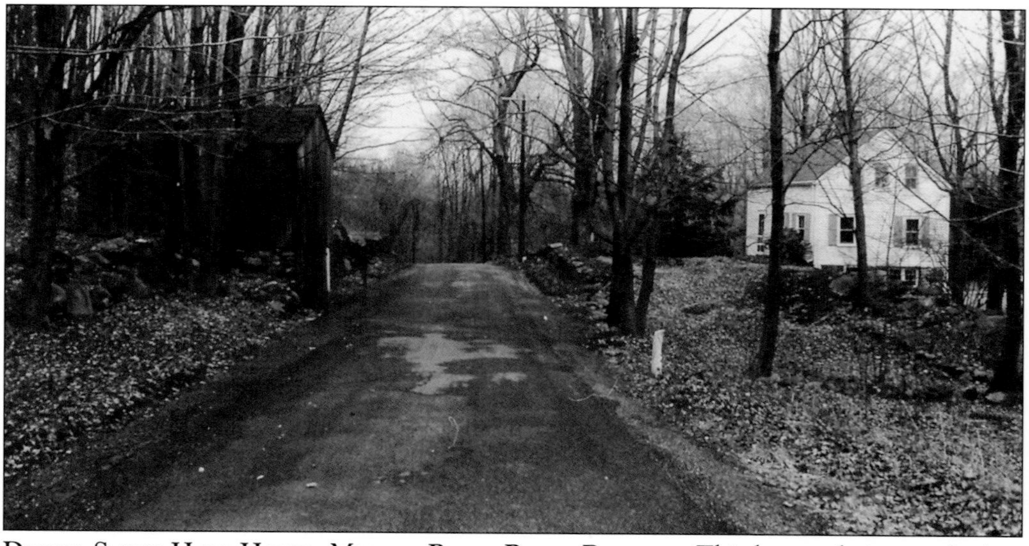

Daniel Smith Half House, Mianus River Road, Bedford. This house, dating to the late 1700s, embodies the town's small, unpretentious farming roots. In 1816, Daniel Smith deeded the farm of about 150 acres to his son, Daniel L. Smith. George Hall, who died in 1933, lived here. Later, Lucia Turner Faithful owned it. Jean-Paul Valles faithfully restored it in 2007 and donated it with about three acres to the Mianus Gorge Preserve.

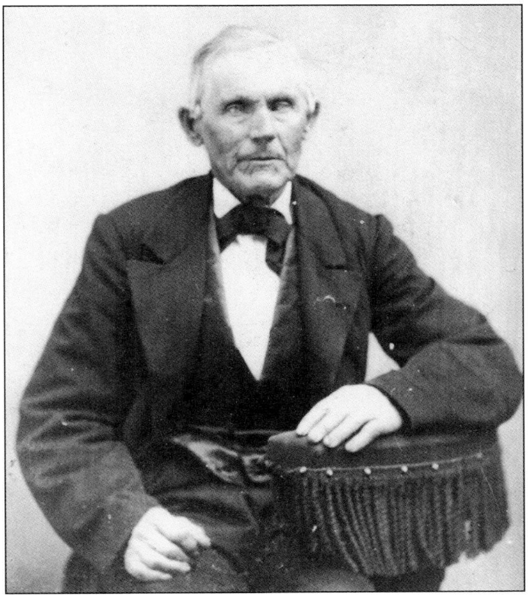

Farmer Walter Banks (1798–1882). Banks was affiliated with the large Jay farm in Bedford, which had been inherited by the son of John Jay, the great statesman and first chief justice of the US Supreme Court. Banks married Mary Dayton. His granddaughter Ella, daughter of David Clausen Banks and Sarah Ann Field, married William Sutherland Finch of the Finch's Country Store family in Banksville.

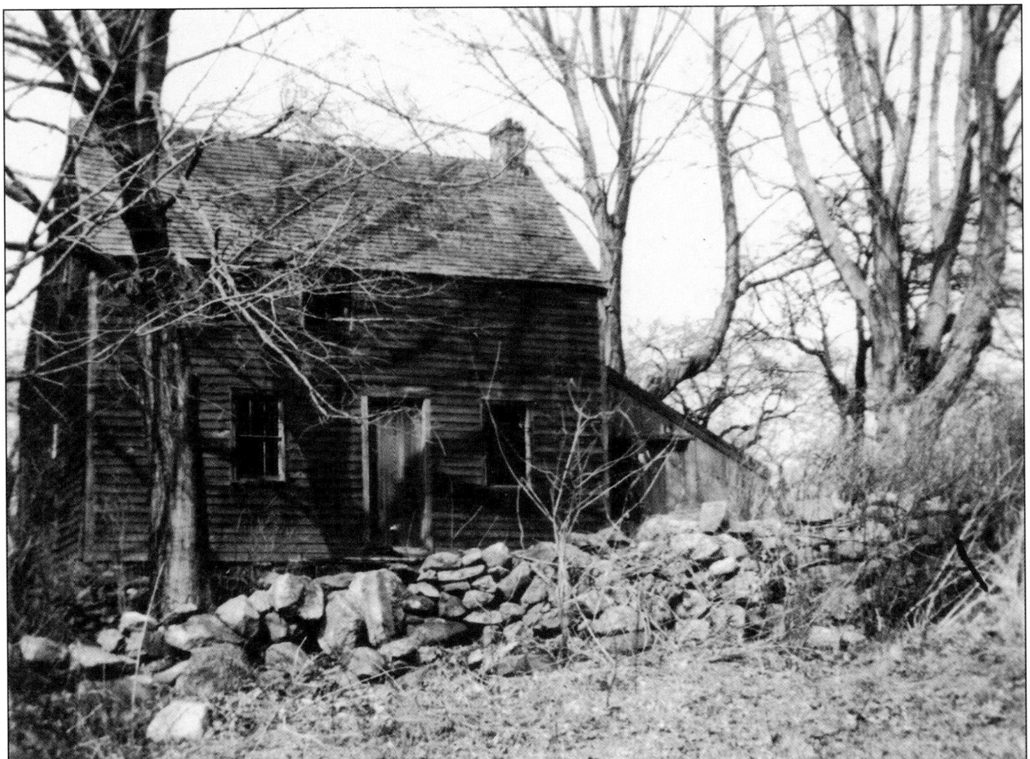

Hiram Lounsbury Farm, Dating to the Early 1800s, Bedford. This early salt-box farmhouse is typical of a less prosperous farmer. Jessop Reynolds, who died insolvent, owned the farm in 1822. His administrator sold to David Hobby Jr. (1768–1829), who rented the farm to others. When Hobby died, his son-in-law Samuel P. Smith bought it for speculation. In 1844, Smith sold to Hiram Lounsbury (1797–1872), who lived there until his death. The farmhouse was torn down in 1985.

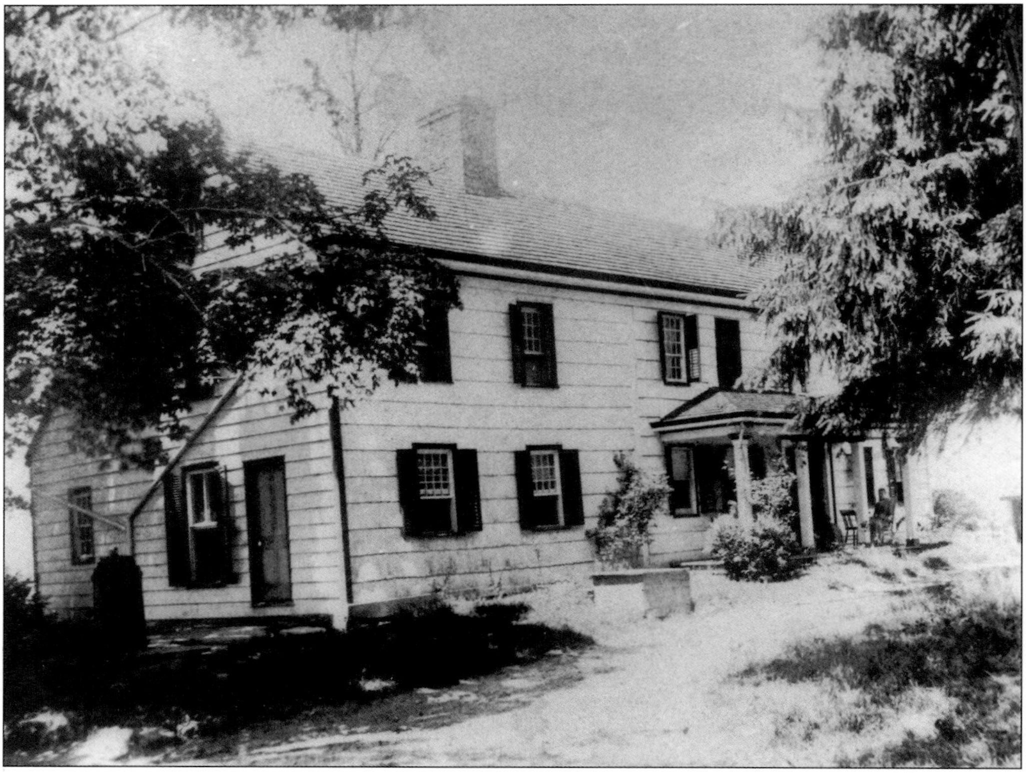

ROBERT FIELD FARM, DATING TO THE EARLY 1800S. The Field farm was located in the extreme southeastern portion of North Castle, within sight of the shores of Big Rye Pond. Field (1769–1836) was a well-to-do Quaker farmer and commissioner of highways for North Castle from 1823 to 1828 and 1830 to 1834. In later years, Daniel Tripp owned this farm.

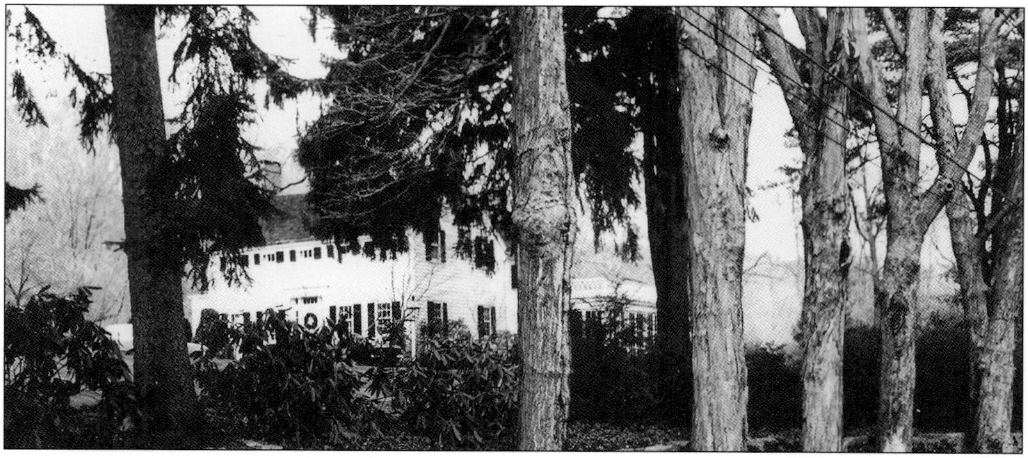

HOBBY HILL FARM, BEDFORD. When Albert Hobby died in 1911, estate records listed "3 young cattle, 8 cows, 2 pair oxen, 2 horses, 4 wagons, 5 pigs, 50 chickens, miscellaneous farming implements and 400 gallons of vinegar." This pre-Revolutionary farmhouse, boasting eight fireplaces, is on today's Mianus River Road. Jonathan Finch, Jehial Worden, and Stephen Worden all owned the farm before Hobby.

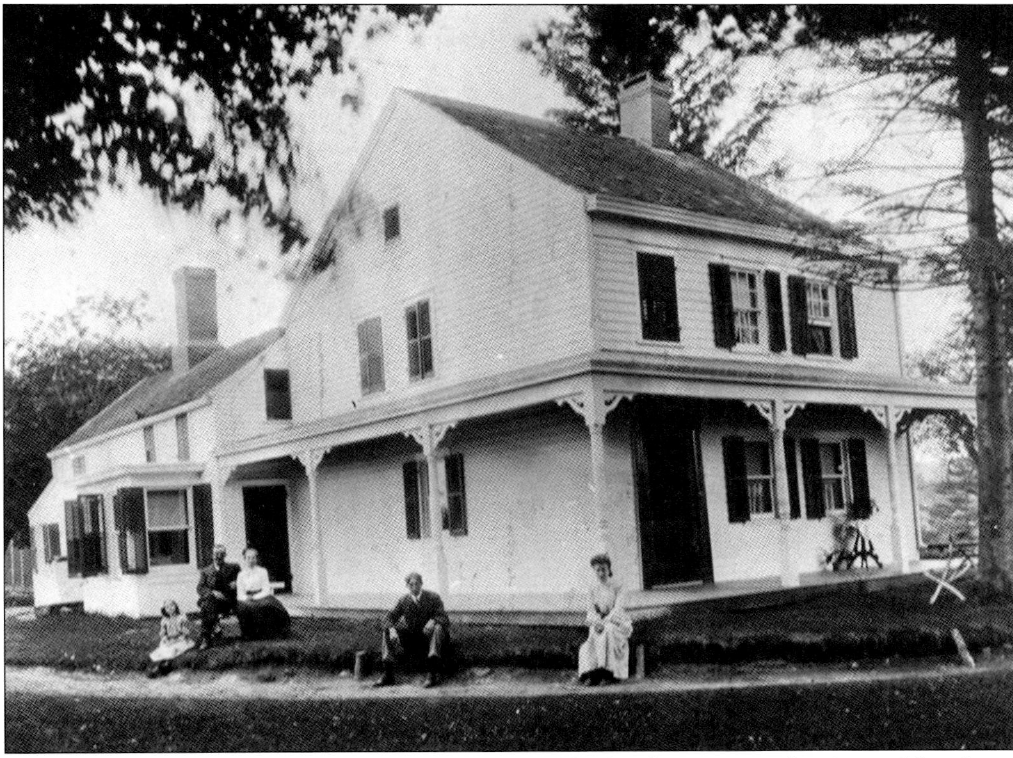

Abram Smith Hopkins House, c. 1905. Members of the family are pictured in front of their home Fair View, also called Pleasant View, which stood on the hill above present-day Byram Brook Place on the east side of today's Route 22 in Armonk. From left to right are daughter Gertrude Hopkins, born 1896; father A. Smith Hopkins, born 1852; mother Anna Maria (Flewellin) Hopkins, born 1855; son Niles Smith Hopkins, born 1882; and daughter Eulaila Hopkins, born 1888.

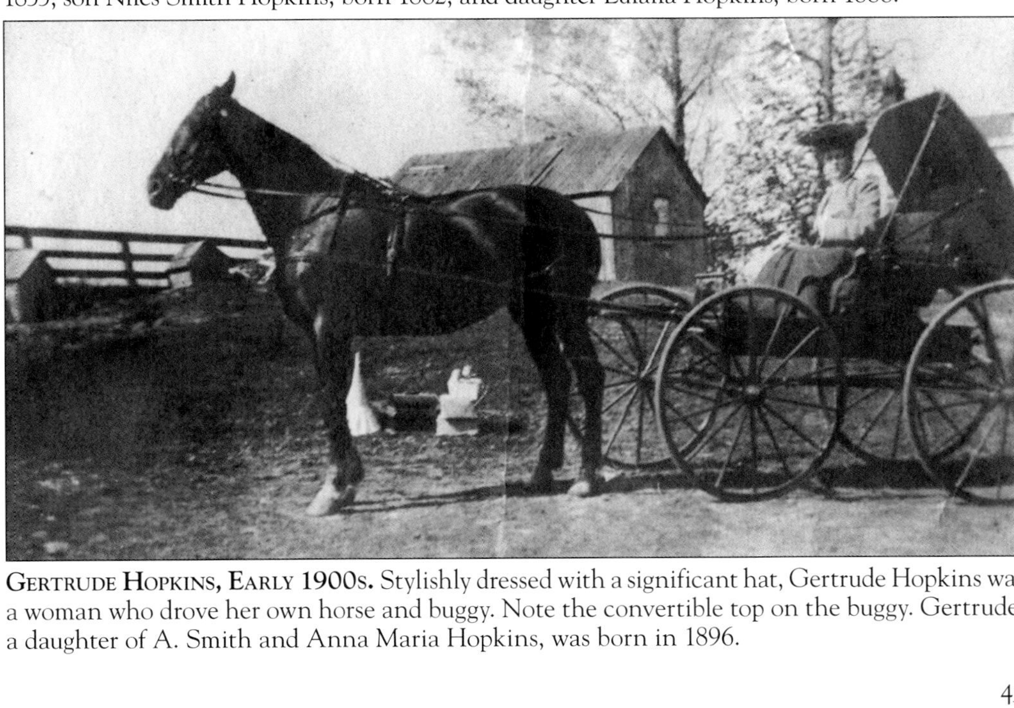

Gertrude Hopkins, Early 1900s. Stylishly dressed with a significant hat, Gertrude Hopkins was a woman who drove her own horse and buggy. Note the convertible top on the buggy. Gertrude, a daughter of A. Smith and Anna Maria Hopkins, was born in 1896.

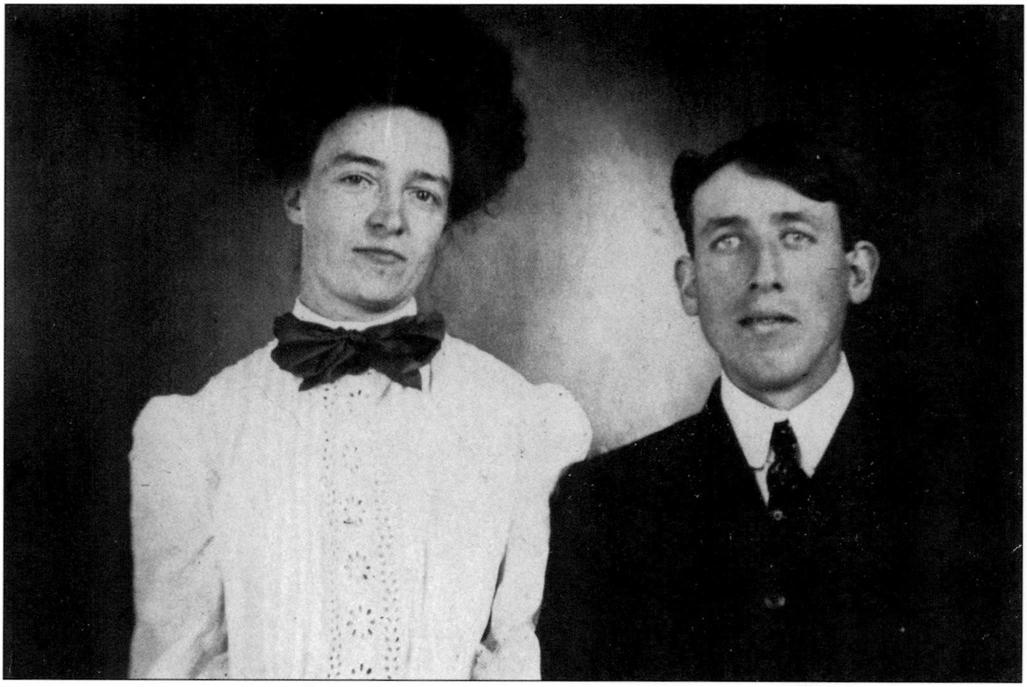

Niles and Kathryn (Kate) Ryan Hopkins, Early 1900s. Niles, son of A. Smith and Anna Maria Hopkins, died in 1949. He was a realtor and insurance broker. He and his wife, Kate, had two children, Marguerite (1915–2002) and James (Jimmy) Daniel (1912–1996), who was a noted lawyer, town supervisor, county legislator, and New York Supreme Court justice.

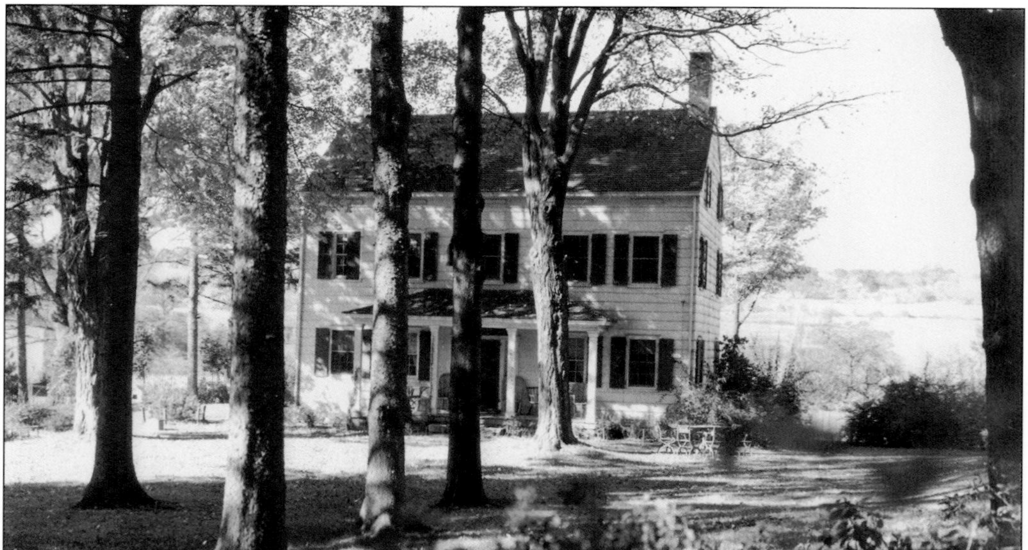

Benoni Platt Farm, Dating to c. 1760. The back and right wing are later additions. Platt served as captain in the 2nd Regiment, Westchester County Militia, under the command of Col. Thomas Thomas. He also owned grist and sawmills located just south of this farm, both on the present Bedford-Banksville Road, Bedford. Later, the Samuel Knapp, Emmet Smith, and Percy Limburg families lived here.

William Emmet Smith (1849–1924). According to a family genealogy by Everett Reynolds Close Jr., Emmet and his wife, Amanda, moved to the Benoni Platt House in the late 1870s. They called their home The Pines and raised pigs, chickens, and cows. They grew rye and buckwheat and kept a large vegetable garden.

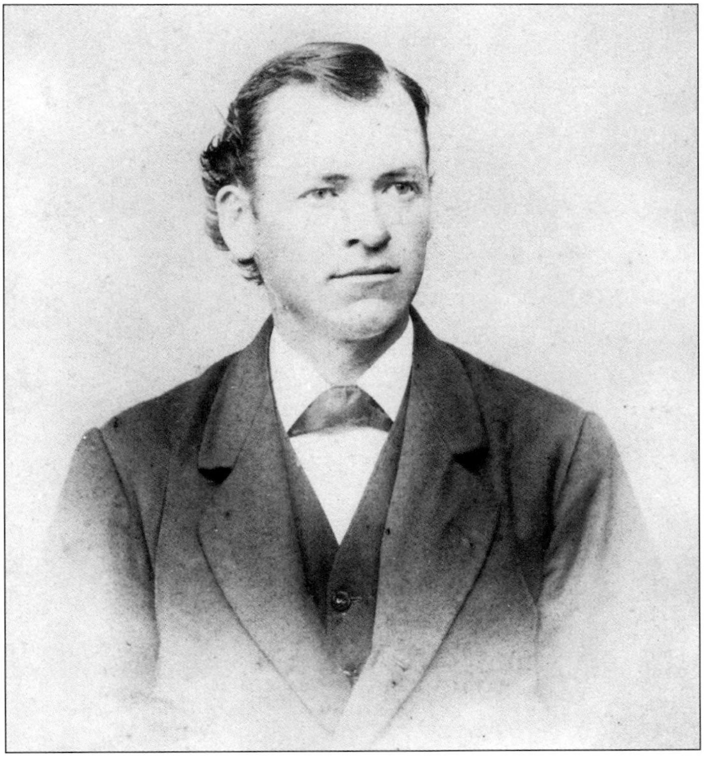

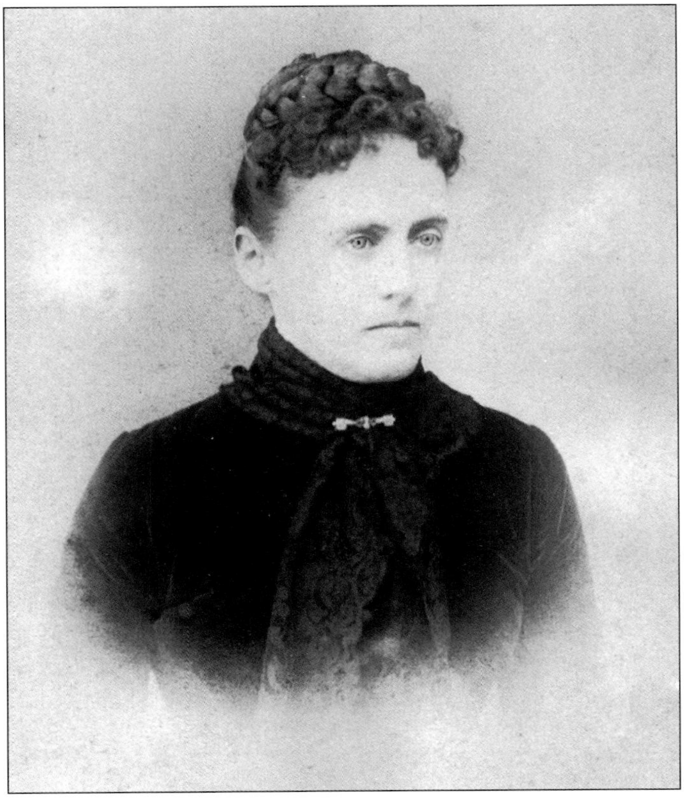

Amanda Jane Banks Smith (1845–1924). Amanda was a noted artist and also authored the *Grandma Country Life Stories for the Children*. She married William Emmet Smith.

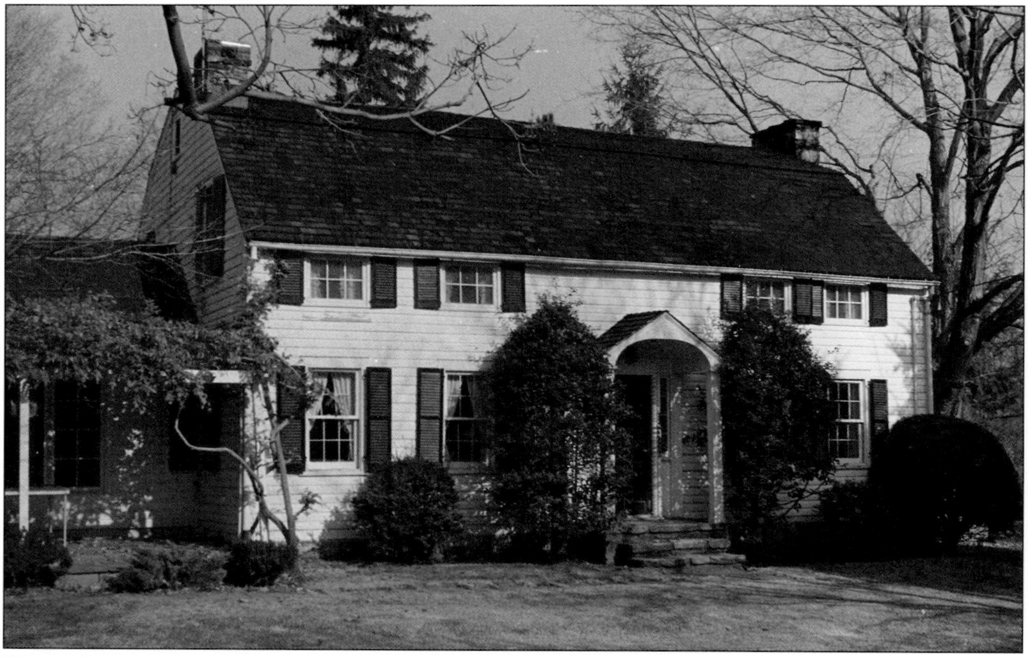

Winus Palmer Farm, Dating to the Late 1770s. Winus Palmer lived on this farm on today's Round Hill Road, Armonk, in 1787. His son Gideon farmed here until his death in 1878. Next it passed to William Biddolph, who was the last to farm the property. Several owners and real estate companies owned the property thereafter. It was probably once a half house, and another part was added exactly matching the first half.

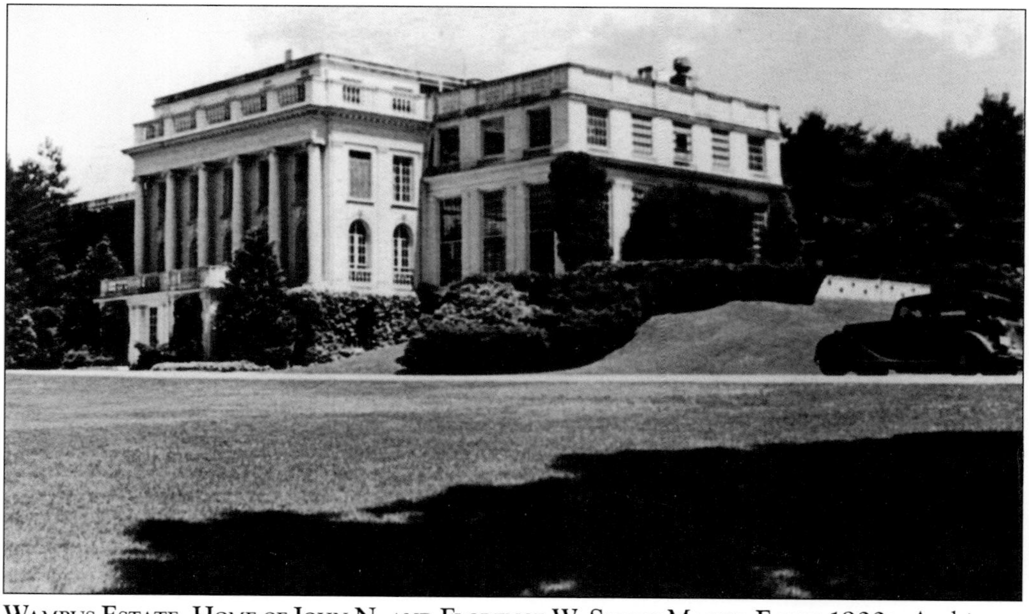

Wampus Estate, Home of John N. and Florence W. Seeley Magee, Early 1900s. Architects Whitney Warren and Charles D. Wetmore, who helped design Grand Central Station in New York, designed the residence, garage, and gate lodge in 1907. Overlooking Wampus Pond, the 250-acre estate consisted of a 27-room residence, five cottages, a greenhouse, and a farm building. Eldon Bisbee destroyed the mansion in 1937 and later sold the property to the Labriola family.

Wampus Estate, Garden View. This view of one of the gardens shows the trellis wing with a large decorative figure above a large window. The outdoor dining area, bordered by tulips and boxwood, is seen at lower left. A statue appears behind the marble bench with carved figures on the supports.

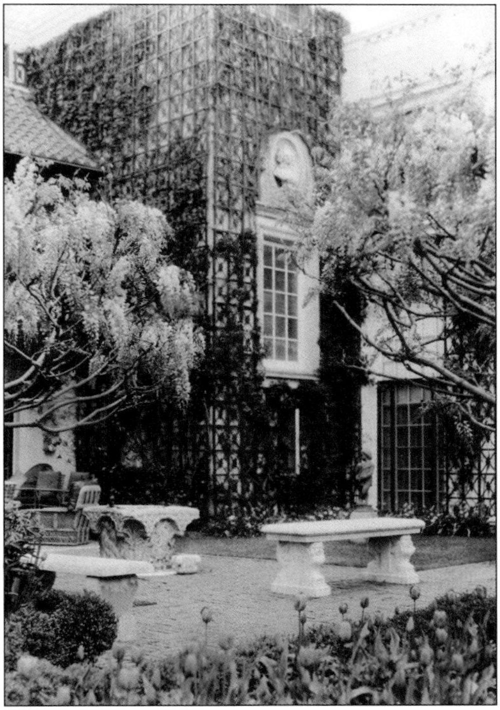

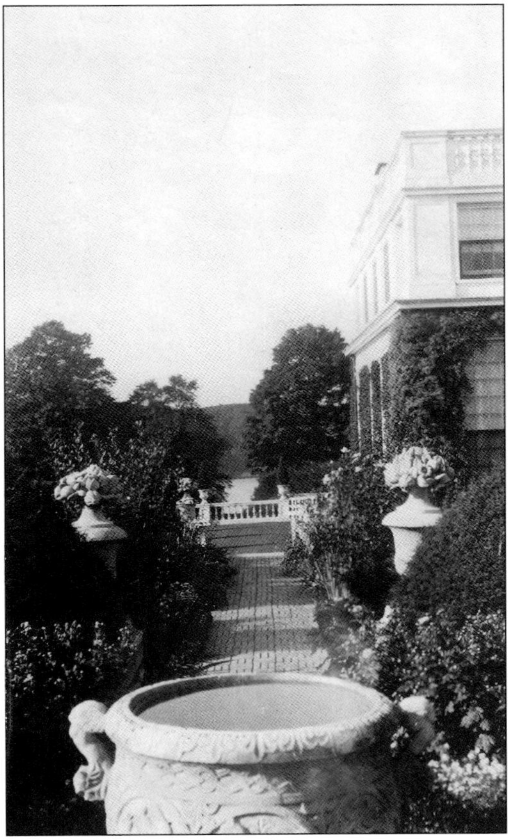

Wampus Estate, Italian Gardens with View of Wampus Pond. Robert Pippet and members of the Farquhar, Ferris, and Ringwood families were employed on the estate. Their houses were on Whippoorwill Road, Armonk, and now are part of the Whippoorwill Club property. The brick path led to an overlook of Wampus Pond (center).

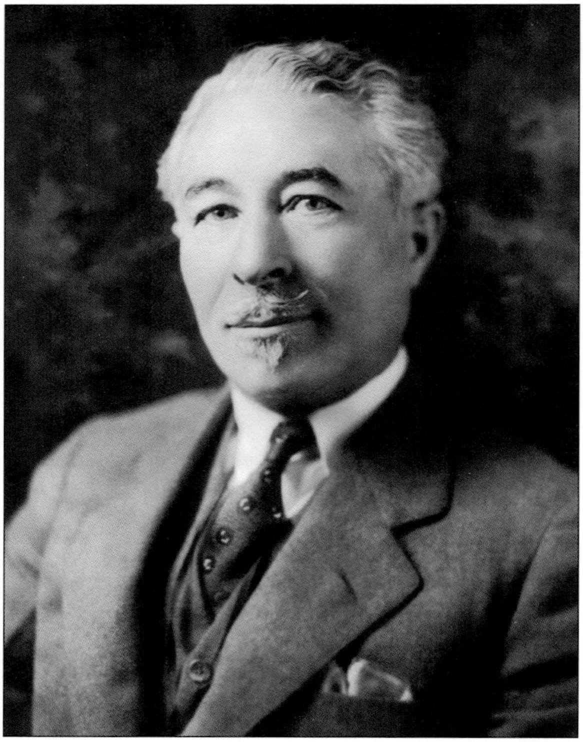

Dr. Charles V. Paterno, Early 1900s. In 1921, Vanderbilt Avenue Realty Corporation, with Paterno as president, purchased about 260 acres from Arrow Holding Corporation, with Frederick Brown as president. The acres had been Elijah Watt Sells's North Castle Farm, and before Sells's ownership, the property had been the farms of Norman Lander, William Eugene Rich, Enoch Sniffin, Will Biddolph, and Jennie B. Moody.

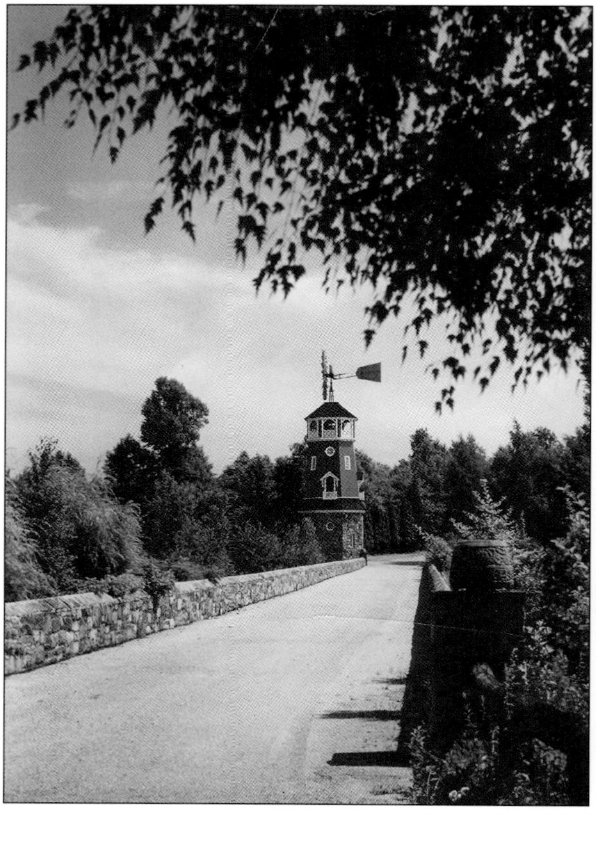

Windmill Farm, Mid-1900s. Paterno planted evergreen seedlings and sold Christmas trees. He acquired more land and added large new dams, creating four beautiful artificial lakes, and built a boathouse, new wells and working windmills, farm buildings, bridle trails, and miles of stone walls. Son Carlo subdivided, built a water system and roads, and established Windmill Farm Inc., which he sold in 1954 after constructing about 60 houses. Windmill images symbolize the community and its club.

Four

STANDS AND STORES

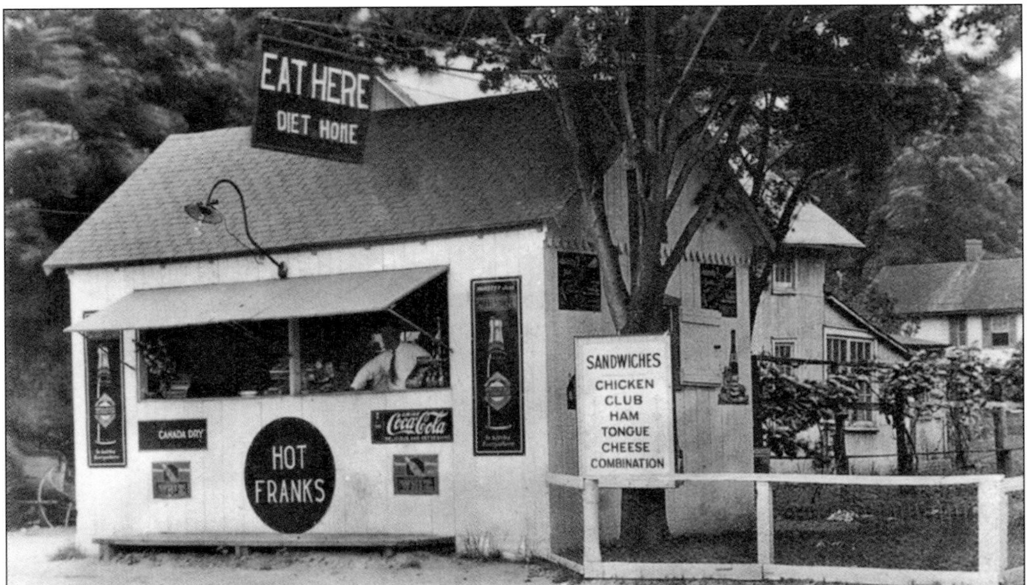

BROOKER'S MAPLE SHADE, MID-1930S. Fred Brooker operated this little wooden food stand during the 1930s. It stood facing Main Street in front of today's 410 Main Street, Armonk. The sign at top center reading "Eat Here, Diet Home" quickly came to be read as "Eat Here, Die at Home." Relative Mae Brooker ran Old Town Tavern next door.

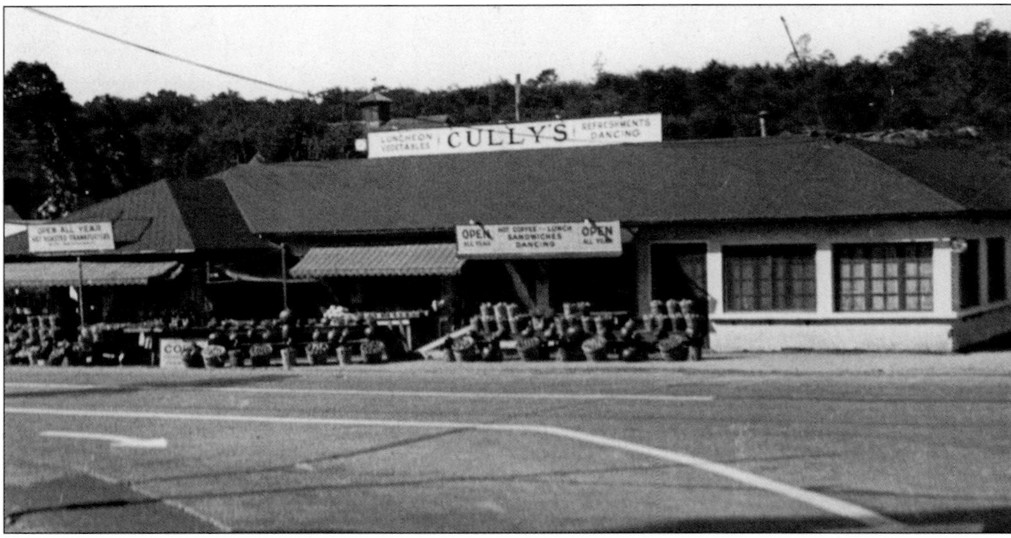

CULLY'S IN ARMONK, 1931. This farm produce stand also offered dancing and refreshments and was open all year. Constantine Filardi donated this 1931 photograph to the historical society.

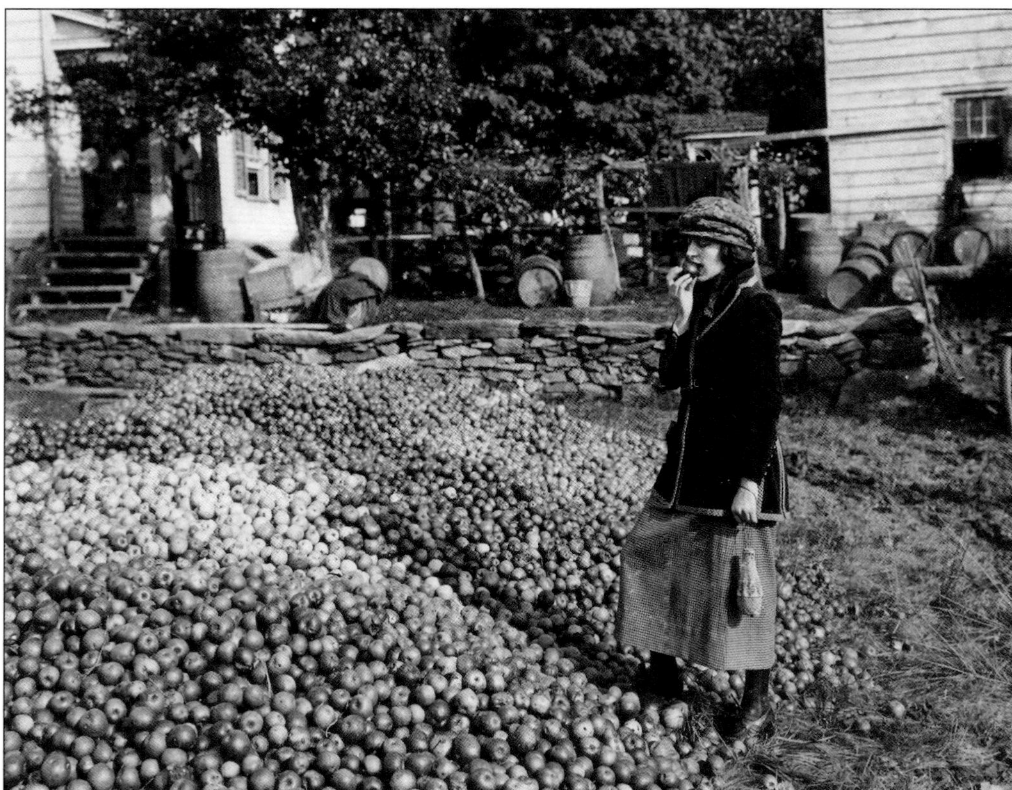

RAVEN'S CORNER, ARMONK, SELLING APPLES, EARLY 1900S. When Julius A. Raven's family farm and hotel were sold for Kensico Reservoir, he moved to Armonk and operated this produce stand in front of his home and restaurant. The nicely dressed young woman sampling the apple is unidentified. Today's Bedford Road and Main Street intersection, this dirt-road corner was later known as Kromer's, Miles Corner, and Olive Branch.

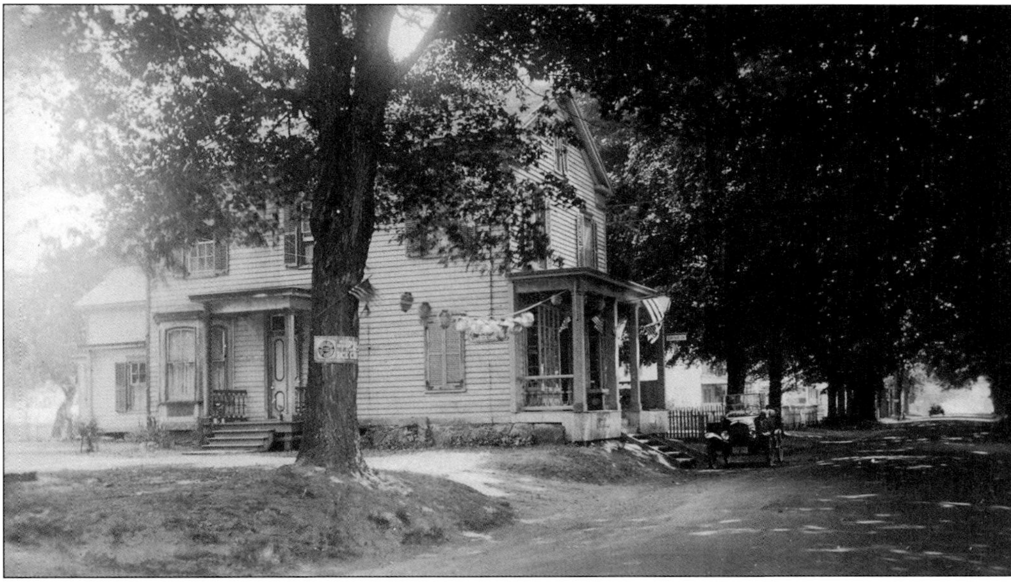

RAVEN'S CORNER, ARMONK, HOUSE AND RESTAURANT, EARLY 1900S. Raven was town assessor from 1917 to 1919 and town justice from 1931 to 1970. His office was in his home. He reportedly married over 6,000 couples. Sherman Billingsley, the owner of the famous Stork Club in New York City, is said to have sent couples—including baseball legend Dixie Walker and Estelle Shea—to Judge Raven in Armonk. Raven died on October 6, 1976.

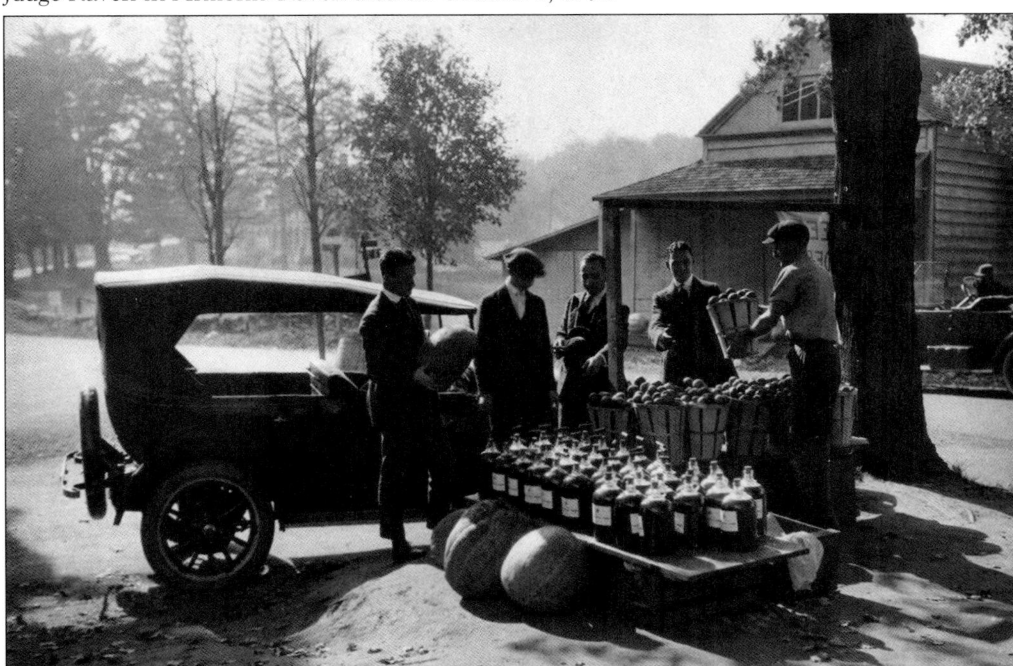

RAVEN'S CORNER, ARMONK, CIDER, APPLES, AND PUMPKINS, C. 1920. Although the patrons are unidentified, Raven is shown handing a basket of apples to a customer. The produce stand and restaurant are behind the photographer. Shown across today's Main Street, about where Kent Place is today, is an old building from before 1850 that was a stagecoach stop, store, post office, and butcher shop. It was torn down in 1922.

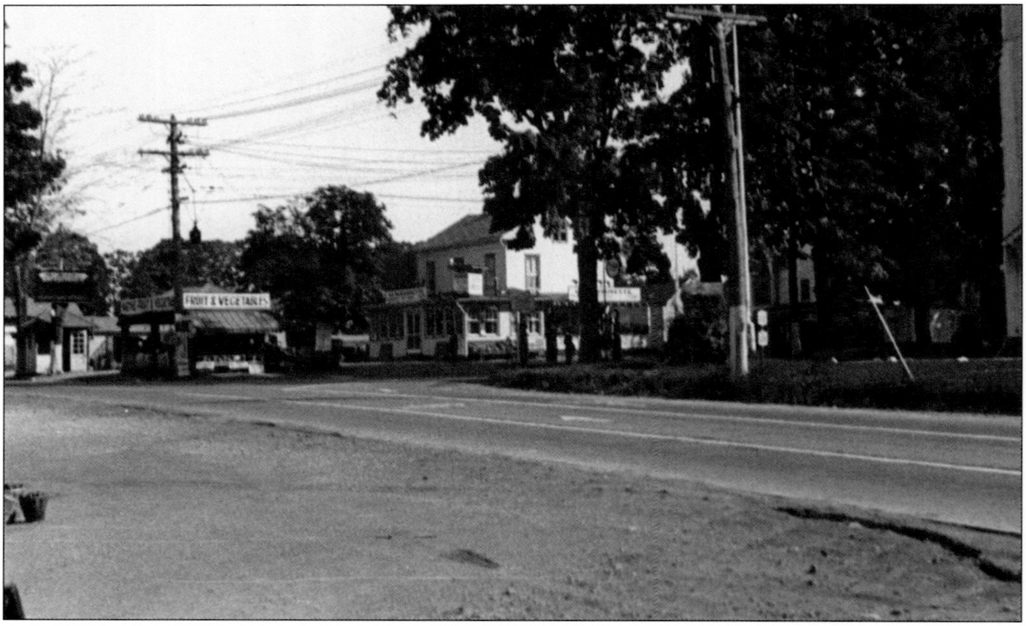

RAVEN'S TRIANGLE, ARMONK, 1929. Approaching today's Armonk village heading north, the restaurant and fruit and vegetable stand are seen in perspective. The front edge of the old Methodist church building shows on the right. By 1929, the road was paved, a closed front room had been added to the restaurant, and the intersection was renamed Raven's Triangle.

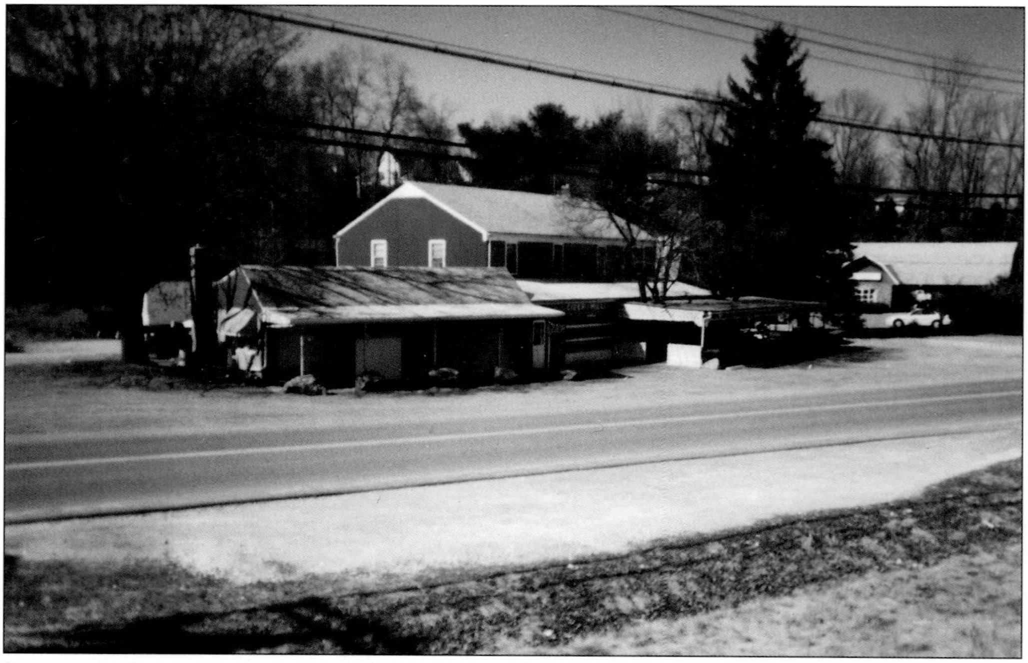

SCHULTZ'S CIDER MILL. A family business established in 1951 provided two rites of passage to every North Castle child: fresh-pressed cider in the fall and homemade donuts year-round. Parents Edwin and Mary, sons Bud and Donald, daughters Rosemary and Joan, Joan's husband, Peter, and Bud's wife, Ree, gave the community quality products and services and wonderful memories for 51 years from their stand on today's Old Route 22, Armonk.

SCHULTZ'S CIDER MILL, "LEAVE THE BAG OPEN." Fresh homemade donuts were cooked and conveyed to delivery behind a glass wall and were available in three flavors: plain, cinnamon, or powdered for $5 a dozen, and purchasers were limited to a dozen. Customers were warned to "Leave the bag open."

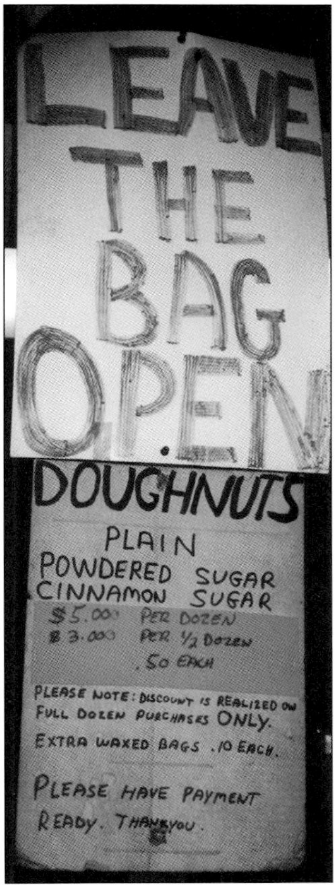

SCHULTZ'S CIDER MILL, CLOSING DAY PARTY, 2002. An Armonk tradition for more than half a century closed in March 2002. Cider Mill, a gated development of 27 houses and townhouses, was built on the property.

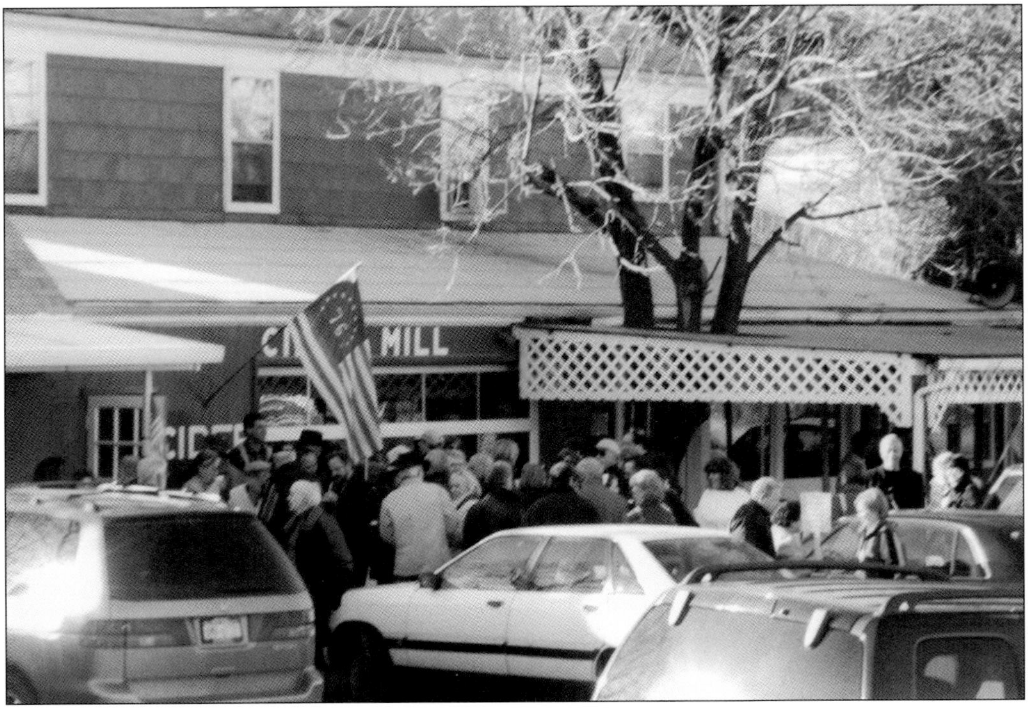

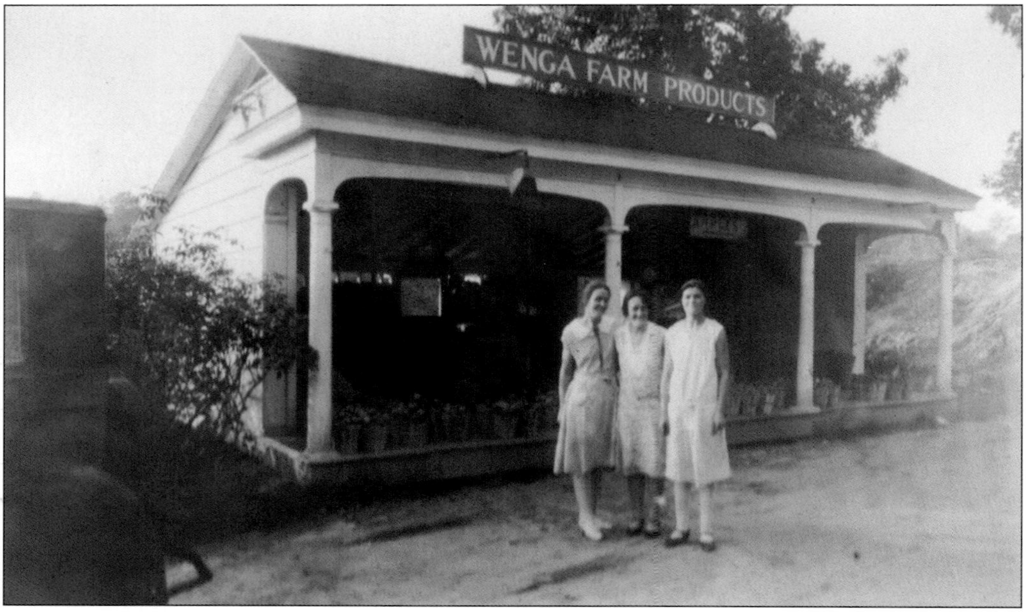

WENGA FARM PRODUCTS EXTERIOR, MID-1900S. From left to right, Emma Tompkins, Mildred Bell, and Sadie Holman sold farm products at a stand located at today's 69 Old Route 22, Armonk. In the early 1900s, Cornelius Rea Agnew built a large mansion and farm in Armonk. During the first half of the 20th century, his 550-acre Wenga Farm (Agnew spelled backwards) was a working farm producing products for sale. Agnew died in 1954.

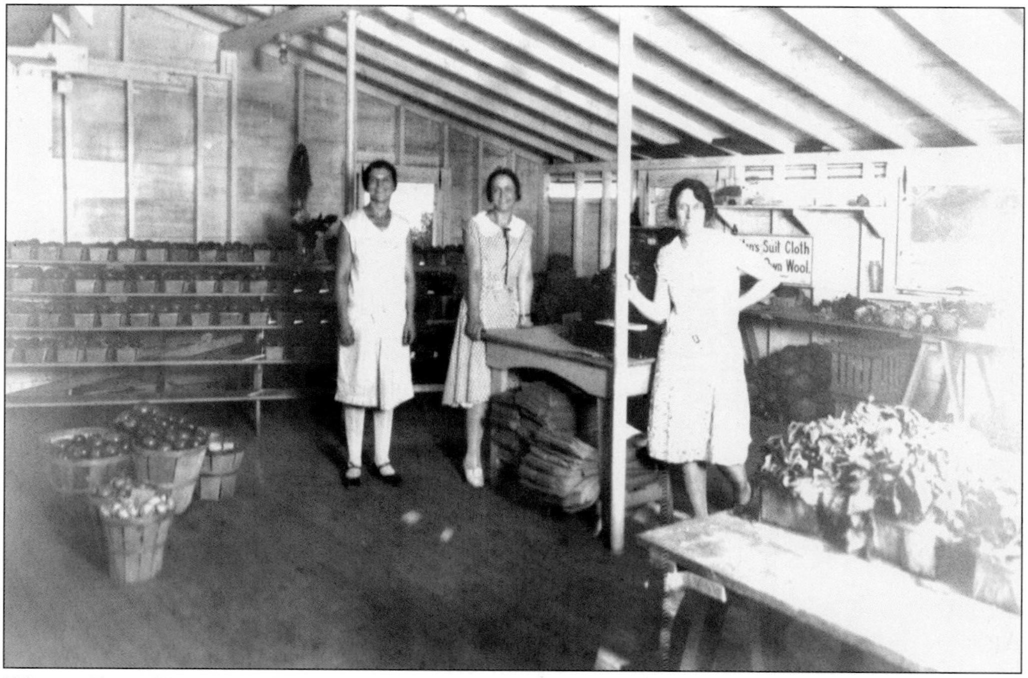

WENGA FARM PRODUCTS INTERIOR, MID-1900S. From left to right are Emma Tompkins, Mildred Bell, and Sadie Holman. Many local people worked on Wenga Farm through the years, including William Carpenter, Frank Holmes, George Light, Charlie Caston, and George Coupe. The stand also offered "Men's Suit Cloth, Our Own Wool."

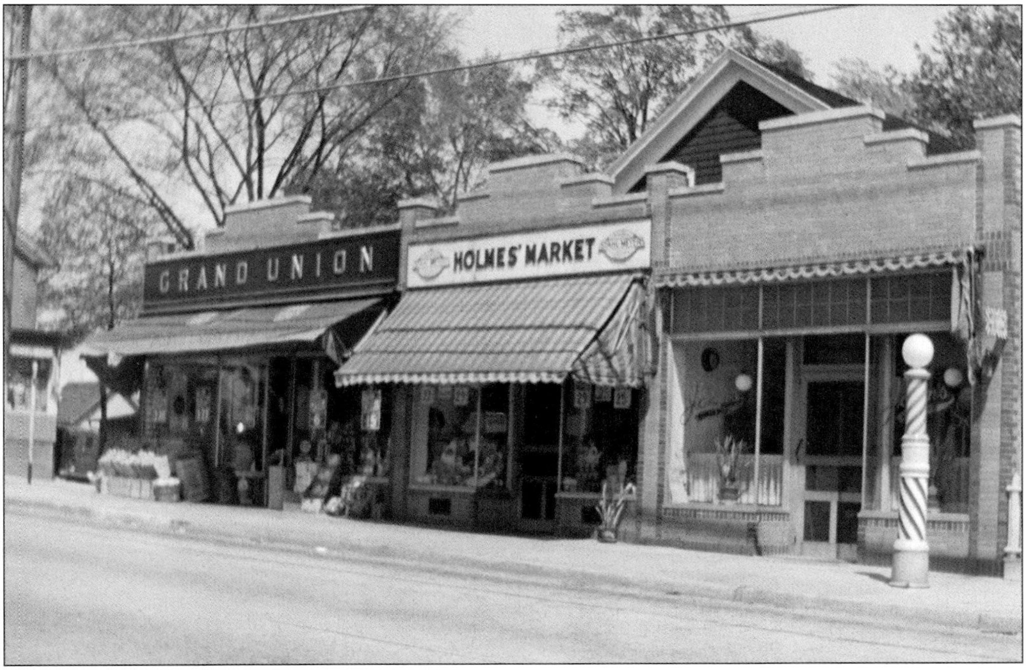

Main Street Stores at Maple Avenue, Armonk, Mid-1900s. From left to right, these stores at today's 420, 418, and 416 Main Street are the Grand Union grocery store, Holmes Market, and John's Barbershop. John's Barbershop was John Trerotola's barbershop in the early 1900s, later Scotty Farquhar's, and is still a barbershop today.

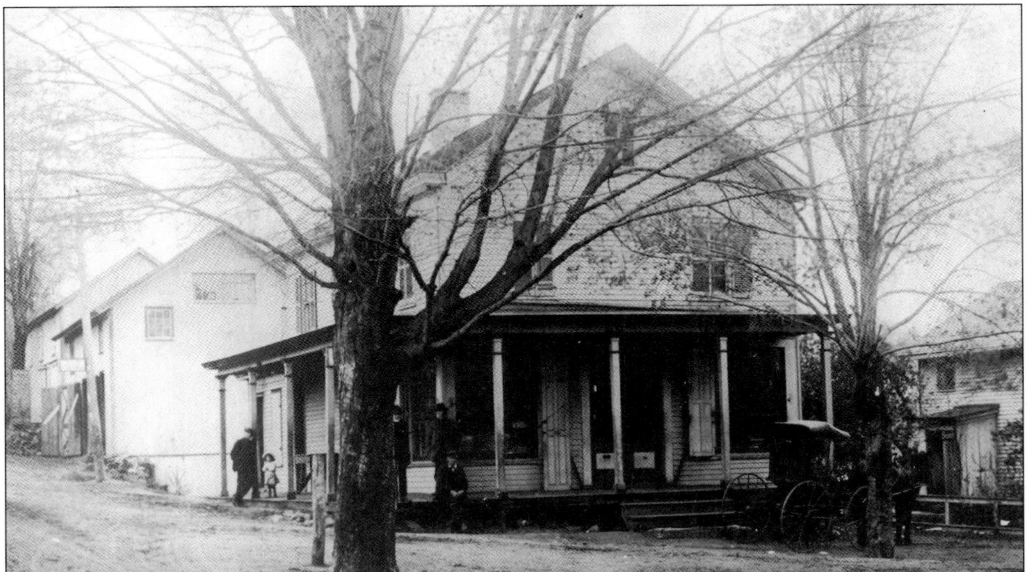

Armonk Store and Post Office, Early 1900s. From left to right are Harry Wayne and child, Jim Angevine, George Lander, and Zeke Flewellin (seated). About 1881, James Hopkins moved his store and post office here. Ezekiel Flewellin and William F. MacDonald, joined by James Lovelett, operated here by the late 1800s, and by 1929, members of the Lander family kept a store and post office here. The building, on the northeast corner of Main Street and Maple Avenue, houses a realty office today.

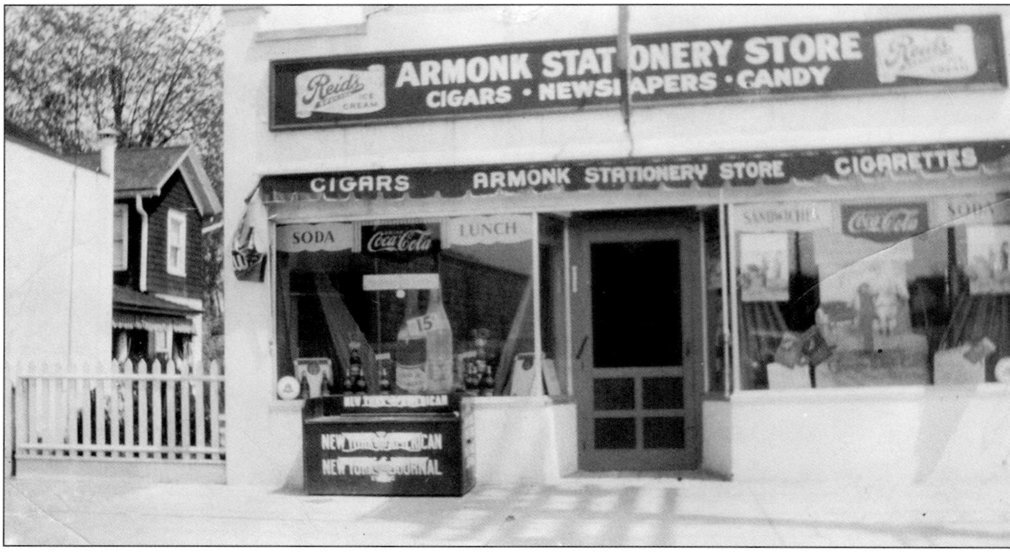

Armonk Stationery, Armonk, c. 1940. This old building on Main Street with a tin ceiling, wood floor, wainscoted walls, and a potbelly stove offered display cases and shelves filled with newspapers, tobacco, and candy. Armonk Stationery was established in 1934 by Richard and John Schnoor. It was then owned by Al Trela, George Abrams, and Arthur (Art) L. Nicholas. Many people have fond memories of Art's store. The building was demolished to make way for today's Armonk Square development.

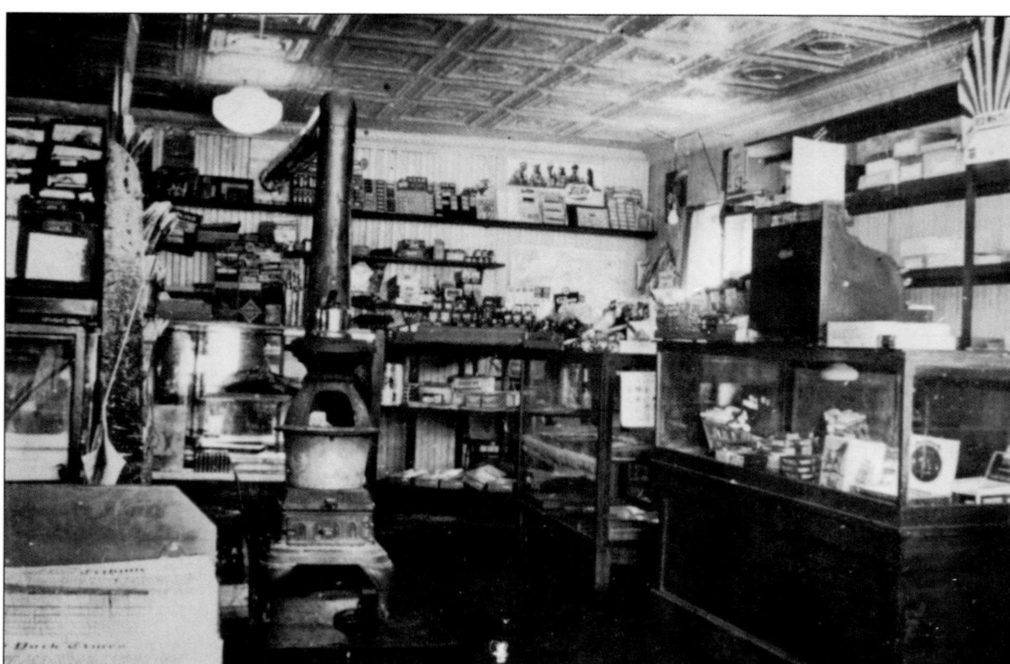

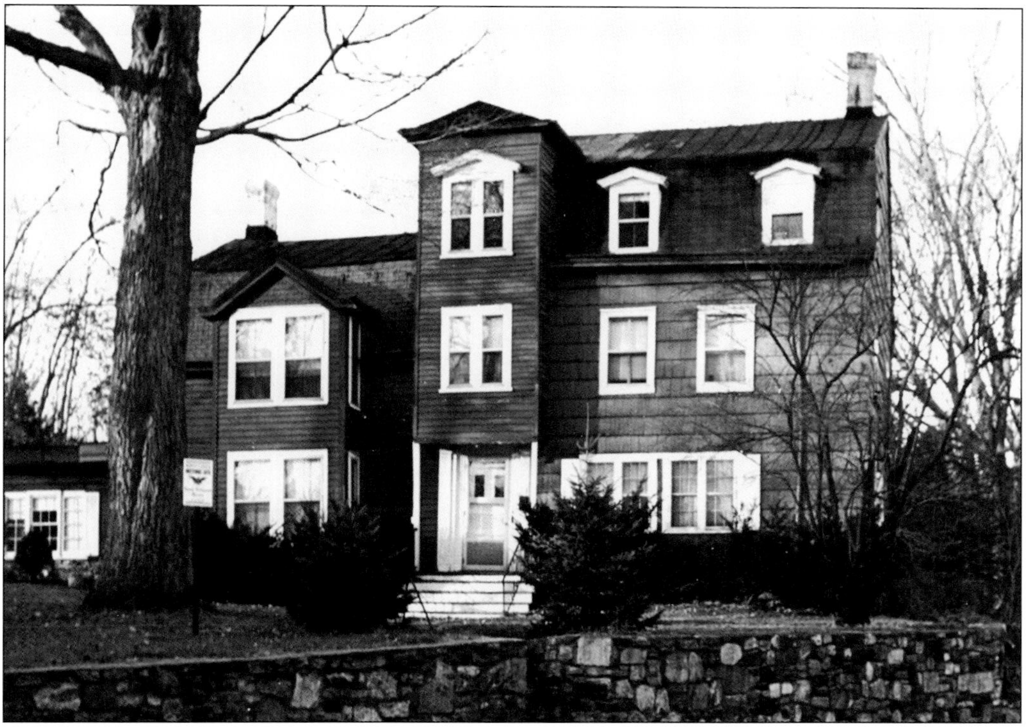

Israel Townsend House, Late 1700s. Israel, born in 1742, and Phoebe Townsend, born in 1752, had 10 children. They were buried in their small family cemetery, where other members later joined them. This house had 16 rooms, was unusually large for its time, and reflected the economic and social status of the family. At today's 495 Main Street, Armonk, it has been extensively remodeled and is now retail space.

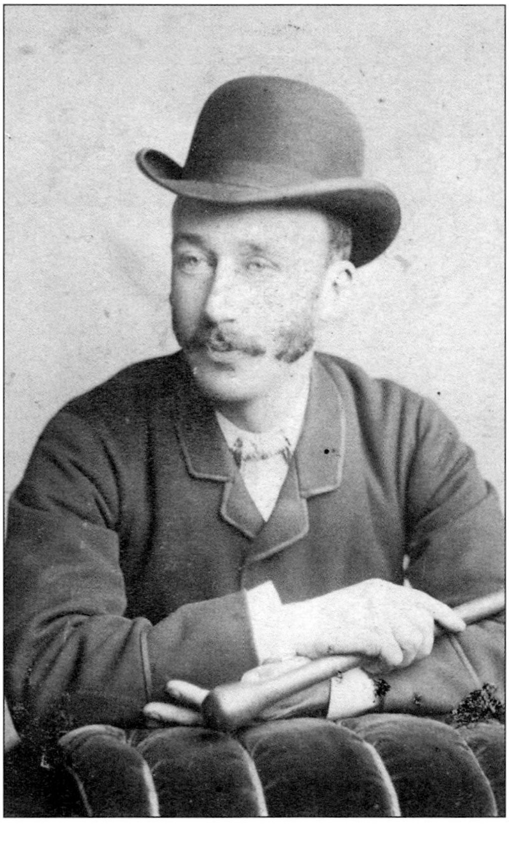

John H. Troy, Troy's Garden Nursery, c. 1930. An acclaimed early horticulturist, Troy owned a garden nursery business on Bedford-Banksville Road in Banksville. Due to complications brought about by a fall onboard a ship, he died in 1931. The fourth generation of the family owns and operates the business today.

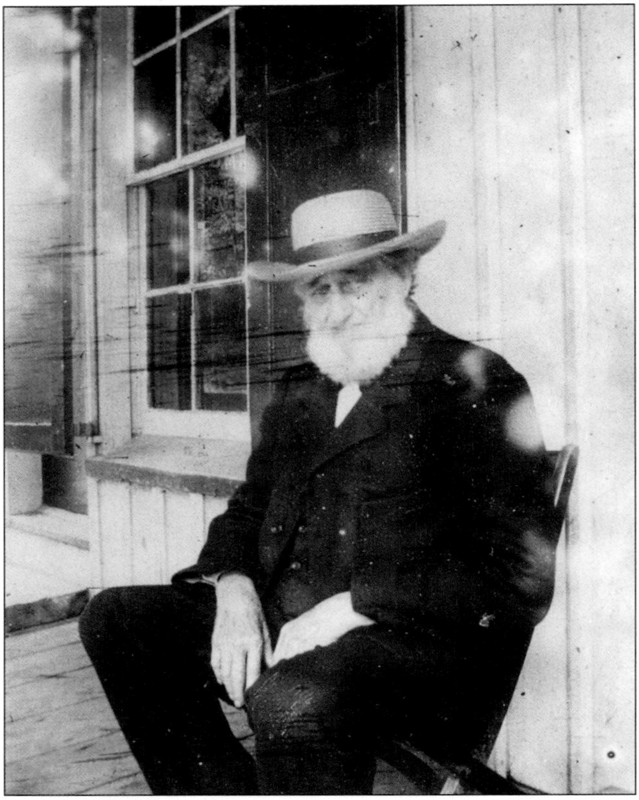

Finch's Country Store, Established 1860. Marvin N. Finch bought the business owned by Joseph Silkman Hobby, F.H. Van Ranst, and Lewellen N. Parker in 1860. He operated a general store, selling shoes and boots, in the center of Banksville. He constructed a new building in 1929 (restored after a 1980 fire) that housed a family business for five generations. Today it houses a delicatessen, and the older building houses an automotive repair shop on Banksville Avenue, Banksville.

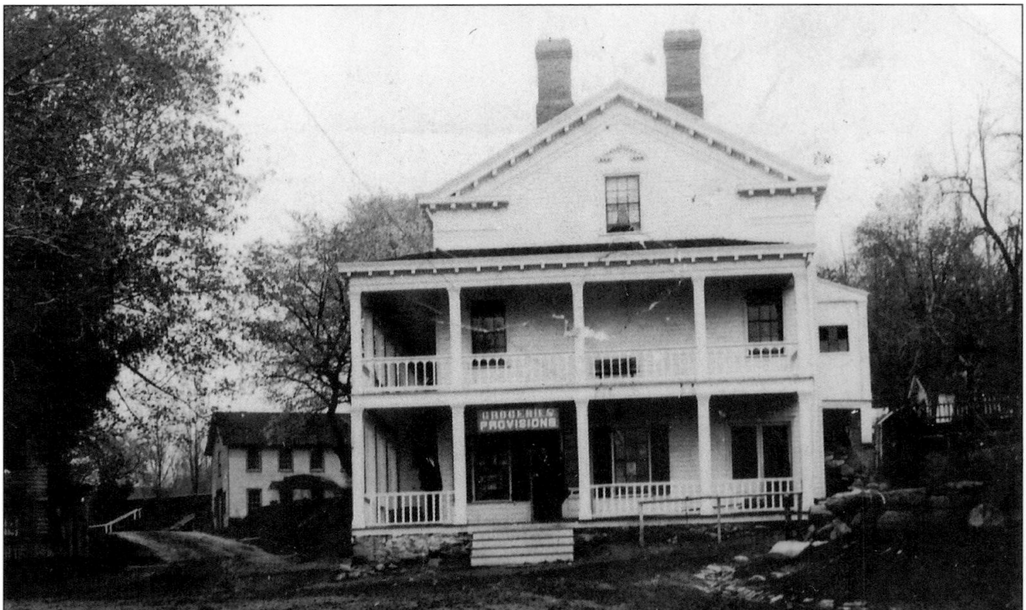

Jacob Pfister's Store and Post Office, c. 1900. The horse-drawn stage stopped twice a day in each direction bringing passengers, packages, newspapers, and the US mail. This store, known as Bang's before Pfister bought it, was a place to visit and pick up needed supplies. Outgoing letters were postmarked "Kensico, N.Y." This property was inundated by Kensico Reservoir.

Five

Hotels, Restaurants, Bars, and Dance Clubs

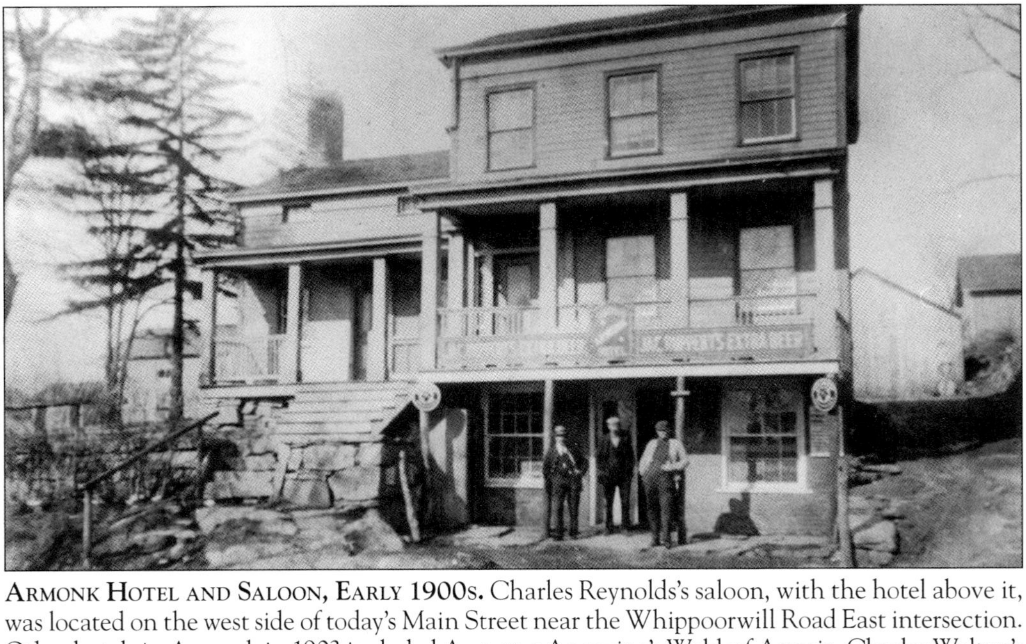

Armonk Hotel and Saloon, Early 1900s. Charles Reynolds's saloon, with the hotel above it, was located on the west side of today's Main Street near the Whippoorwill Road East intersection. Other hotels in Armonk in 1903 included Augustus Angevine's Waldorf-Astoria, Charles Walton's Brookside, William Ackerly's Road House, and Daniel C. Merritt's Pig Street Hotel.

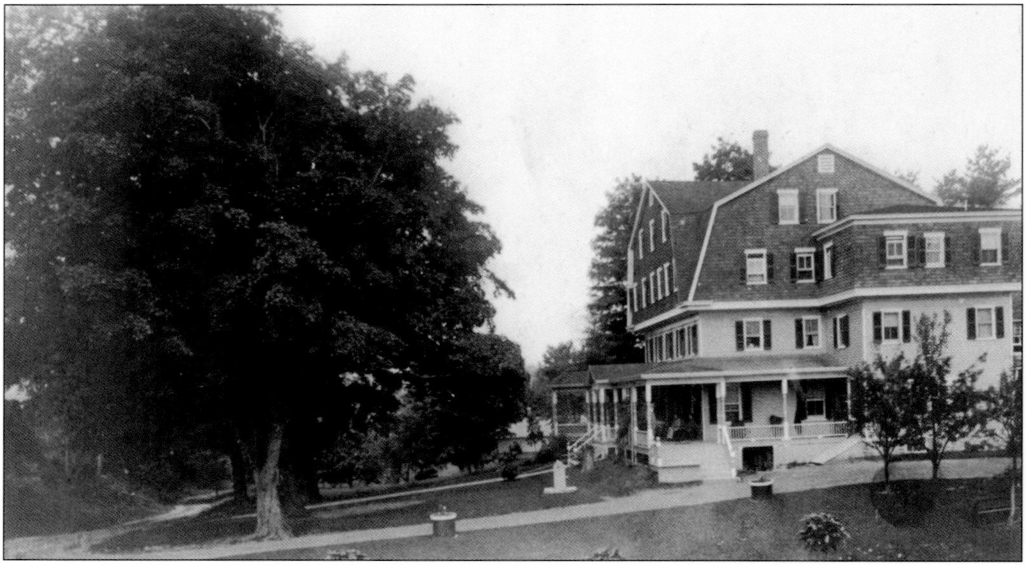

SUMMIT VIEW FARM, COX'S BOARDINGHOUSE, C. 1914. J. Hobart Cox, later town supervisor, operated this boardinghouse as Summit View Farm in the early 1900s. Henry E. Tredwell owned the property by 1925 and advertised the "best of foods in the heart of the lake region." Later, Jean and Beatrice Laurain operated a summer hotel colony called Breezemont. Today it is a children's day camp called Breezemont. The building, at today's 62 Cox Avenue in Armonk, has landmark status.

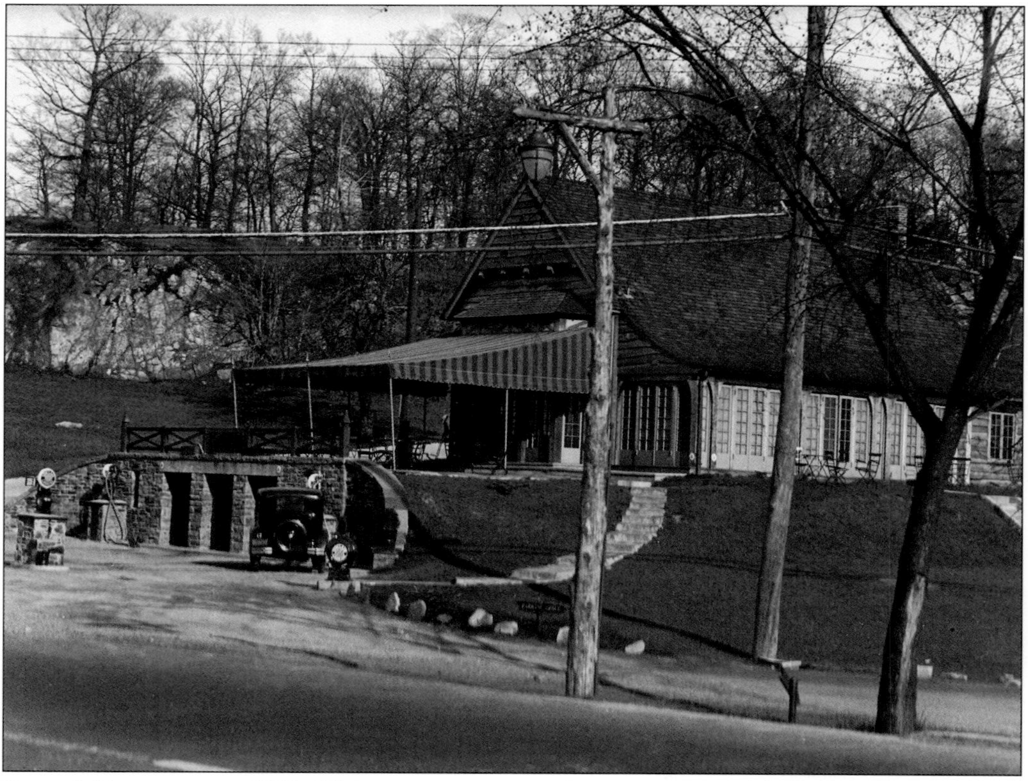

CRAFT'S RESTAURANT, 1929. This restaurant was at the intersection of the Bronx River Parkway and Washington Avenue in North White Plains.

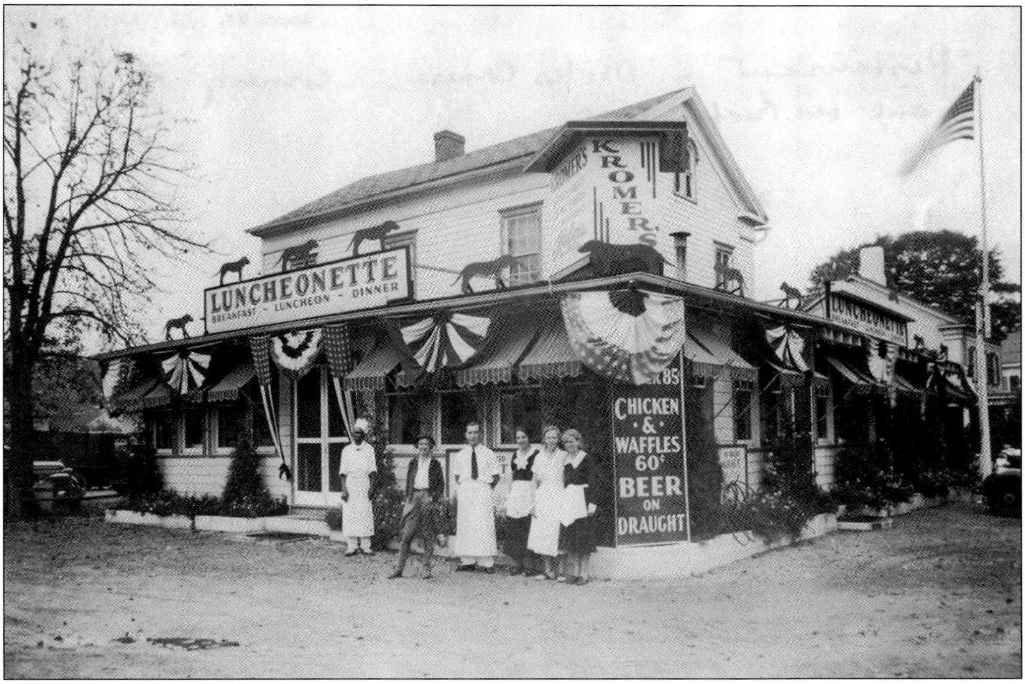

RICHARD (DICK) KROMER'S CORNER, ARMONK, C. 1928. Kromer took over from Raven, and in time the corner was called Kromer's. In a 1936 advertisement in the *North Castle Sun*, Kromer offered a quart of rye each week for the largest trout weighed at the restaurant.

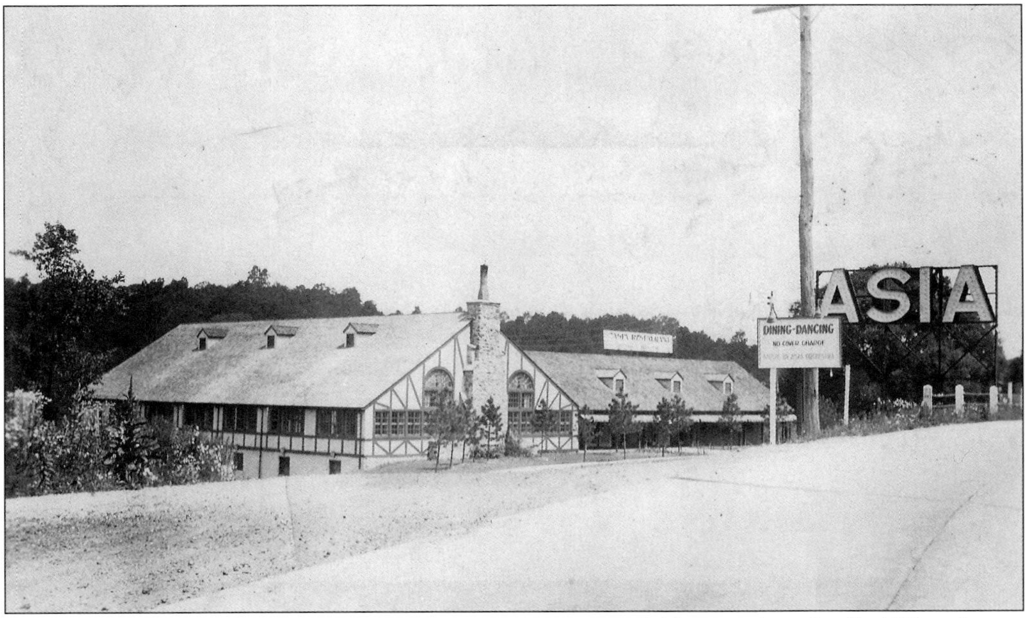

ASIA RESTAURANT, C. 1930. Built by attorney Lorenzo Landolfe in 1927 and called Westchester Palais D'Or, the building on today's Old Route 22 in Armonk near Kaysal Court accommodated about 600 patrons and had a large multifaceted chandelier that reflected bits of colored rays throughout the room. It closed in 1929 and soon reopened as a Chinese restaurant called Asia, which closed in 1931. Both restaurants employed house bands for dancing.

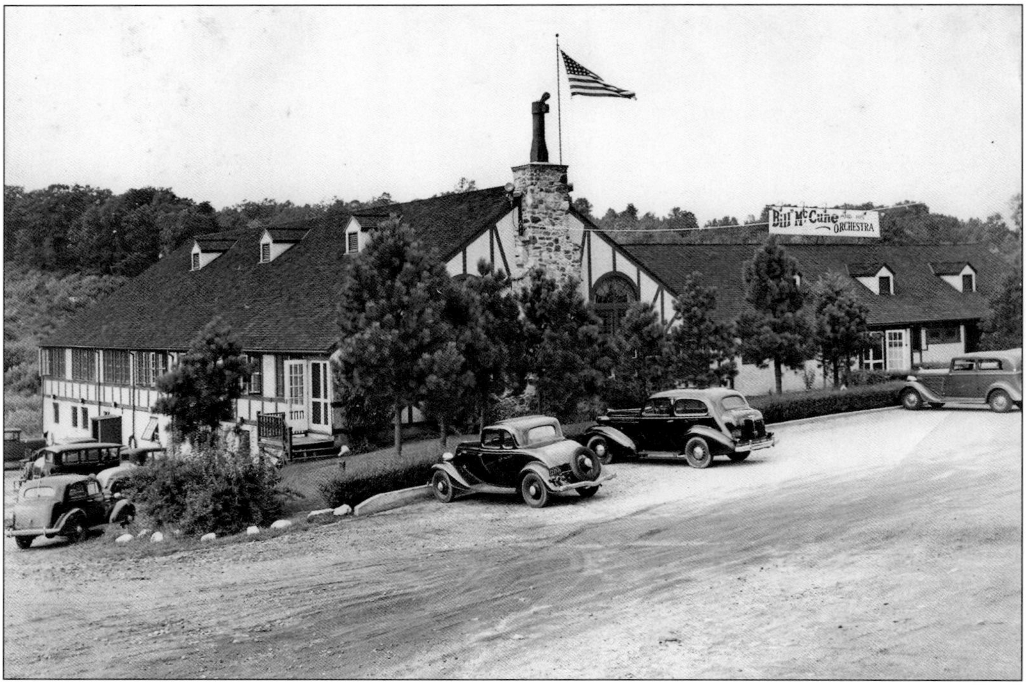

Rhineland Gardens Night Club, 1936. In April 1932, Bill Reiber took over from Asia Restaurant and opened Rhineland Gardens. He had an orchestra and a floor show. Reiber brought in name bands and broadcast them live on the radio. He discontinued his operations in Armonk in 1939.

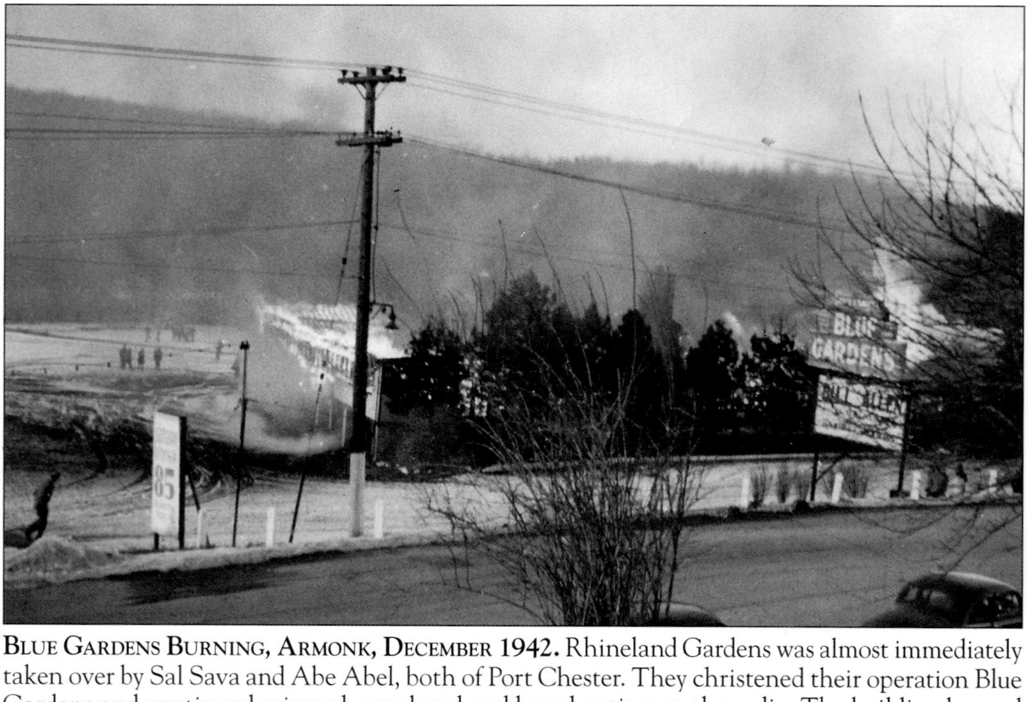

Blue Gardens Burning, Armonk, December 1942. Rhineland Gardens was almost immediately taken over by Sal Sava and Abe Abel, both of Port Chester. They christened their operation Blue Gardens and continued using a house band and broadcasting on the radio. The building burned to the ground at the end of 1942 when an oil-burning kitchen range exploded.

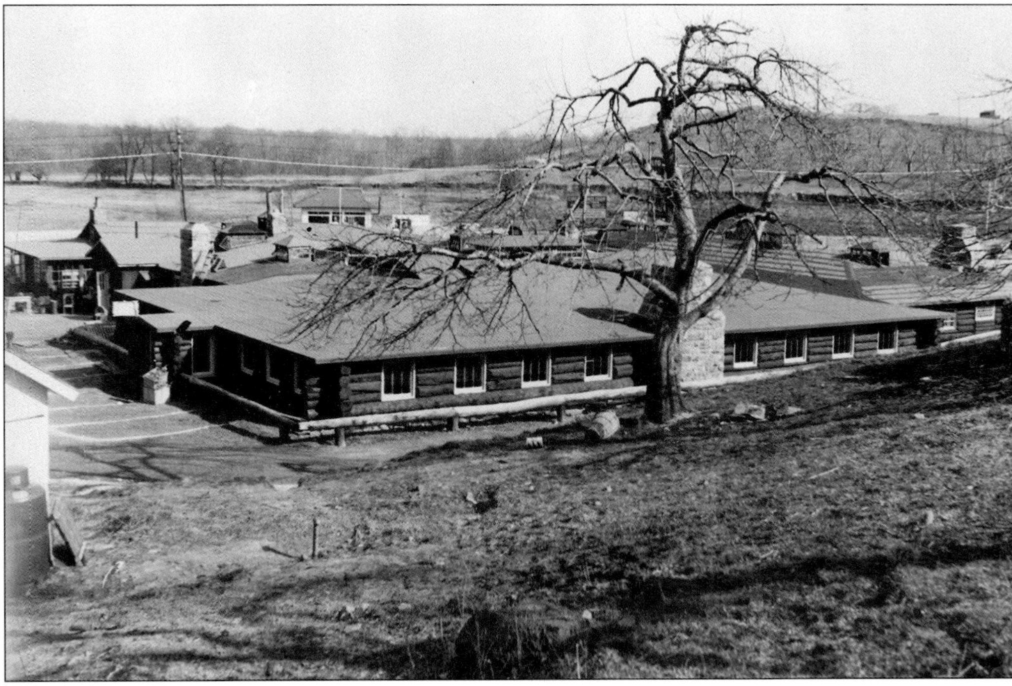

Log Cabin Restaurant, Armonk, Rear View. House bands, beginning as early as 1934, included Bill Whelpley, Parker Lee, and Ray Schafer. In May 1940, owner August Hussar began broadcasting band music live on radio stations. Orchestras playing here included those of Ray Herbeck, Herbie Holmes, Les Brown, Bob Chester, Teddy Powell, Joe Marsala, Lawrence Welk, Tommy Dorsey, Gene Krupa, Eddie Condon, Buddy Rich, and Alvino Rey.

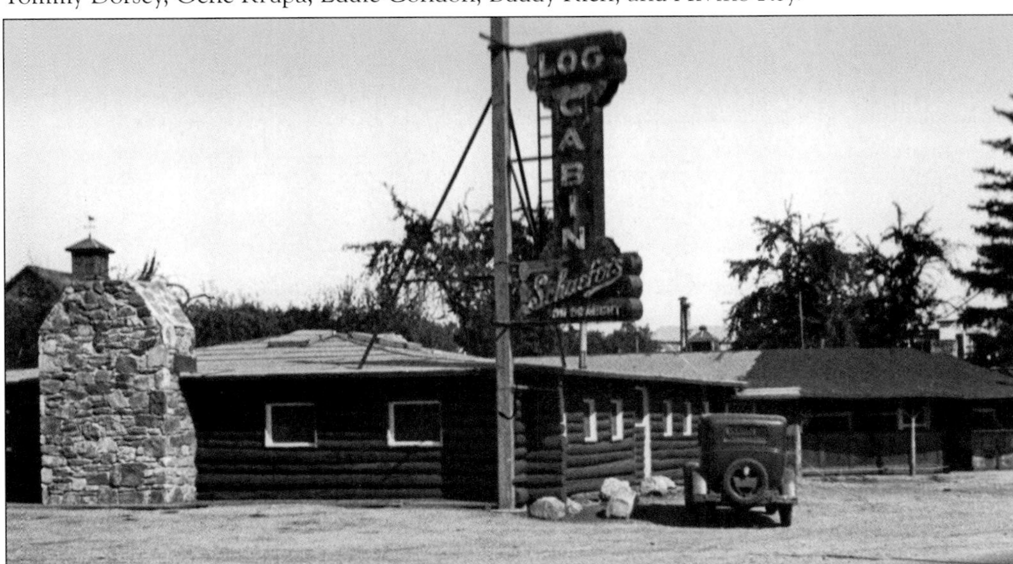

Log Cabin Restaurant, Armonk, 1931. Frank Webster began selling cider, cake, coffee, and honey from a stone wall in front of his house and progressed to a farm stand offering local produce in 1916. His nephew Webster Schmaling built a small log cabin in 1921 in which he sold cider, farm produce, and homemade desserts. In 1929, he sold to August Hussar, who expanded the restaurant and dancing business.

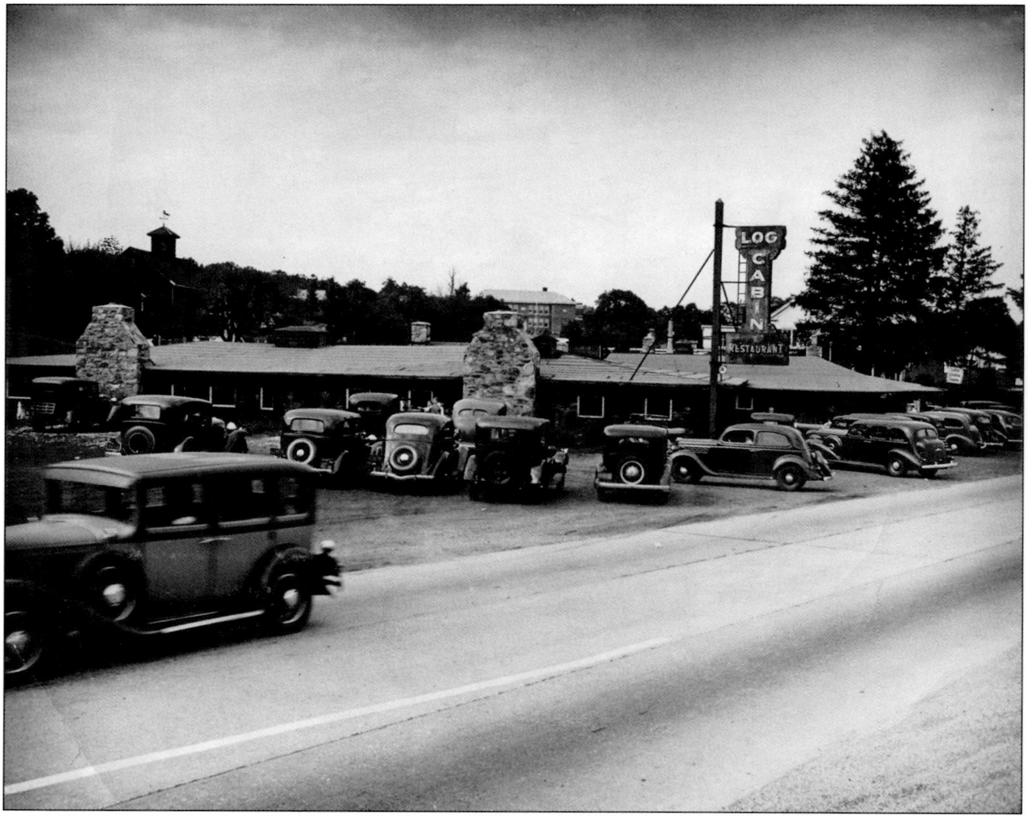

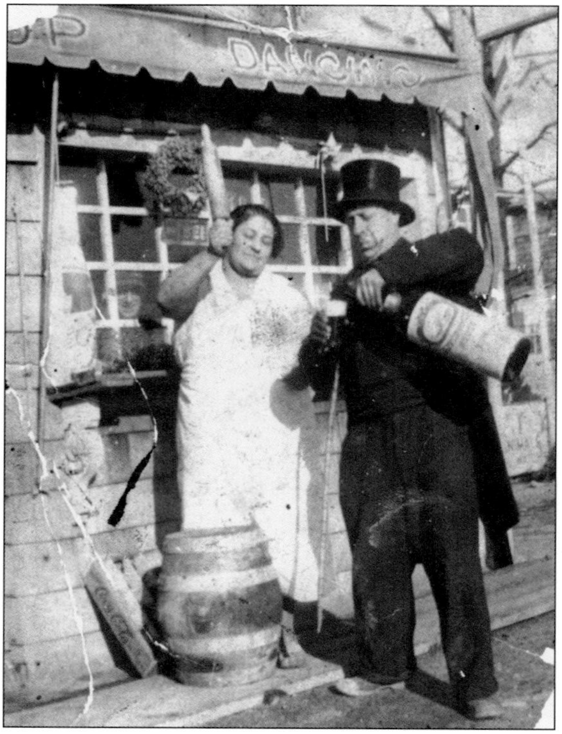

LOG CABIN RESTAURANT, ARMONK, C. 1930. The building faced today's Main Street just south of today's Kent Place. The Log Cabin, owned by the Schmaling, Webster, and Hussar families, burned to the ground on December 19, 1965. Whippoorwill School, which opened for classes in December 1924, is visible at center behind the restaurant.

VETERANS STOP, ARMONK, 1932. Rebecca and Fred Calabrese owned Veterans Stop across from Westchester Airport on what was then Route 22, now Bedford Road, Armonk. They are clowning for the camera, she with a rolling pin held ready and he with a very large bottle of spirits. They offered food, beverages, and dancing and kept an animal zoo that included monkeys and a bear.

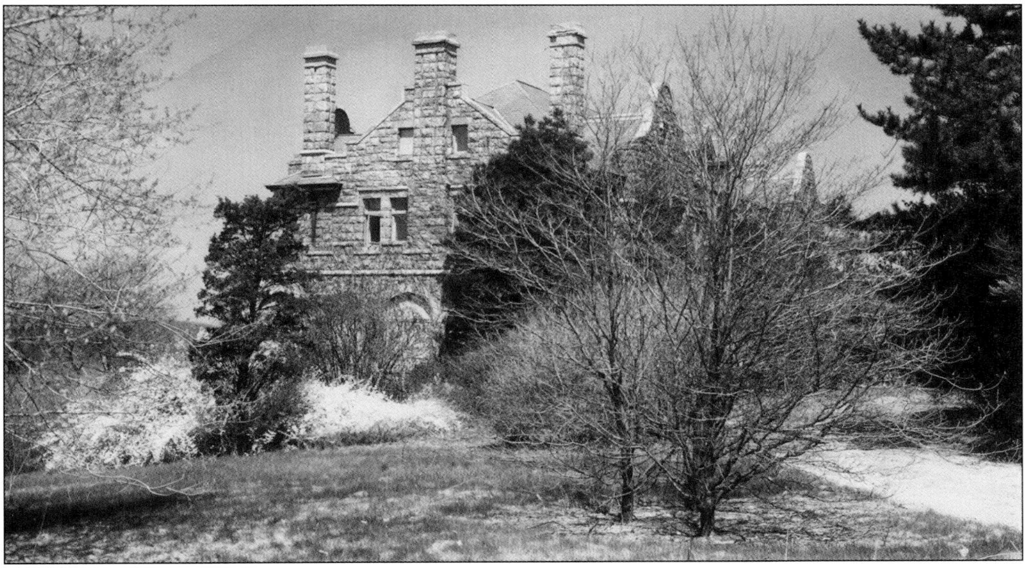

WESTCHESTER EMBASSY CLUB STANDING VACANT, MID-1900S. John H. Watkins built his home on today's Route 22 north of Armonk village about 1900. He sold to Hugh Prichitt, who lived there in the 1910s and 1920s and sold in 1928. North Castle Golf and Tennis Club offered swimming, trap shooting, horses, and Saturday evening dinners and dances.

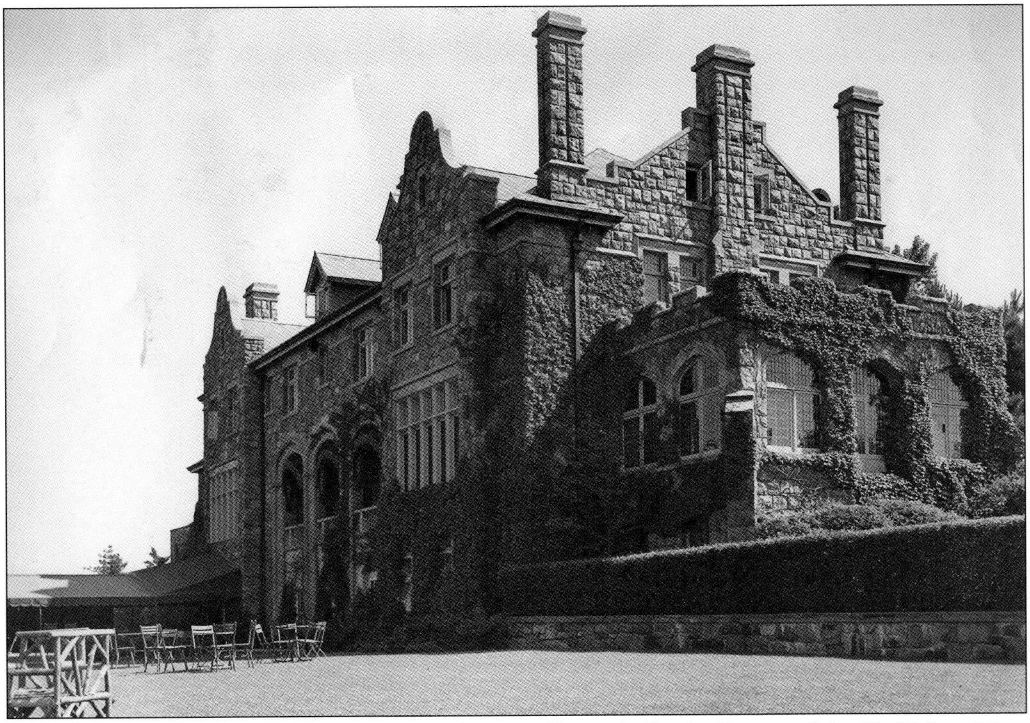

WESTCHESTER EMBASSY CLUB, C. 1931. Jack Kreindler and Charlie Berns, of the 21 Club in New York City, operated here in 1931. The building was destroyed by fire in 1953. In 1931, the *North Castle Monitor* reported, "We must admit that science has worked wonders on the farm; yet believe that dry enthusiasts possess as great a charm. Just look at these fanatics and thank them for the boon; Armonk has ten 'speakies' now where once was one saloon."

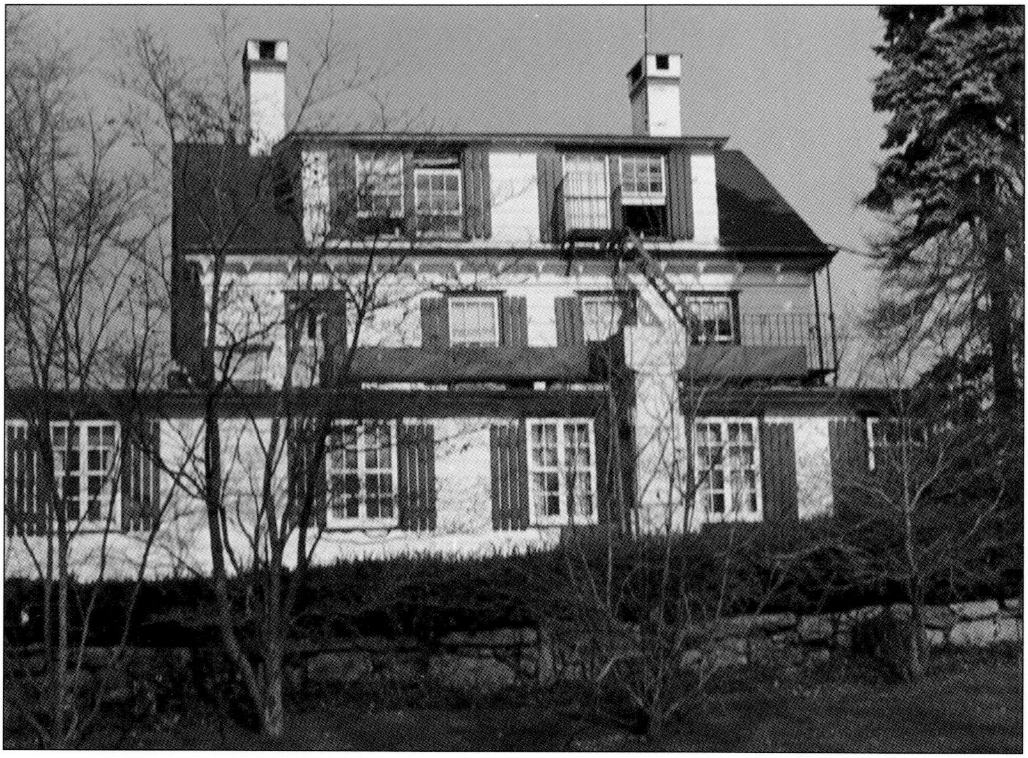

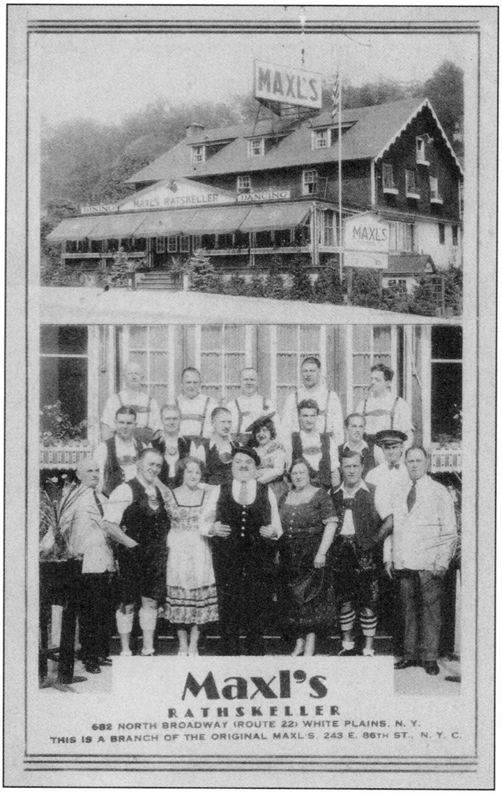

WIDOW BRUSH'S HOUSE, EARLY 1700S. This house passed into the Hobby and Brundage families. William Jackson acquired it in 1925 and formed the Westchester Women's Golf and Tennis Club, which was followed by the Middle Patent Golf Club (open to women and men). Wings and porches were added and enclosed, but the stately twin end chimneys still overlook this fine old building. Today it is home to the famous La Cremaillere Restaurant of Banksville.

MAXL'S RATHSKELLER, NORTH BROADWAY, NORTH WHITE PLAINS, 1934. Although unidentified, the group pictured includes the owners (center front). The restaurant offered lunch for 75¢ and dinner for $1, and there was dancing. In 1936, the owners staged a lavish Fourth of July fireworks display in which an American flag, formed by fireworks, floated several hundred feet through the air before descending.

Six

Kensico Dam and Reservoir

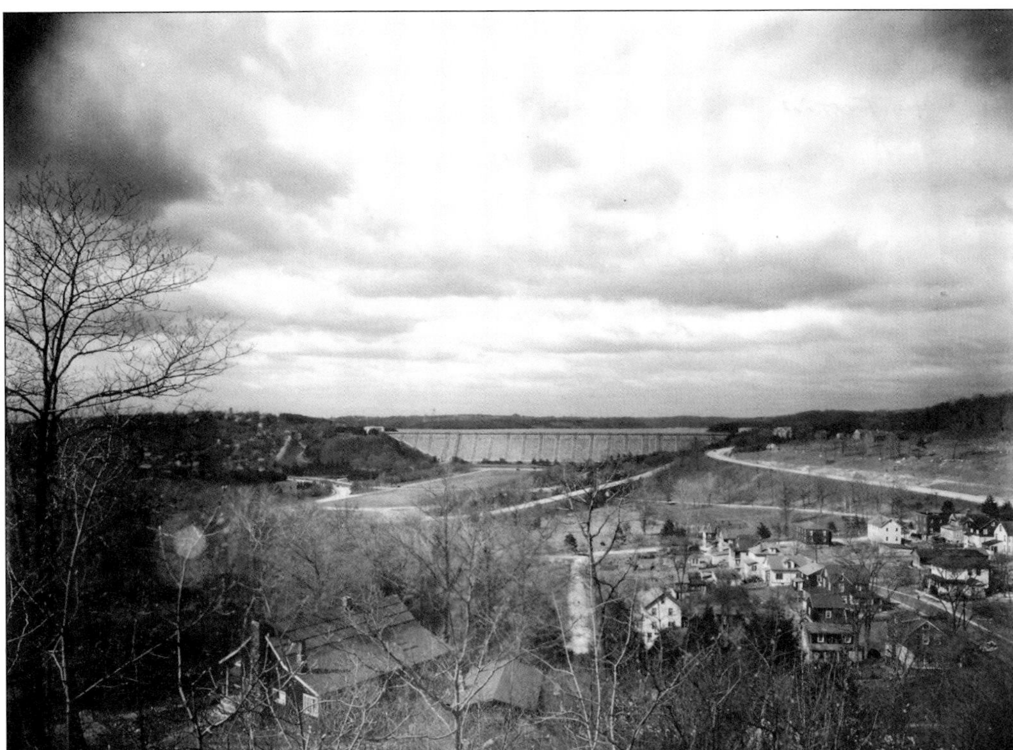

Kensico Dam (after Completion) with North White Plains Homes, Early 1900s. After years of acquiring property, diverting water, and relocating highways, construction began on the dam in 1913. North Castle granite from today's Cranberry Lake Preserve decorates the surface of the dam. The reservoir itself covers approximately 2,145 acres, divided about equally between the towns of North Castle and Mount Pleasant.

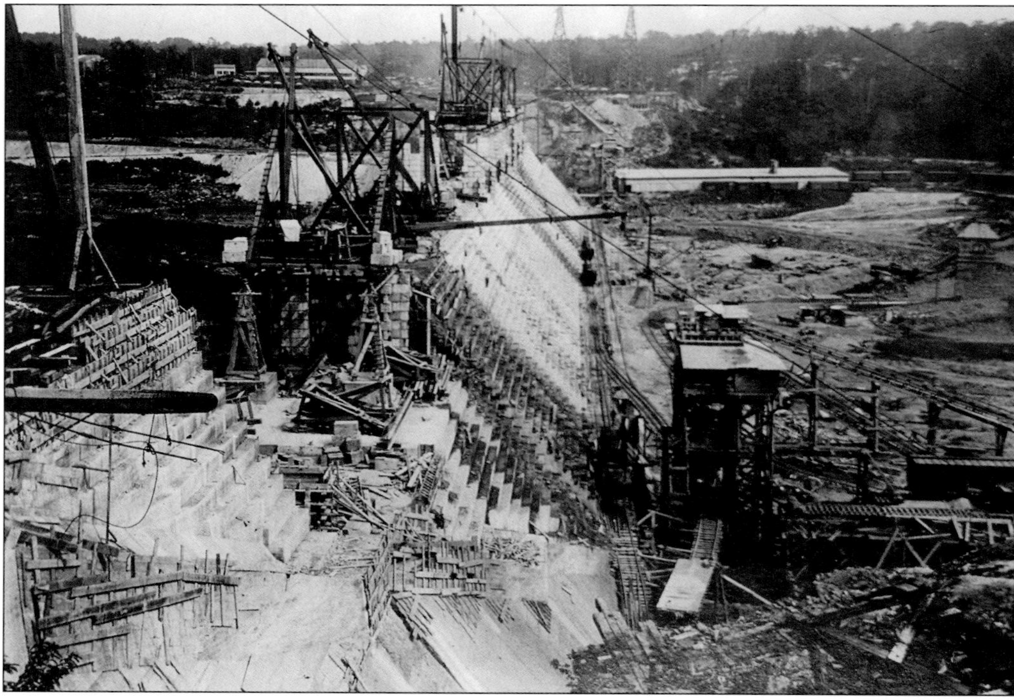

KENSICO DAM CONSTRUCTION, BETWEEN 1913 AND 1917. As the masonry rose, derricks were used. Concrete was laid between bulkheads at the bottom of the gorge, and guy derricks on each side placed the buckets of concrete and huge stones for the masonry work.

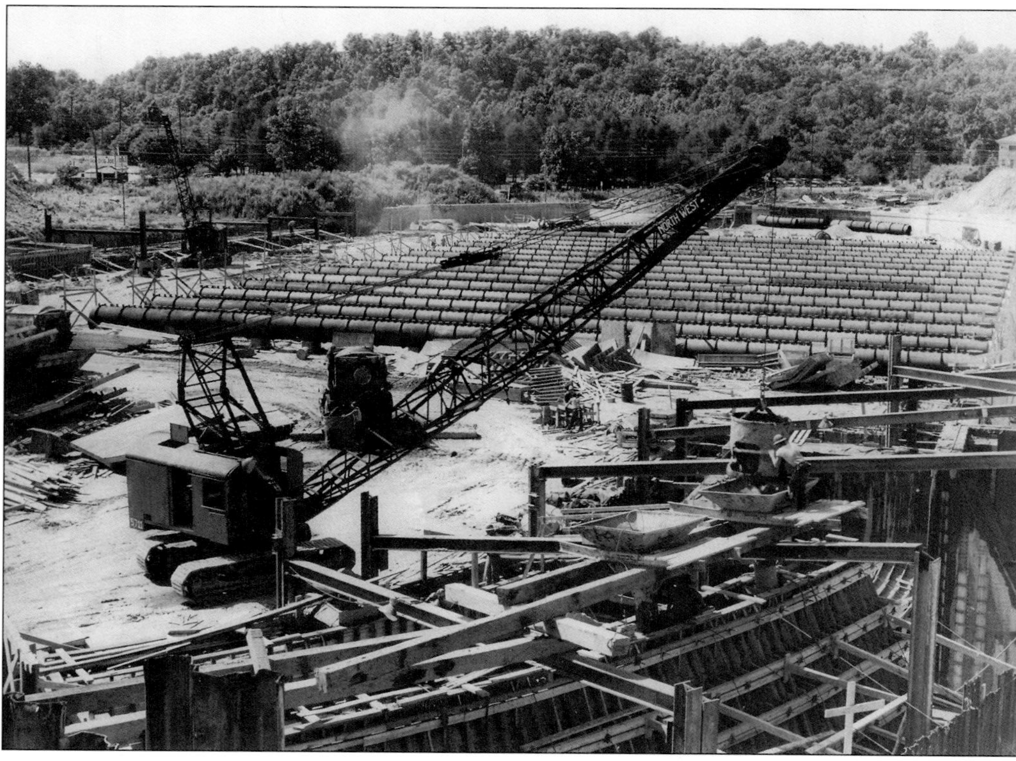

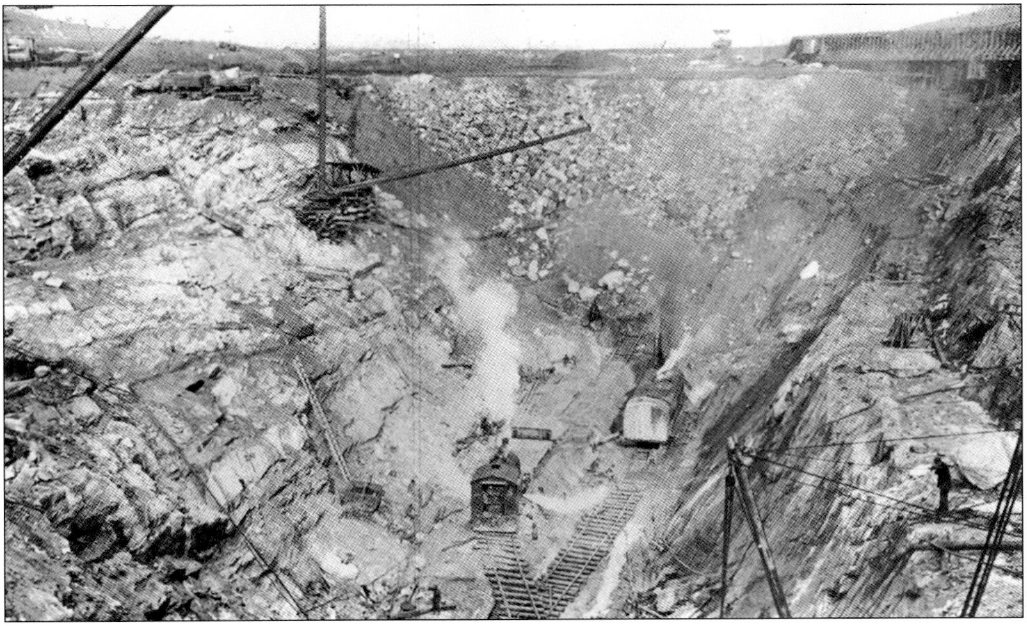

Excavating for the Foundation of Kensico Dam. There was an extensive cableway system used for hoisting the derricks and excavating the bottom of the gorge. Supporting towers at each end were 50 feet by 100 feet at the base and 125 feet high from the top of the rail. (Courtesy of the Board of Water Supply, New York City, 742, Contract 9.)

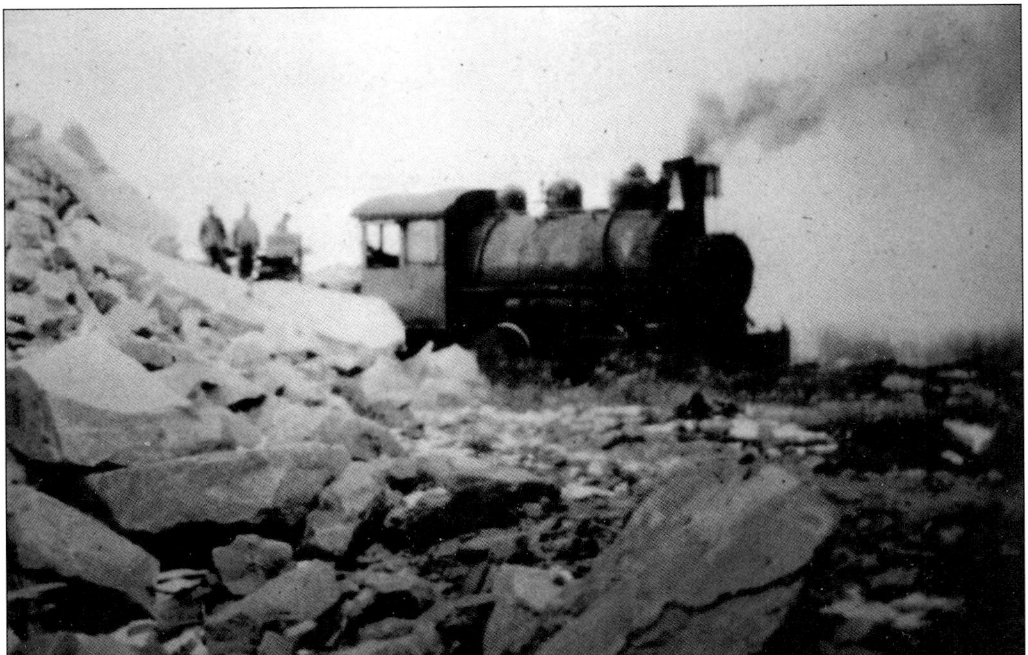

Kensico Dam Construction, Train Picking Up Stone in the Quarry. The quarry in the present area of Quarry Heights in North Castle and Harrison was the source of stone. Trains picked up the stone and conveyed it to the crusher and then to the construction site or the mixing plant.

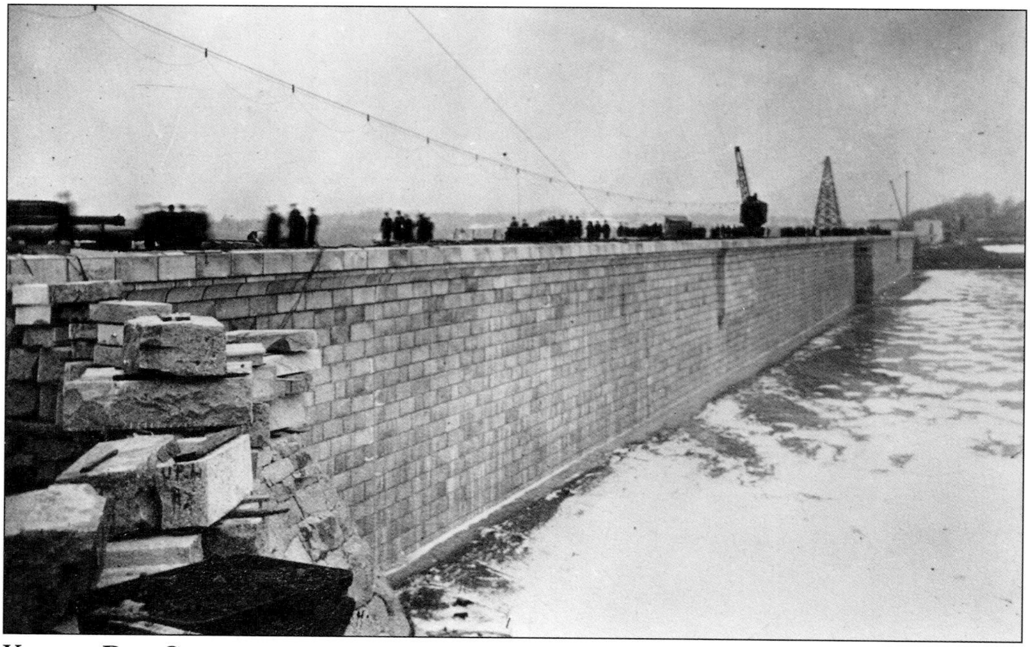

Kensico Dam Construction, Setting the Blocks. A seasoning period was necessary before the huge blocks could be used; each block had to be date-marked. Sand pits were located at the west end of the lake, where the sand was excavated and transported by conveyors. A North Castle quarry supplied the stone used for the concrete work, dimension stones, and facing stones on the front of the dam.

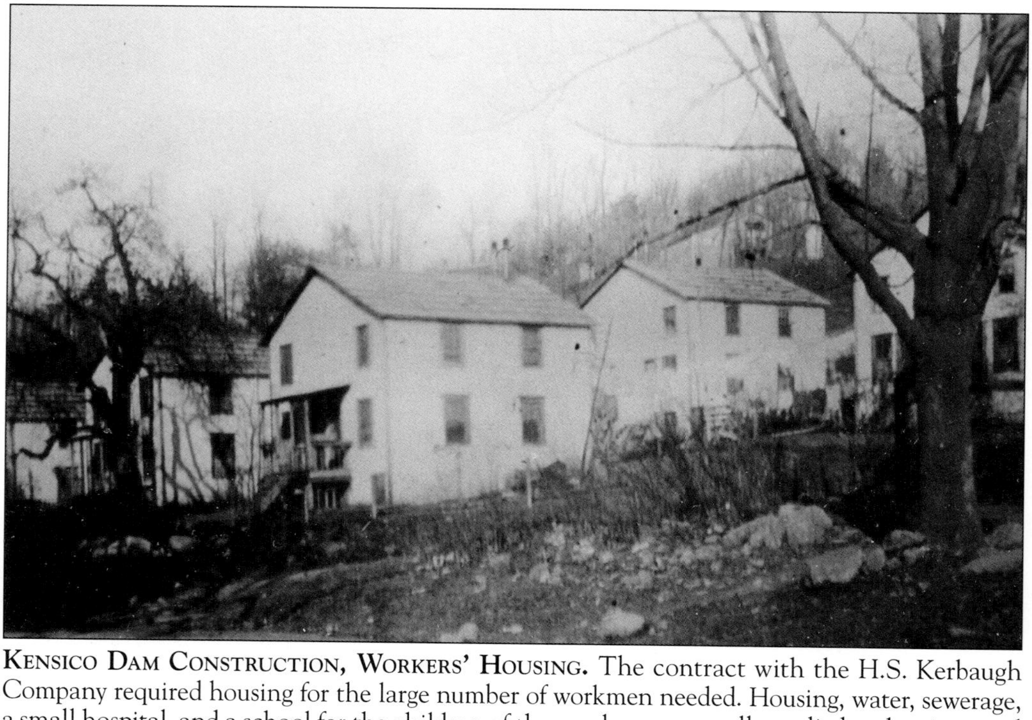

Kensico Dam Construction, Workers' Housing. The contract with the H.S. Kerbaugh Company required housing for the large number of workmen needed. Housing, water, sewerage, a small hospital, and a school for the children of the employees were all supplied and maintained in North White Plains.

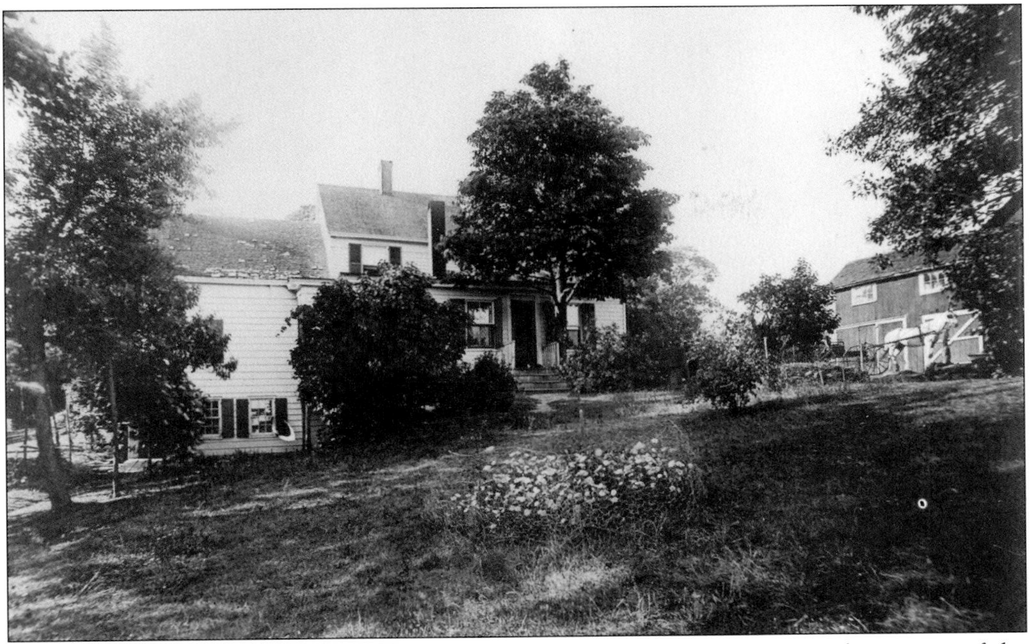

ARTHUR PIETSCHKER HOUSE AND BARN, KENSICO, C. 1910. Pietschker served as justice of the peace for North Castle from 1913 until 1932. He was active in the Kensico Methodist Church and served as a pastor of the Castle Heights Methodist Church from 1921 to 1924. Some Kensico families stayed in the area, settling in Valhalla, North White Plains, or Armonk, where they began new lives.

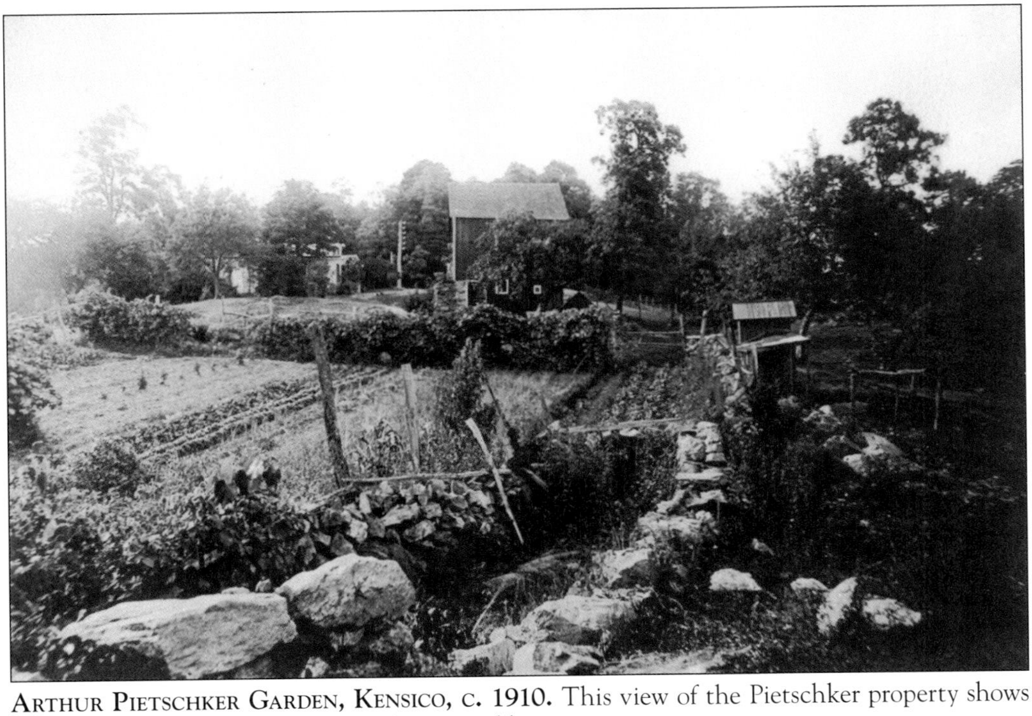

ARTHUR PIETSCHKER GARDEN, KENSICO, C. 1910. This view of the Pietschker property shows the family garden to the side of the house and barn.

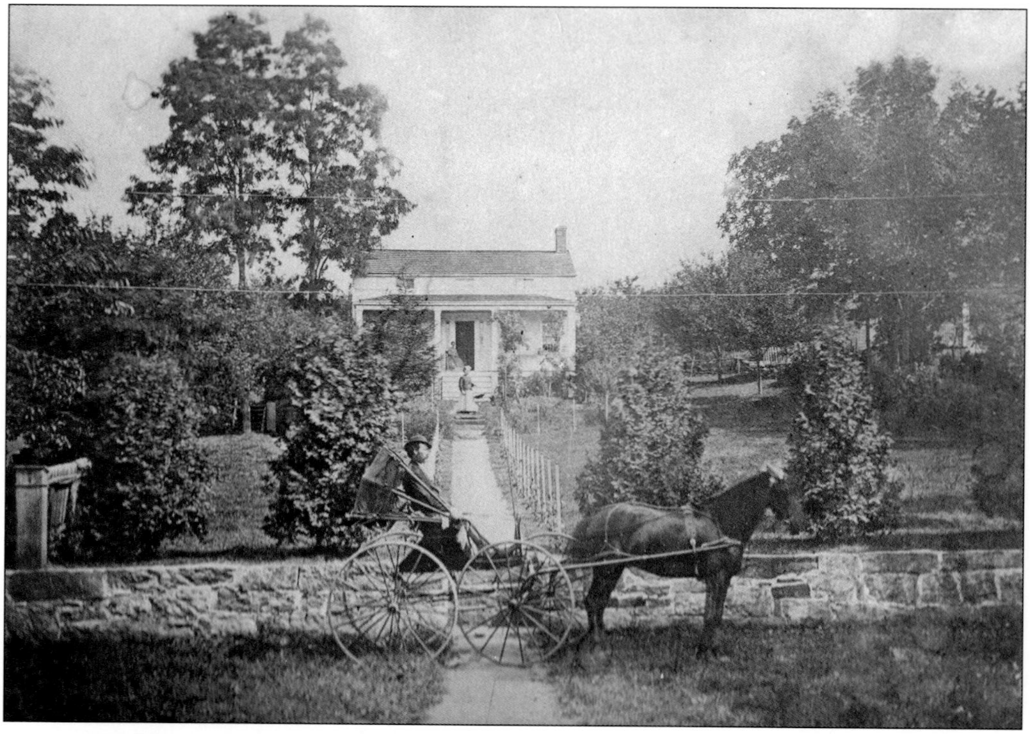

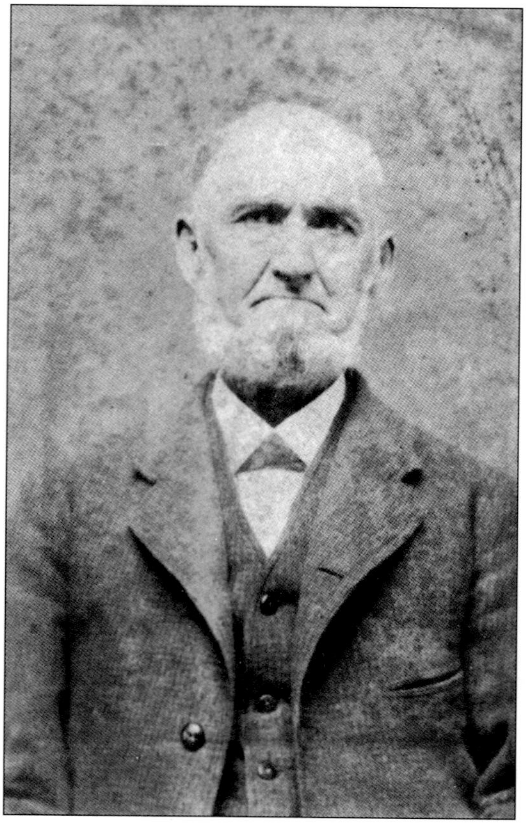

JUDGE JOHN B. WYCKOFF HOME, KENSICO, INUNDATED BY KENSICO RESERVOIR. When the original earth dam was completed in 1885, most of those affected simply moved to higher ground. But, in 1907, New York City Water Supply decided to enlarge the original Kensico Lake and dam. Hundreds were displaced and their ways of life destroyed when the present Kensico Dam and Reservoir were constructed.

JOHN B. WYCKOFF (1818–1895), KENSICO. Wyckoff was a US postmaster, owned a general store, and was a justice of the peace for North Castle. The first Kensico post office (1849) was in the Wyckoff store. According to family genealogy, he married Elizabeth Fisher, and they had four children: Charles Fisher, Frances Estelle, William J., and Daniel Hatfield Fisher Wyckoff. The family moved to Connecticut.

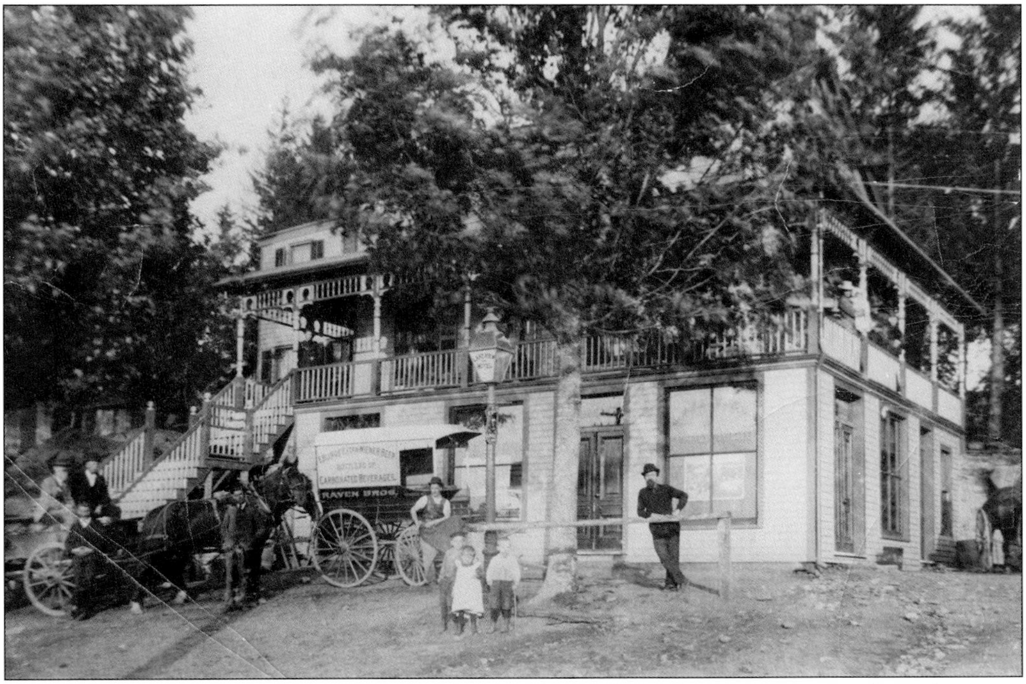

Raven's Kensico Lake View Hotel, c. 1900. John and Caroline Raven came from Germany about 1870. They owned a hotel near today's Orchard Street in North White Plains. Their family grew to include 11 children. Locals called Lake View a "rum hole" because beer, wine, and liquor were served there. Sold to the Jennie Clarkson Home about 1904, it was later burned in the course of making a movie; no recorded histories mention the name of the movie.

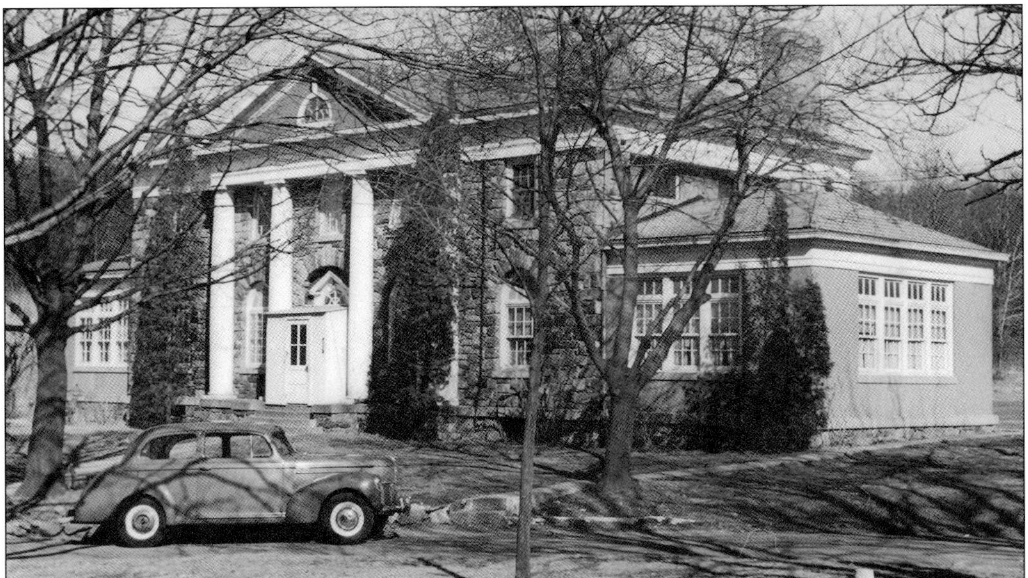

Jennie Clarkson Home, Administration Building, Early 1900s. The *Scarsdale Inquirer* published an annual report in late 1927 stating that the home cared for about 50 children between the ages of 5 and 18 during that year and that orphans and half-orphans were given preference. Dr. Thomas J. Harris was president.

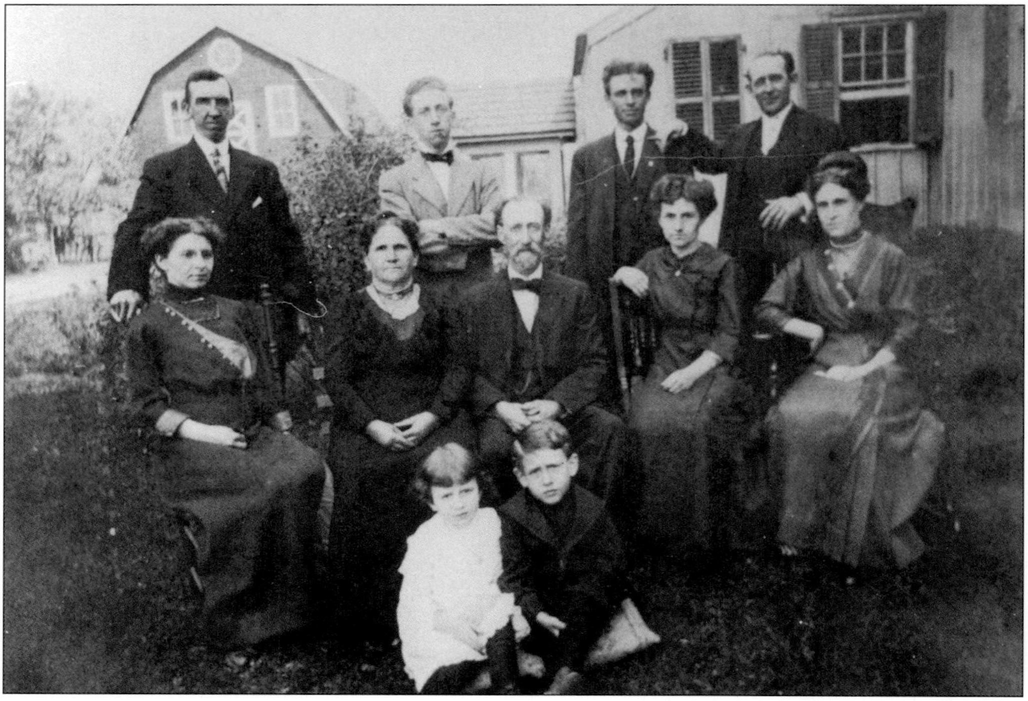

Displaced Kensico Farmer Edgar A. Huestis and Family, c. 1920. This photograph was taken at the Waterbury home, today's 400 Main Street, Armonk. From left to right are (first row) Doris Huestis Cox and Stanley E. Waterbury; (second row) Sarah Elizabeth Huestis Cox, Sara Emma Smith Huestis (mother), Edgar A. Huestis (father), Frances Huestis Waterbury, and Maryetta Huestis Acker; (third row) Raymond H. Cox, Elliott A. Huestis (son), Ernest A. Waterbury, and J. Frederick Acker.

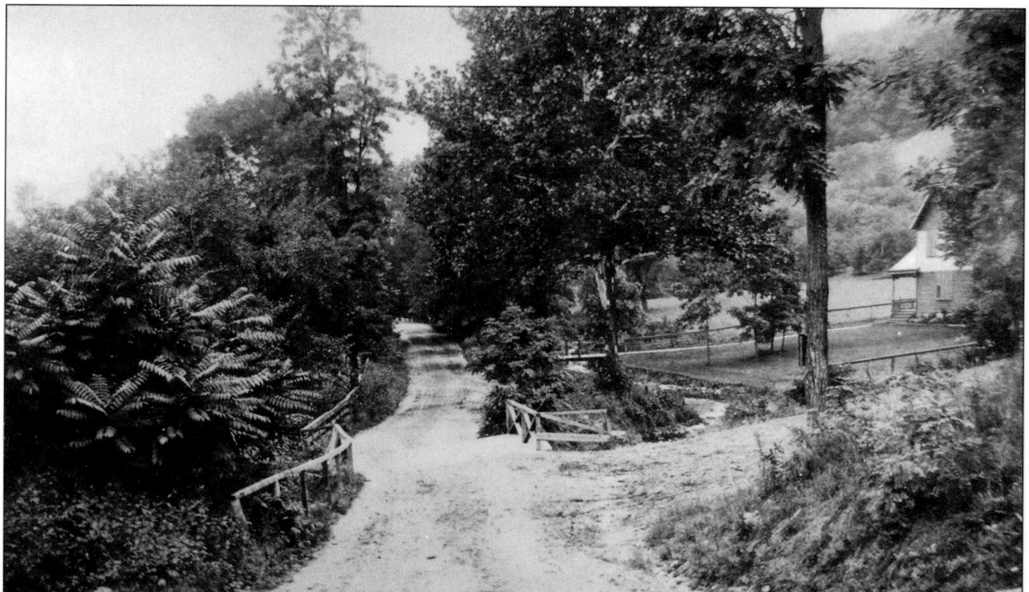

A Kensico Valley Road and Farm, c. 1900. This unpaved country lane and tidy farm in the valley are unidentified. Both were inundated by the waters of Kensico Reservoir.

Seven

TRANSPORTATION

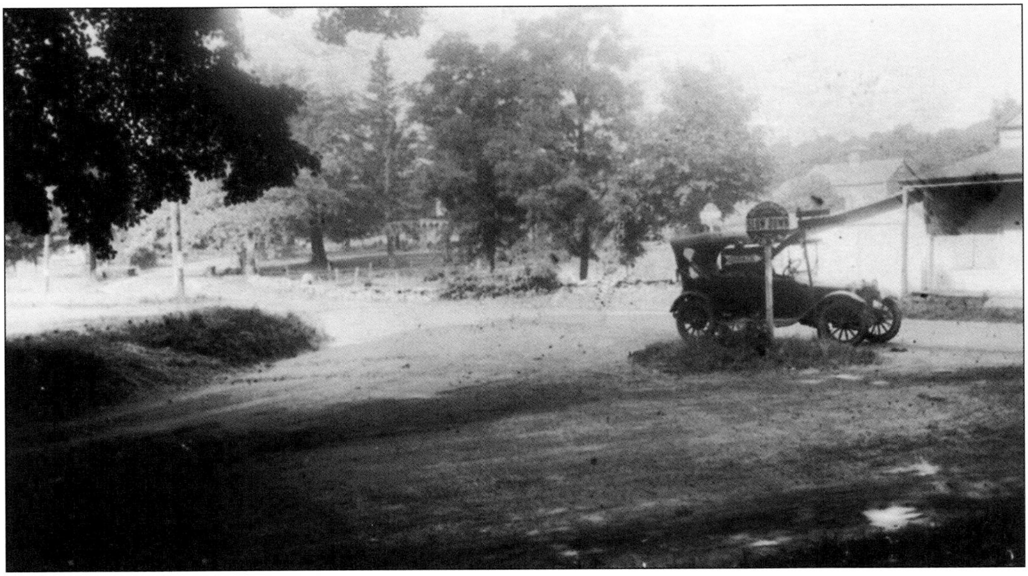

ARMONK CHURCH CORNER (RAVEN'S, KROMER'S, MILES), EARLY 1920S. The sign in front of the car reads "Slow Down." In 1929, the *North Castle Monitor* claimed this road was a "precarious course between refreshment stands and gas stations [and] a very popular parade ground for various kinds of jackasses behind the wheel instead of in front of it with the interior of their gaudily upholstered cars and coupes a popular roosting place for half-dressed chickens."

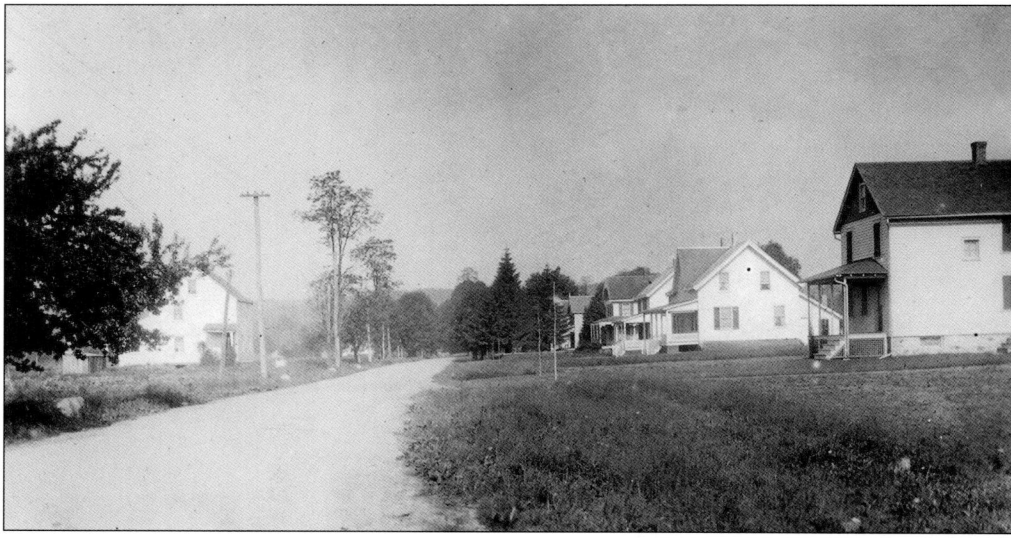

State Road, Armonk, c. 1910. Before the airport started business, Armonk was rural and State Road (today's Bedford Road) was unpaved. The farmhouse on the left is approximately where the airport operations office would later be built. Today the road ends at the I-684 interchange ramps.

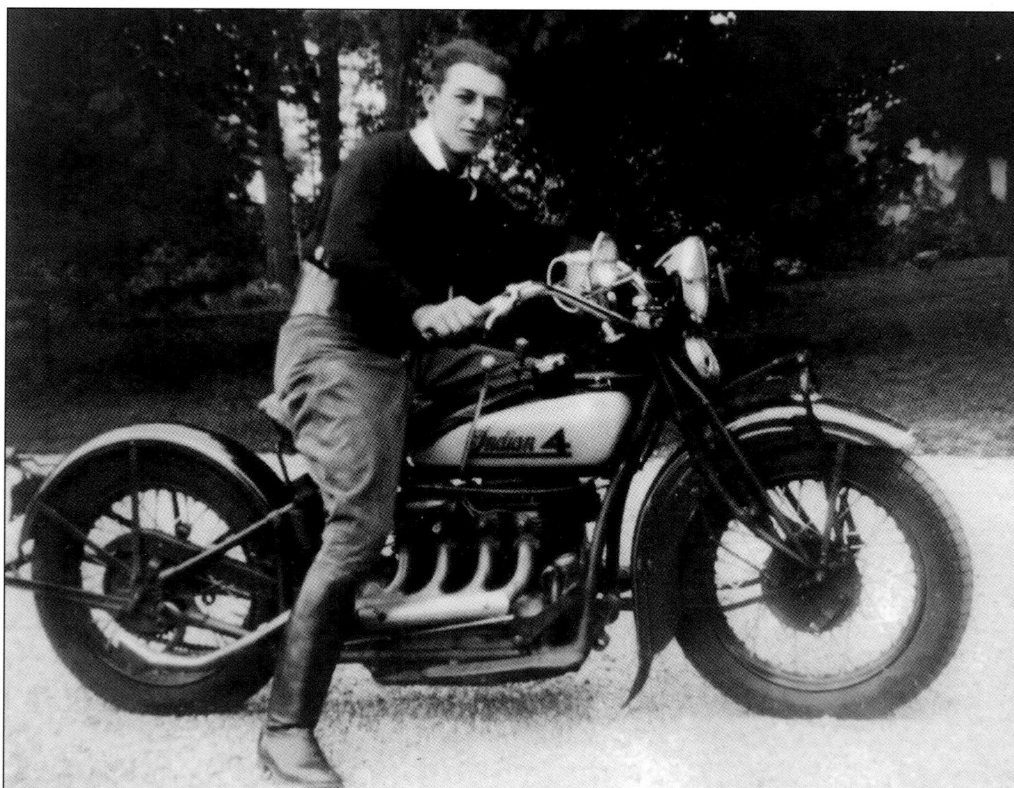

Joseph Wago Jr., Armonk. This picture of Joseph Wago Jr. with his Indian 4 motorcycle was taken in the late 1920s or early 1930s. His daughter Barbara Wago DiGiacinto is currently a member of the North Castle Town Board.

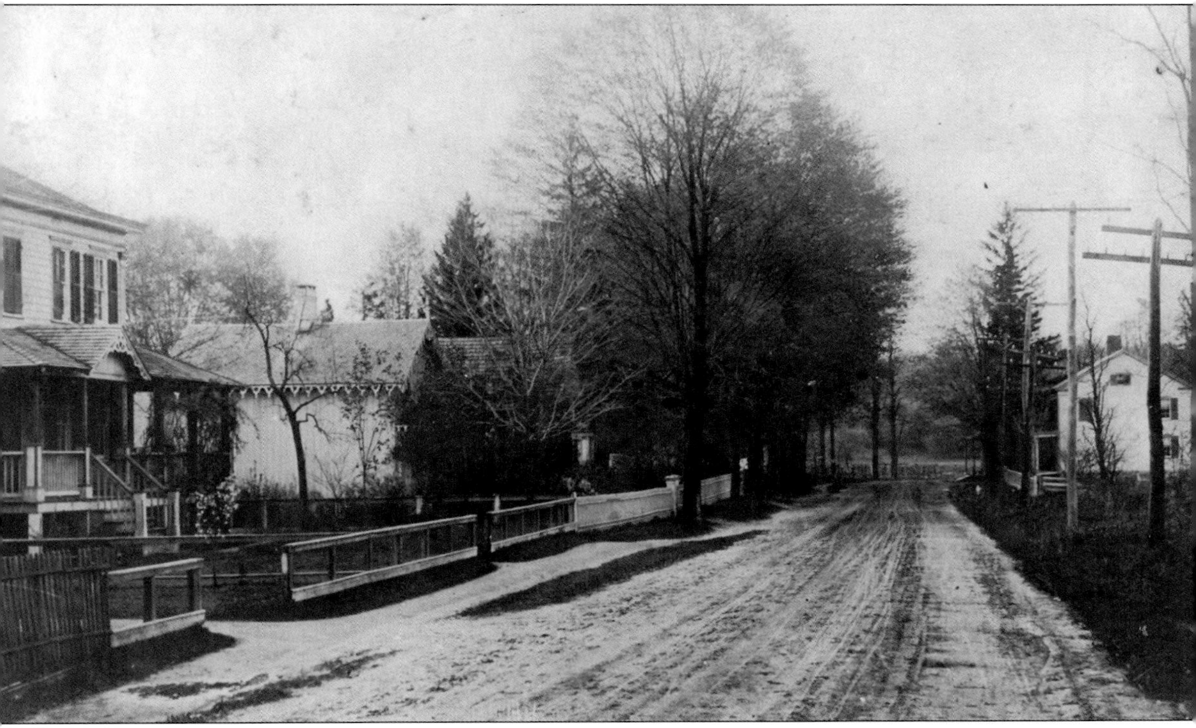

State Road through Armonk Village, Early 1900s. The first building on the left of this unpaved road is today's 410 Main Street. It was home to Charles E. and Julia Remsen Brundage from 1903 until 1908. He was a wheelwright, wagon builder, and repairman. The property was part of the subdivision sold by St. Stephen's Church in 1850. Today, the building is home to a ski and bike shop, Hickory & Tweed.

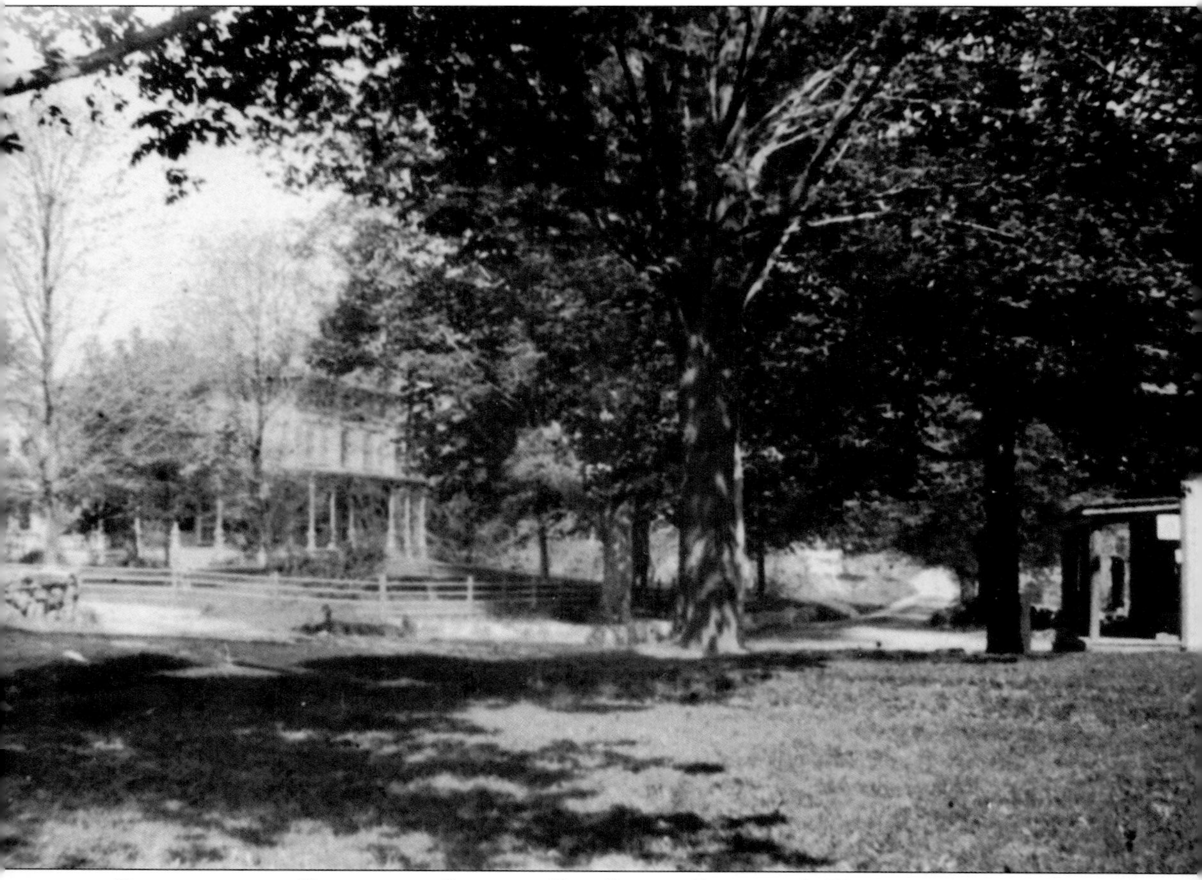

ROAD THROUGH BANKSVILLE SHOWING DR. RALPH GRISWOLD'S HOUSE, 1898. Dr. Griswold provided medical care from 1857 until his death in 1917, first at the round house on today's Round House Road and then in this larger home, built on the site of the old Ezekiel Finch saltbox. Today's Bedford-Banksville Road, passing between the trees and buildings, was little more than a back country lane. Finch's Country Store is the building on the right.

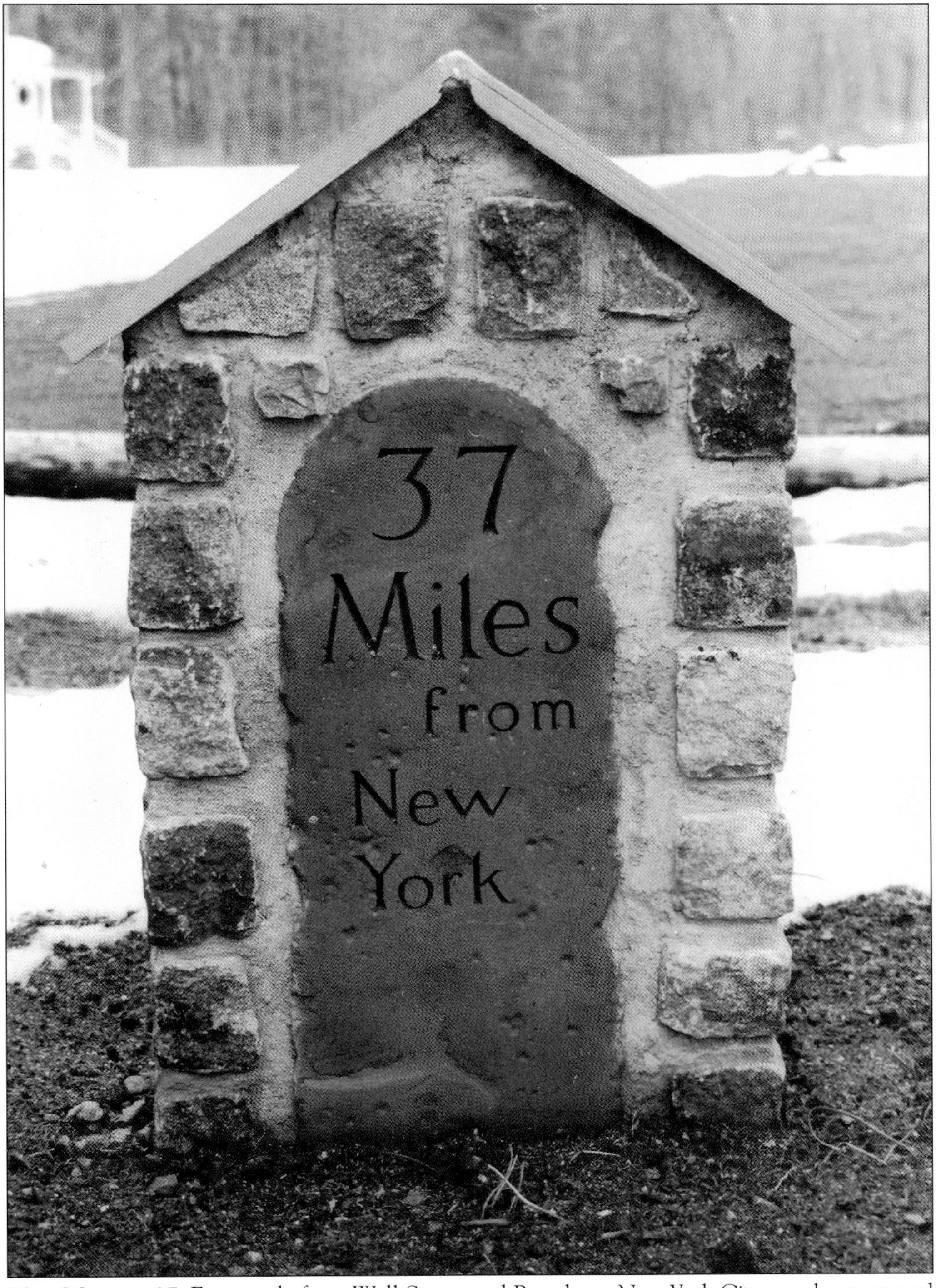

MILE MARKER 37. Every mile from Wall Street and Broadway, New York City, on the post road to Danbury, Connecticut, and Vermont (as the roads were then routed) was marked with a mile marker. This marker is at today's 440 Bedford Road, Armonk (historic Smith's Tavern). After a traffic mishap, it was moved 250 feet west for safety, fitted back together, recut, and encased in this stone "dog house."

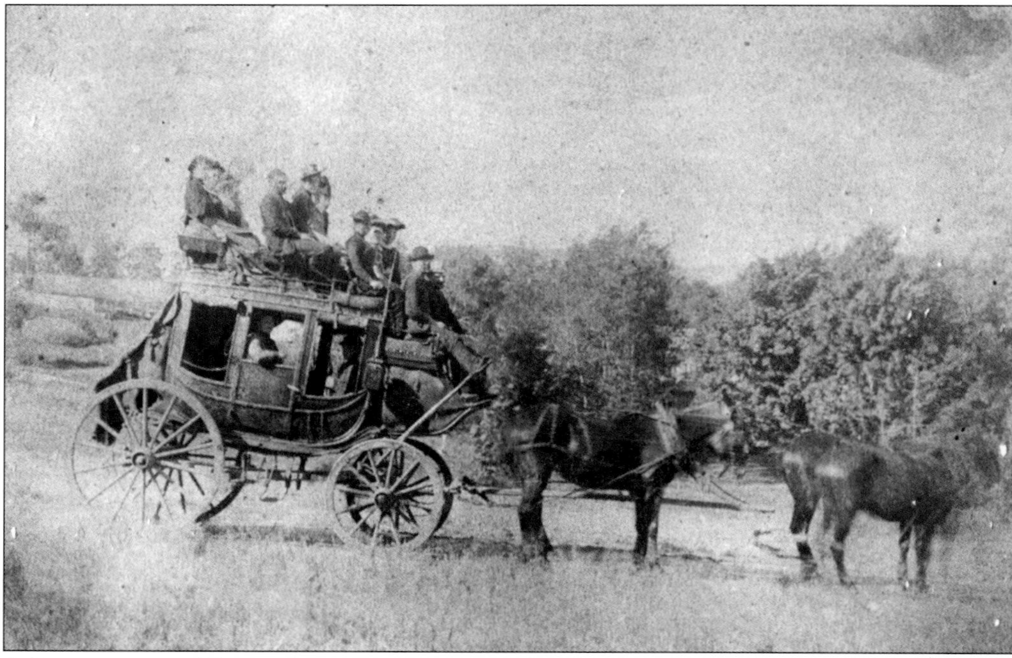

A Stagecoach in North Castle, Mid-1800s. This photograph shows a stagecoach with seating inside and three rows of seating on top plus the two drivers. The stagecoach in 1850 from North Castle Post Office (today's 1 Spruce Hill Road in Armonk) to Port Chester, New York, cost 37 ½¢ one way and took three and a half hours.

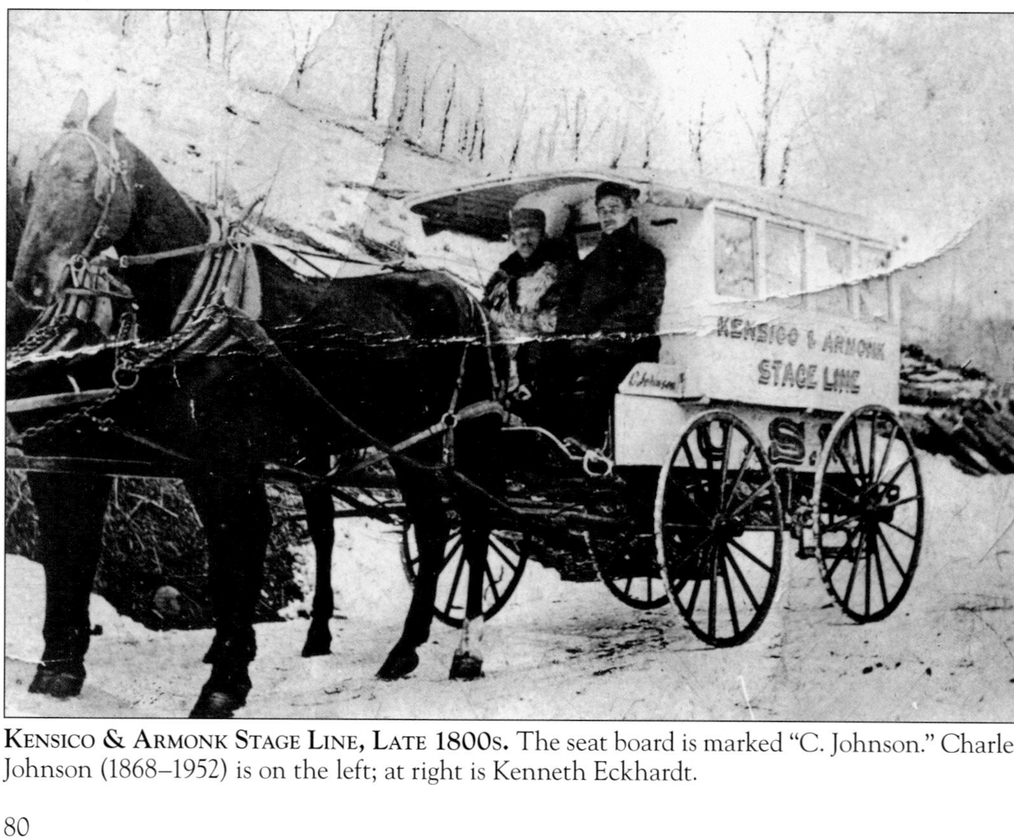

Kensico & Armonk Stage Line, Late 1800s. The seat board is marked "C. Johnson." Charles Johnson (1868–1952) is on the left; at right is Kenneth Eckhardt.

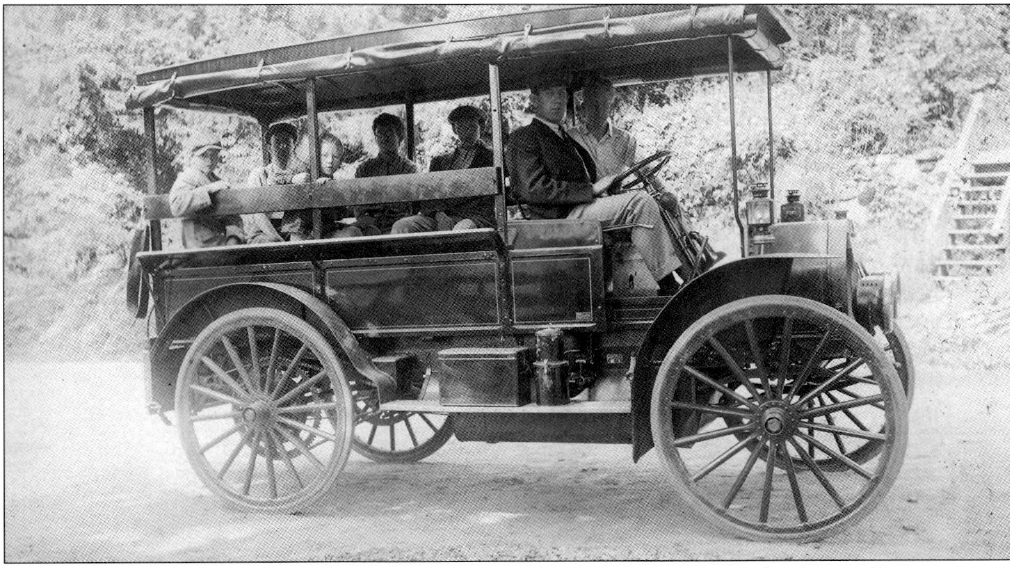

AUTO STAGE BETWEEN VALHALLA AND ARMONK, EARLY 1900S. As the horse-drawn era was coming to a close, this early auto-stage carried the mail and people from Armonk to Valhalla twice a day. The proprietor was Charles Johnson (1868–1952). From left to right in the truck are Clifford Johnson, Reggie Johnson, Stanley Johnson, unidentified, Howard Johnson, Frank Johnson (1891–1973, driving), and Charlie Johnson (front passenger).

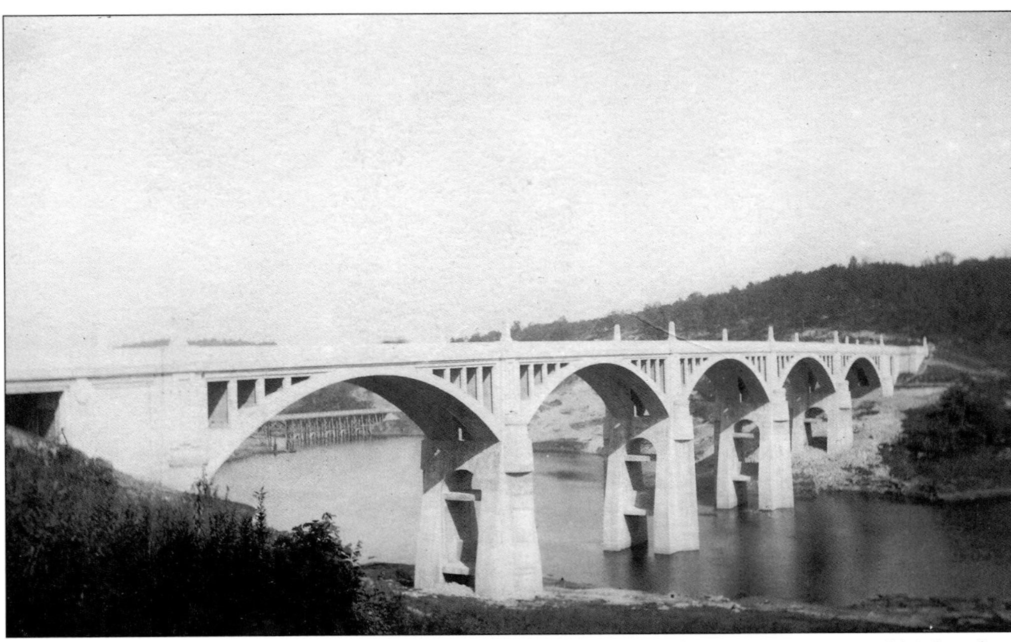

RYE LAKE BRIDGE, NORTH WHITE PLAINS. Initially constructed in 1910–1911 as a 924-foot-long two-lane bridge with five spandrel arches, adding a lane to each side in a cantilevered fashion widened the bridge to four lanes in 1938. Local lore is that one should only use the inside lanes, because the "wings" were added after the bridge was built.

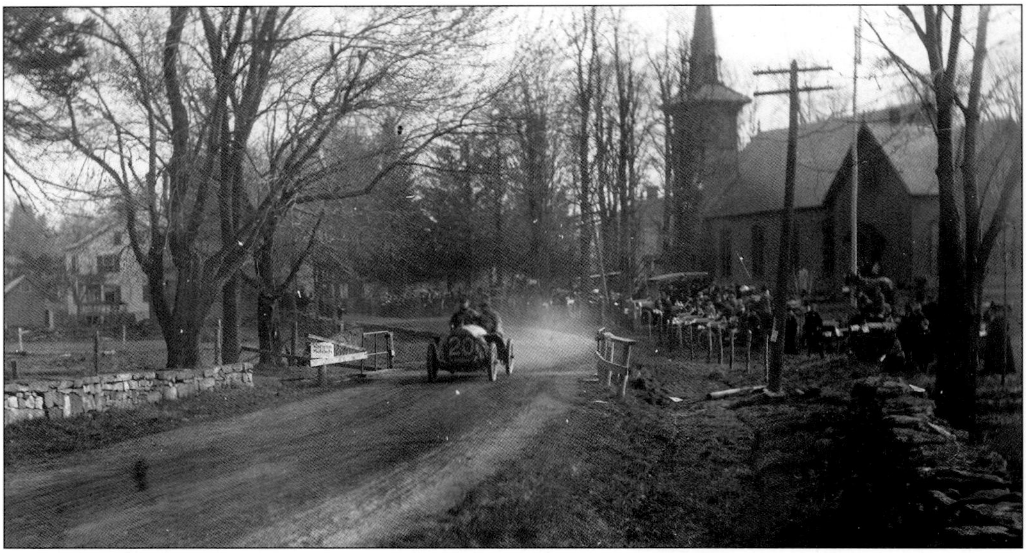

1908 Briarcliff First American International Road Race Speeding through Armonk. The race drew 22 cars from American, Austrian, French, German, and Italian automobile manufacturers and hundreds of spectators. Car no. 20, a Benz driven by L.J. Bergdoll, is shown heading south with the Armonk Methodist Church (today's Westchester Chinese Christian Church at 3 Bedford Road) at right.

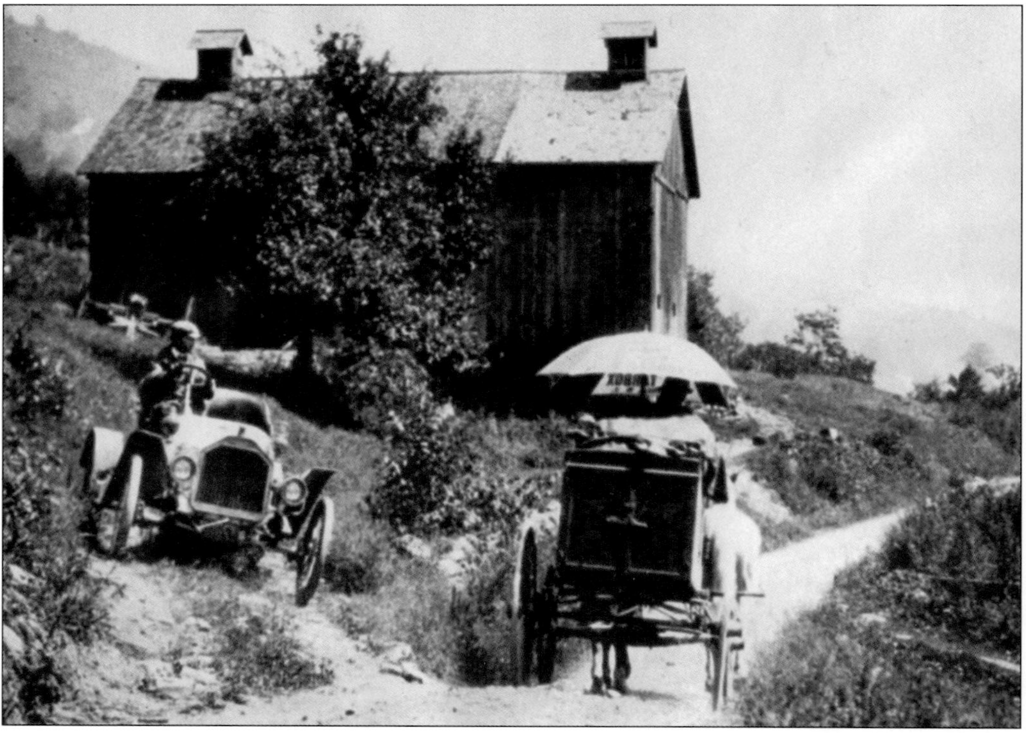

1908 Briarcliff First American International Road Race Drivers Encountered Obstacles. The route began in Briarcliff Manor and called for 10 laps around a 30-mile circle through Westchester County, including North Castle's Armonk hamlet and through Old Kensico Village. A North Castle farmer did not give up the road in favor of this driver.

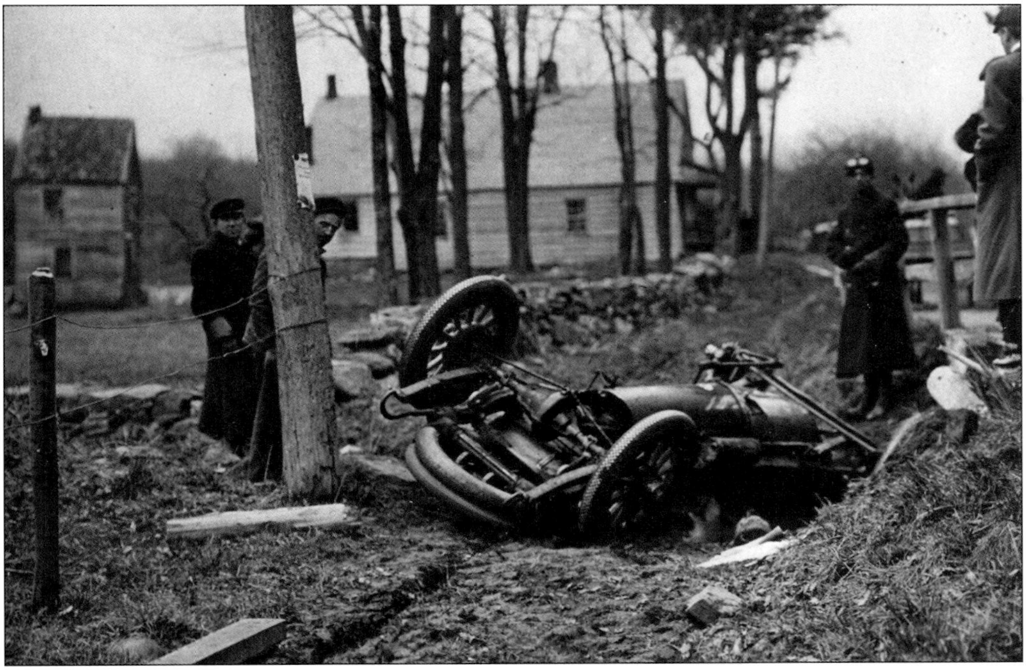

1908 BRIARCLIFF FIRST AMERICAN INTERNATIONAL ROAD RACE, MISHAPS OCCURRED. On April 21, 1908, driver Arthur Campbell was injured in a crash while practicing. Mechanic Ralph DePalma took his place in the race. The *New York Times* reported that more than 300,000 people, coming by car, train, trolley, foot, and horseback, lit fires, camped overnight before the race, and crowded the hillsides overlooking the route.

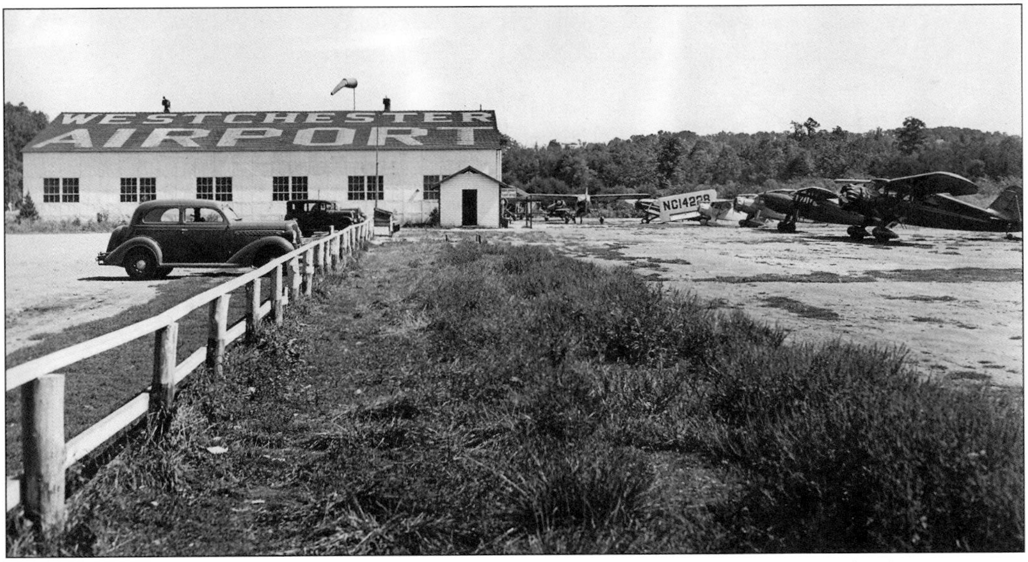

WESTCHESTER AIRPORT IN ARMONK, C. 1930. The heirs of James Hopkins sold the future airport property, about 72 acres, in 1907 to Frederick Schmaling. Ownership of the property and parts of it changed many times over the years. Besides Daniel Barrett, it was owned by various airport and holding corporations until it was purchased by Edward Lashins in 1955. Some of the airport managers and lessees included George Arents III, Spencer Leech, J. Edwin Jones, A.W. Stewart, David Fingar, and Howard "Pappy" Matteson.

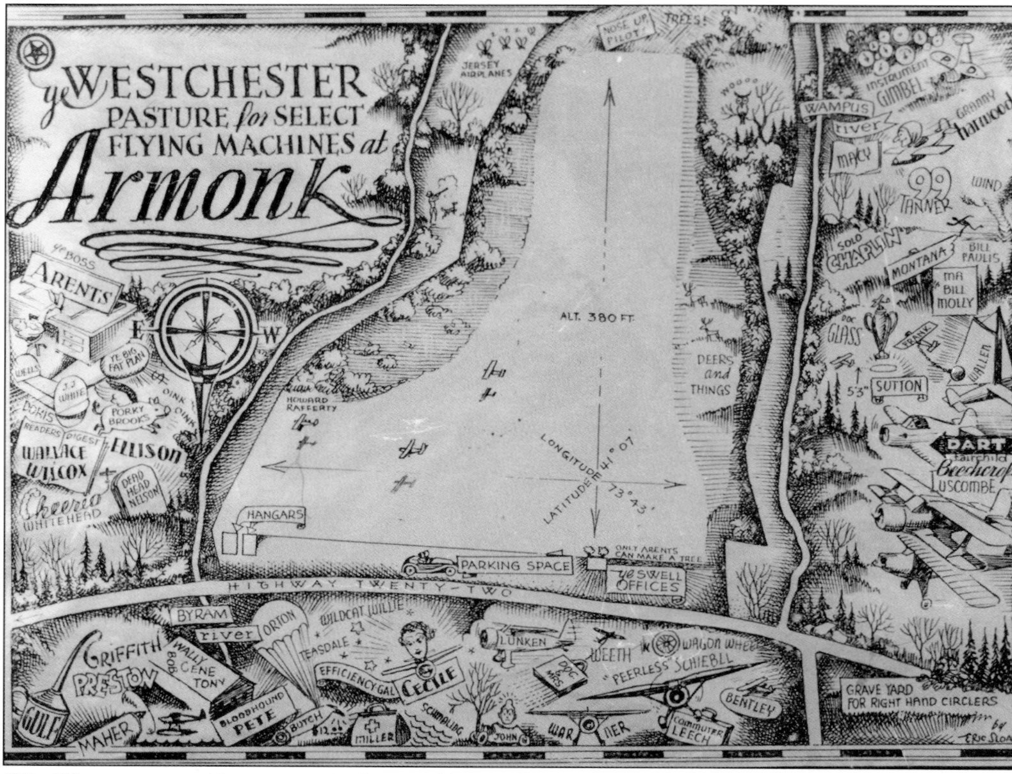

"Ye Westchester Pasture for Select Flying Machines at Armonk." Eric Sloane drew this amusing map of the airport at Armonk. Arents is labeled "ye boss," the compass is backwards, and pilots' nicknames, including Porky Brooks, Dead Head Nelson, Cheerio Whitehead, Granny Harwood, Solo Chaplin, and Commuter Leech, surround the drawing of the landing strip.

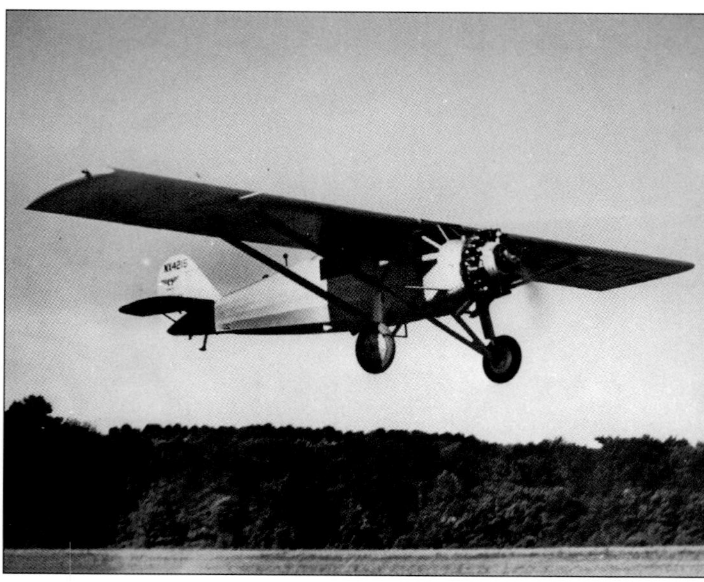

Col. Charles Lindbergh Landing at Barrett Field, Armonk Airport, 1928. According to the *Bronxville Review*, Lindbergh landed at Barrett Field, Armonk, on Sunday, August 12, 1928, and departed Monday morning at 9:00 a.m. He spent the night as the guest of his friend R.M. Lewis of Bedford Hills, New York. Mahoney Aircraft Corporation gave this plane (tail number NX4215) to Lindbergh in 1928.

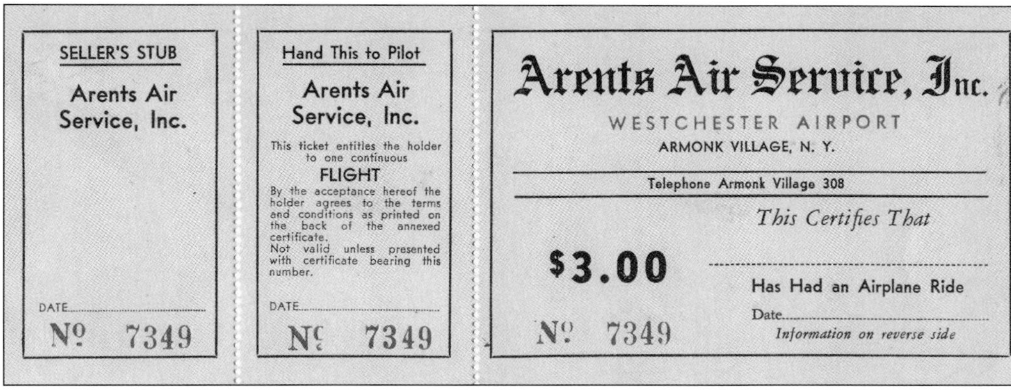
SELLER'S STUB

Arents Air Service, Inc.

DATE

№ 7349

Hand This to Pilot

Arents Air Service, Inc.

This ticket entitles the holder to one continuous

FLIGHT

By the acceptance hereof the holder agrees to the terms and conditions as printed on the back of the annexed certificate.

Not valid unless presented with certificate bearing this number.

DATE

№ 7349

Arents Air Service, Inc.

WESTCHESTER AIRPORT

ARMONK VILLAGE, N. Y.

Telephone Armonk Village 308

This Certifies That

$3.00

Has Had an Airplane Ride

Date

Information on reverse side

№ 7349

ARENTS AIR SERVICE INC. AT WESTCHESTER AIRPORT, ARMONK, LATE 1930S. The price of a ticket for an airplane ride was $3. Arents rented airplanes to pilots and sold rides to the public. Arents operated from November 1938 until late 1941. Armonk Airport was closed for much of World War II.

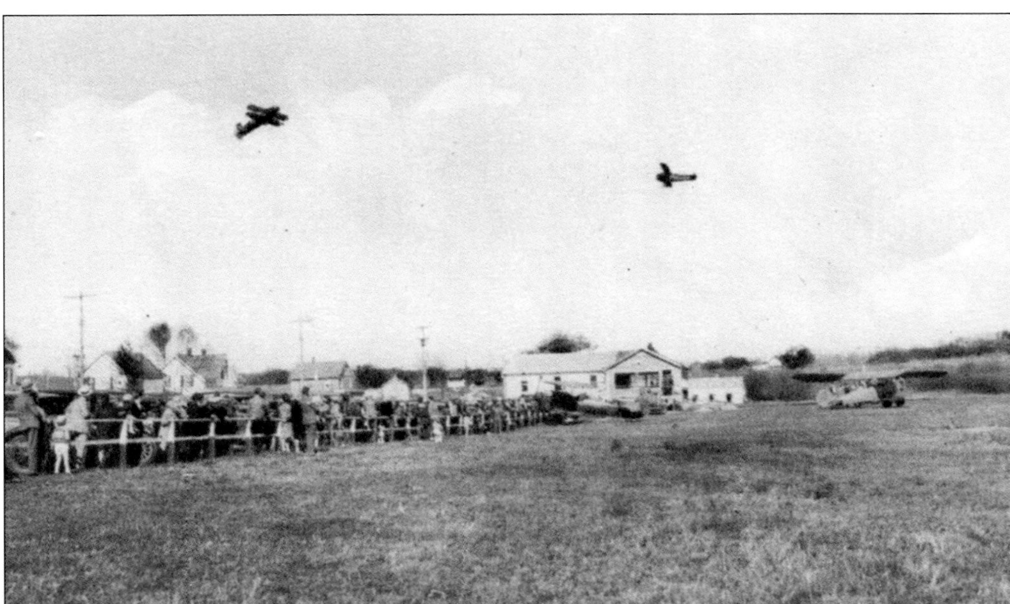

ARMONK AIRPORT AIR SHOWS OFFERED STUNT FLYING, WING WALKING, AND PARACHUTE JUMPING. During the 1930s, automobile traffic in North Castle could be backed up for miles due to Armonk air shows. One of the largest attracted more than 12,000 people. The *North Castle Sun* reported that the May 25 air pageant caused cars to jam local roads and bring traffic to a standstill.

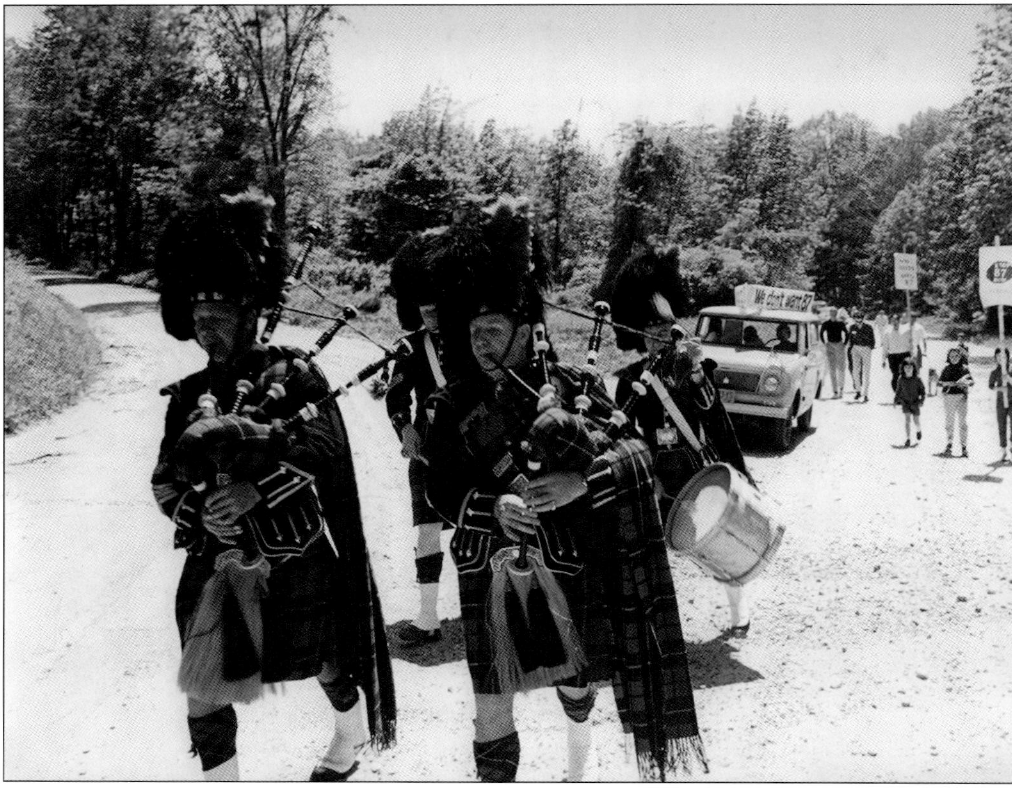

North Castle Protested Route 87 Construction. Plans began in the mid-1950s for a north-south interstate highway through North Castle. Building it took over 20 years, cost about $3.5 million per mile, and produced hours of angry hearings. North Castle protested with bagpipes, baby carriages, and big signs. *Atlantic Monthly* editors wrote that Americans seem to have a "compulsion to become a continent of concrete and monoxide." Today Route 87 is Interstate 684.

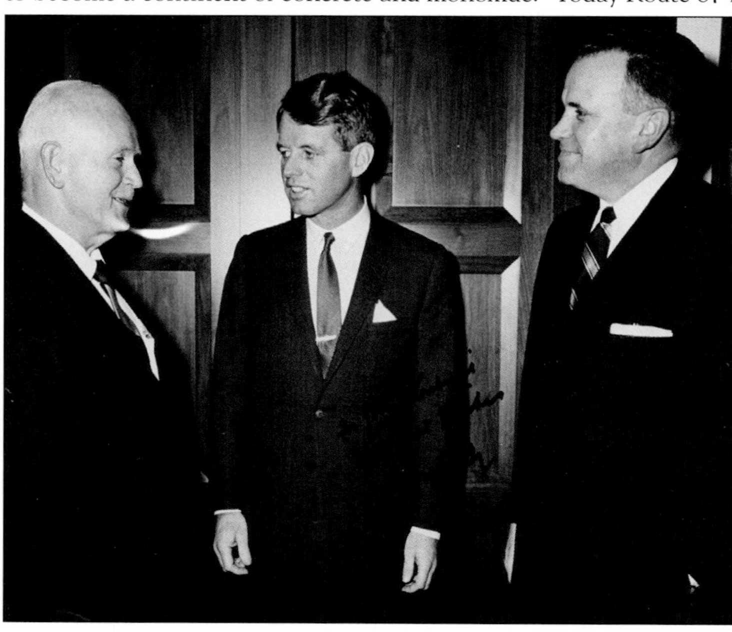

North Castle Went to Washington to Protest Route 87. North Castle supervisor John A. Lombardi (right) and Mount Kisco mayor J. Edward Fox (left) went to Washington and met with Sen. Robert F. Kennedy (center) in 1963. Interstate 684 was completed in 1975 along the route preferred by the Lombardi-Fox protest team.

Eight

Churches and Schools

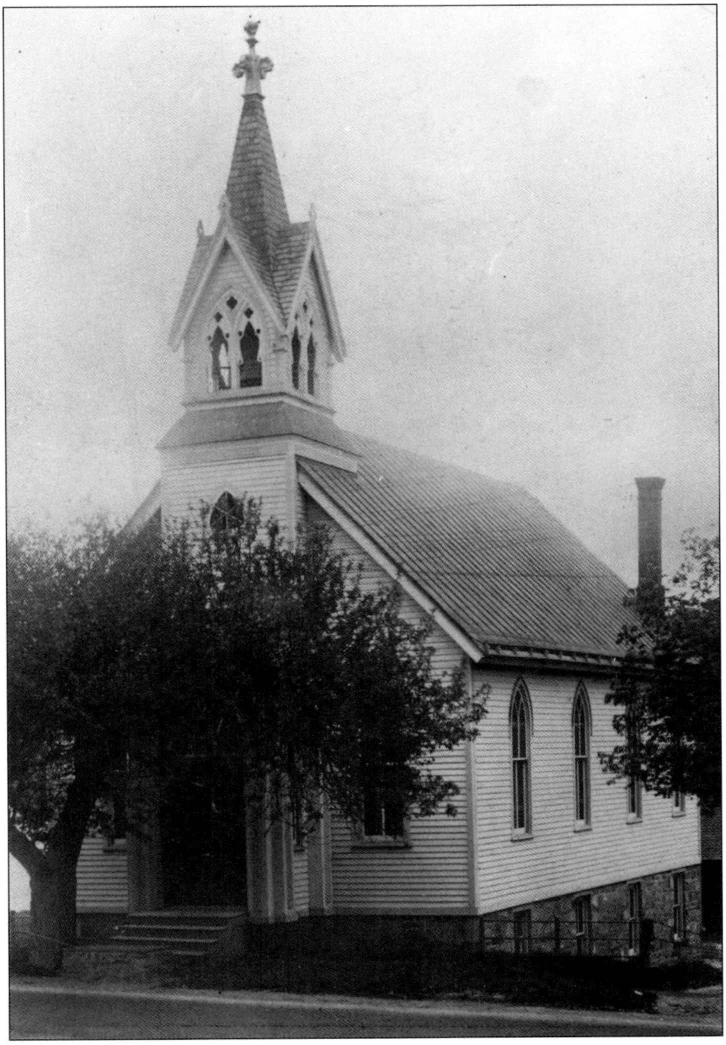

Kensico Methodist Episcopal Church, c. 1900. Judge Arthur Pietschker and Edgar A. Huestis attended the last service held in the Kensico Church and closed the doors for the last time. The building was taken over by the City of New York for the Kensico Reservoir. The congregation then built Castle Heights Methodist Episcopal Church in North White Plains, using the furniture and leaded stained-glass windows from the Kensico Church.

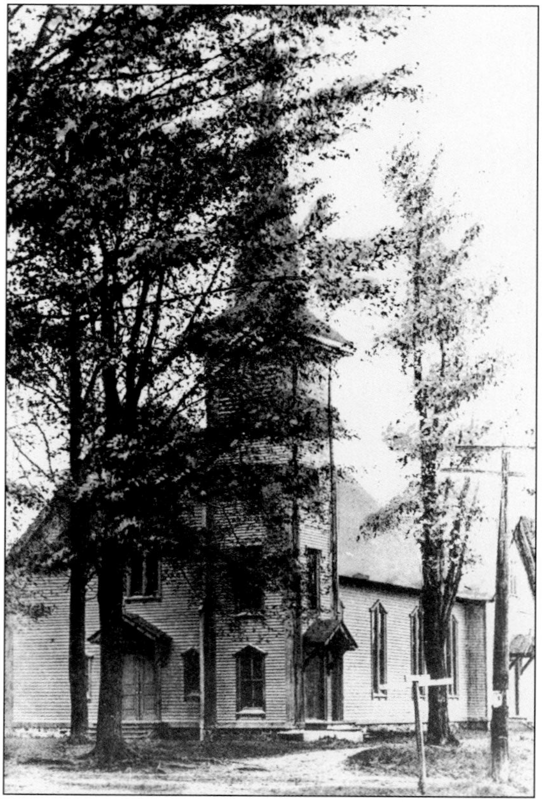

ARMONK METHODIST EPISCOPAL CHURCH (NOW WESTCHESTER CHINESE CHRISTIAN CHURCH). This building at the corner of Main Street and Bedford Road, Armonk, was dedicated in 1872. It replaced the 1787 building that was on today's Cox Avenue at the corner of School Street, where the old cemetery survives.

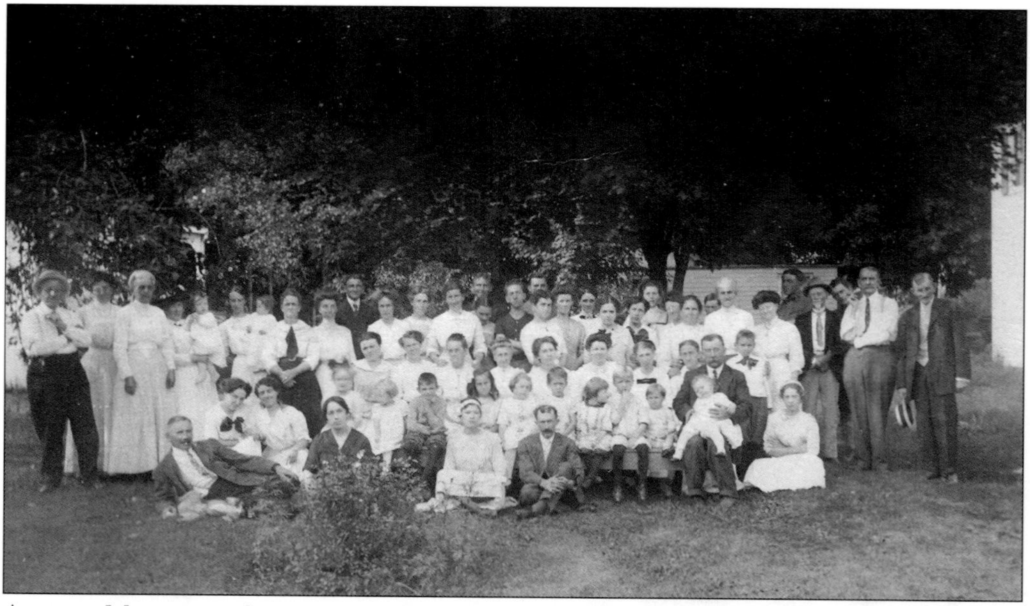

ARMONK METHODIST CHURCH PICNIC, C. 1913. The man standing at left is Judge William Kip Haviland. Among the 60 or so pictured are members of the Acker, Brundage, Lander, Ryan, MacDonald, Waterbury, Cox, Huestis, Finch, Hopkins, Smith, and Lovelett families. By 1916, Haviland was characterized as the "Marrying Justice of the Lake Region" and Armonk as a Gretna Green.

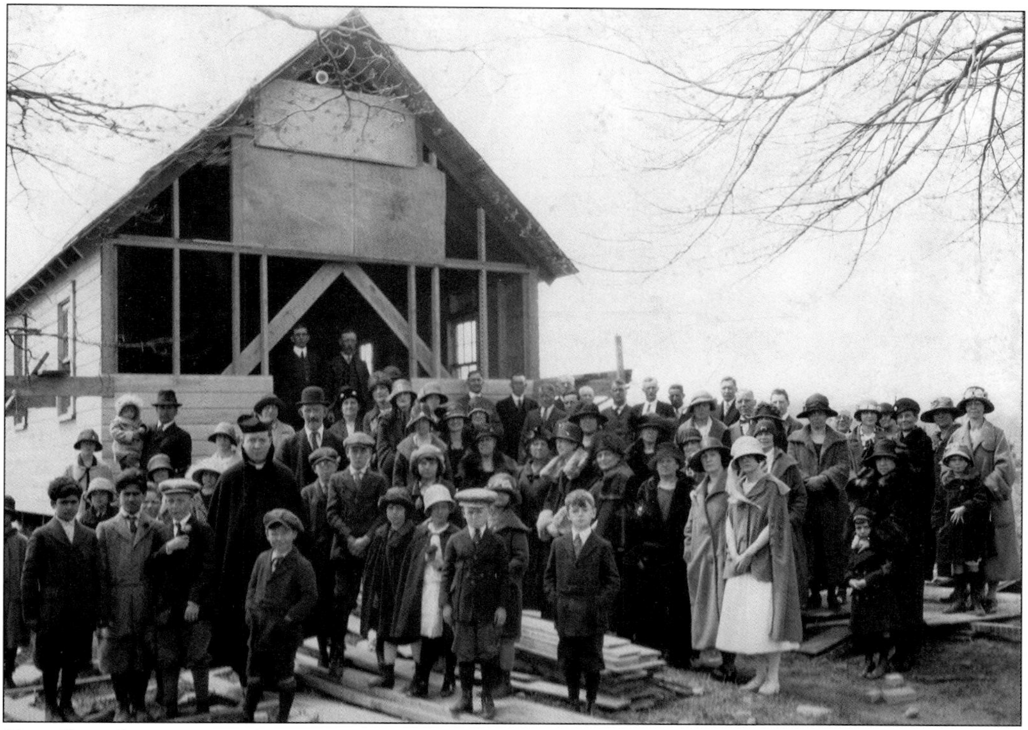

The Old Church of St. Patrick, Bedford Road, Armonk, c. 1924. In January 1924, the Catholic congregation bought two acres from Frederick and Hettie (Webster) Schmaling. Supervised by Harry Schnoor, volunteers constructed the building near today's 111 Bedford Road, Armonk. A large group celebrated the first mass in this far-from-complete building on May 24, 1924.

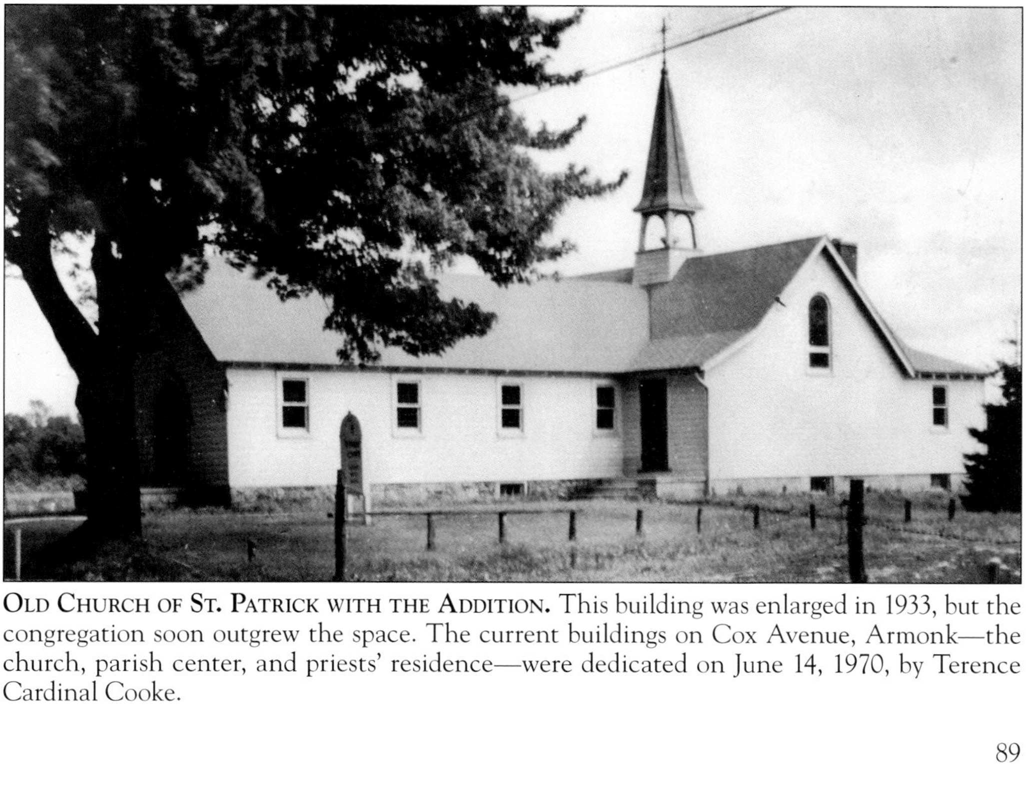

Old Church of St. Patrick with the Addition. This building was enlarged in 1933, but the congregation soon outgrew the space. The current buildings on Cox Avenue, Armonk—the church, parish center, and priests' residence—were dedicated on June 14, 1970, by Terence Cardinal Cooke.

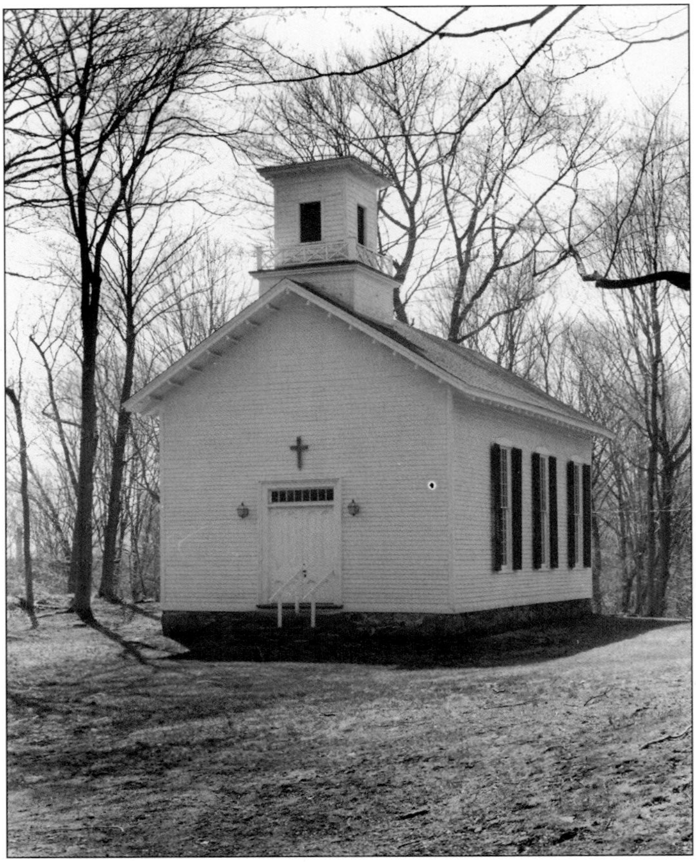

St. Mary's Episcopal Church, Erected 1853. Although the church was incorporated in 1851, the building went up two years later. This building at today's East Middle Patent and Hickory Kingdom Roads, Bedford, figures prominently in Barbara Massi's book *The Diary of Molly Guion Brown.*

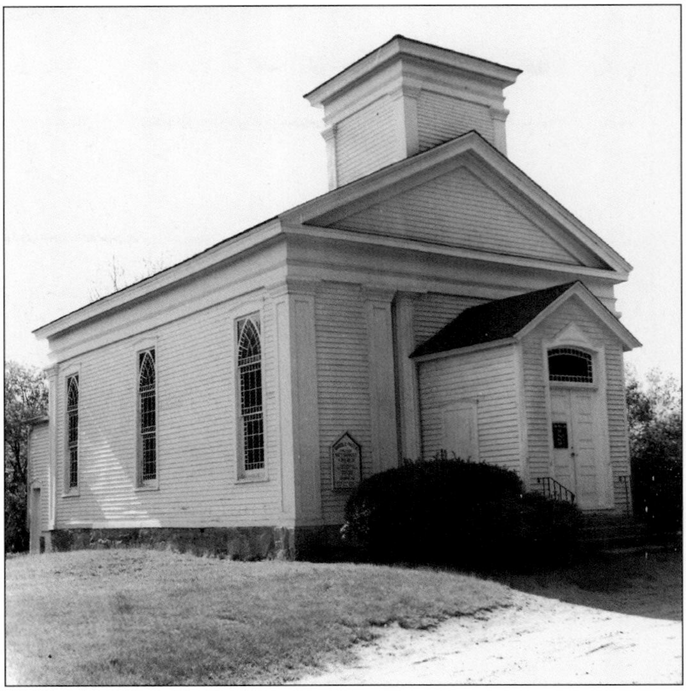

Middle Patent Methodist Church, Bedford-Banksville Road, Bedford. Although the church dates to about 1824, as a result of a fire in 1992, this building is a lovely restoration, faithful to historic details, without any electricity or heating. A period-appropriate, foot-pumped organ was located and installed during the restoration. The beautiful brass kerosene hanging lamps and old stained-glass windows were preserved and utilized in the restoration.

ST. STEPHEN'S EPISCOPAL CHURCH, FOUNDED IN 1842. This early picture of the church at today's 50 Bedford Road, Armonk, was taken before additions were built on the back and east sides of the building.

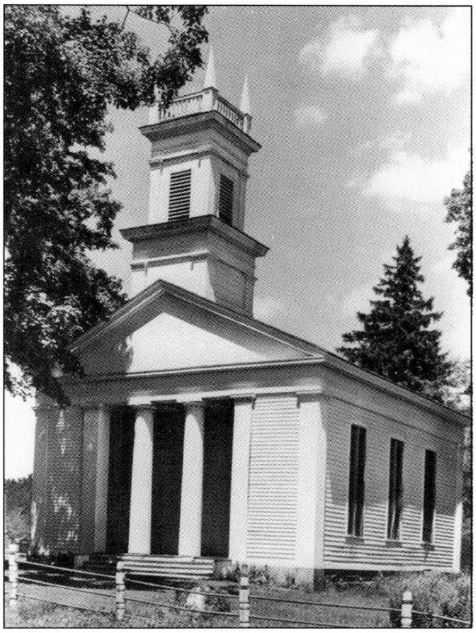

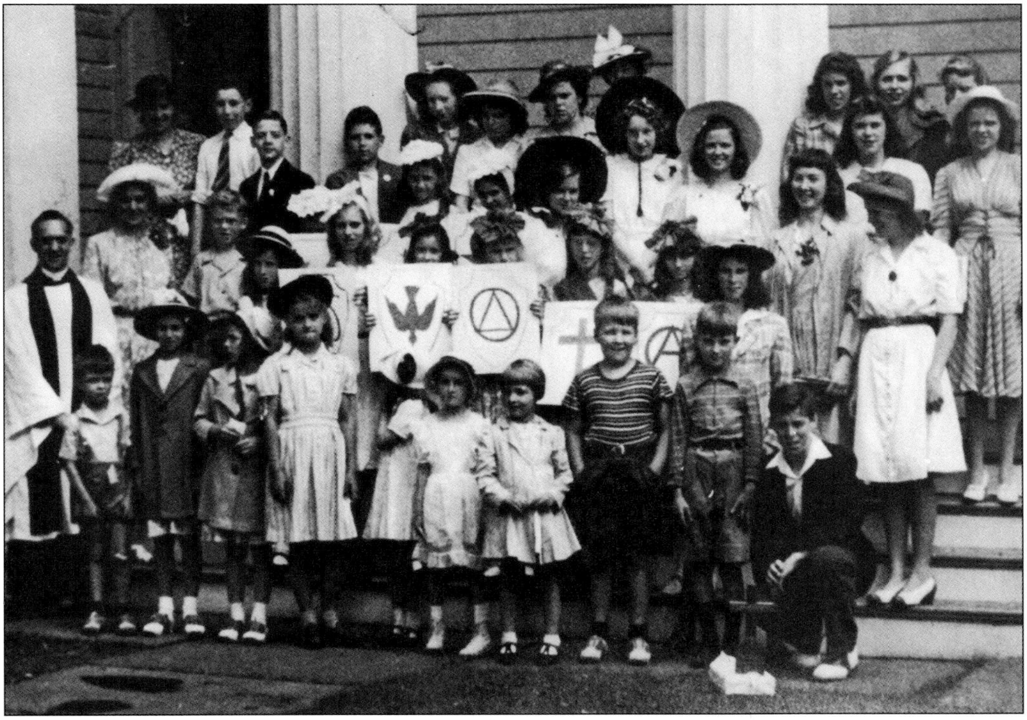

ST. STEPHEN'S EPISCOPAL CHURCH SUNDAY SCHOOL, 1942. From left to right are (first row) Rev. Harold Thelin, James Garvin, two unidentified, Mary Tompkins, two unidentified, Marion Louise Benz, Mark Benz, unidentified, and Norman Holloway; (second row) Pauline Murrah, two unidentified, Kathleen Creed, Janet Curry, Janice Lander, Sally Hendry, unidentified, Beryl Holloway, ? Love, and Doris Lewis Fisher; (third row) Charles Boyd, Elaine Garvin, Sally Tompkins, Helen Kirk, Mary Kirk, Alice Garvin, and Sheelagh Boyd; (fourth row) Margaret Gilbert Benz, Alan Lindsey, Hector Holloway, Eileen Creed, Dorothy Lander, Marian See Craft, Marion Emery, Jean Holloway, Marian Creed, and unidentified.

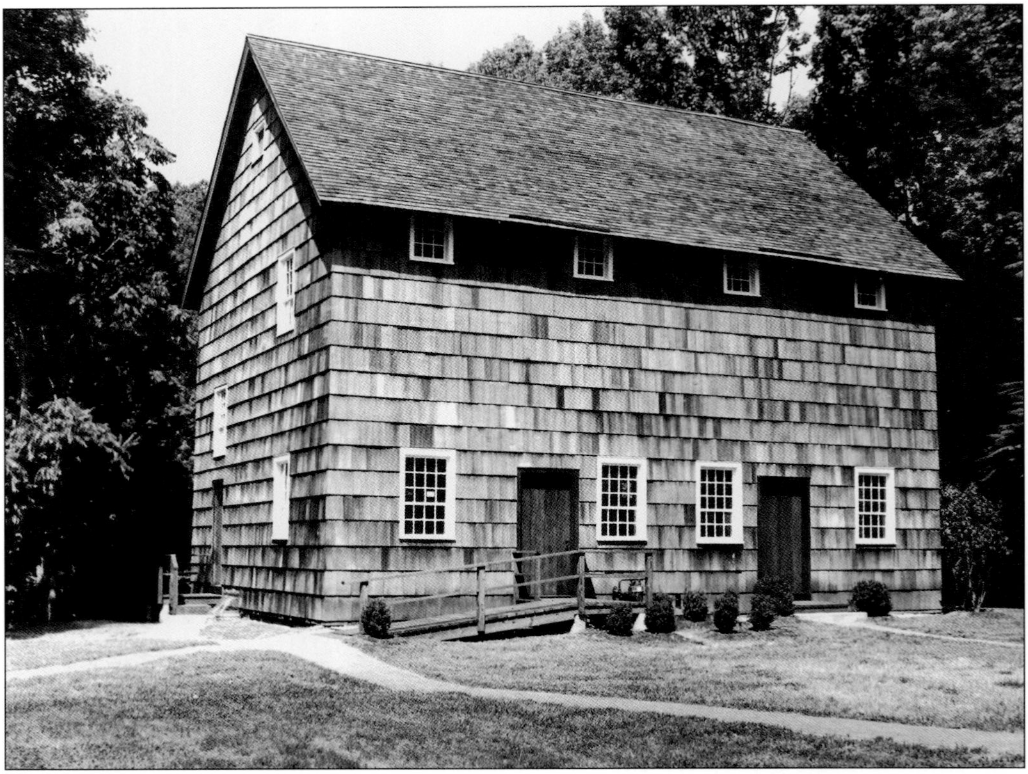

1798 Quaker Meeting House Saved and Restored. The Quakers "laid down" (closed) the North Castle Meeting House and declared the building surplus property in 1875. William Cox bought it. Later owners made significant alterations for farming activities. The North Castle Historical Society saved and moved the building to 440 Bedford Road, Armonk. After four years of detailed restoration, the meeting house was dedicated in 1995.

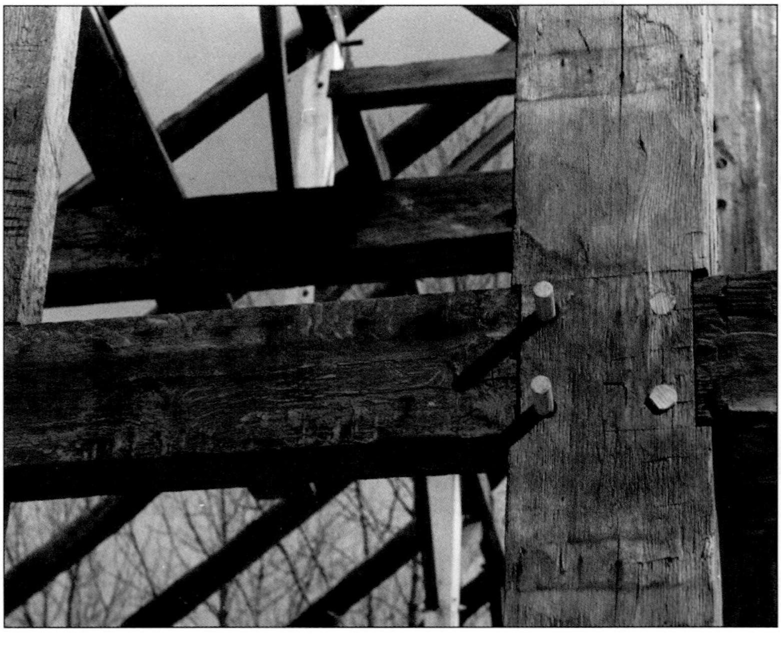

1798 Quaker Meeting House Construction Detail. This close-up photograph, taken during the reconstruction and restoration on North Castle Historical Society property, shows the 1798 timber frame construction. The beams and posts were rough cut, probably by hand. The mortise-and-tenon joints were secured with wooden pegs.

Kensico School Building, Old Kensico Village, Early 1900s. This photograph was taken shortly before the valley was flooded by the Kensico Reservoir.

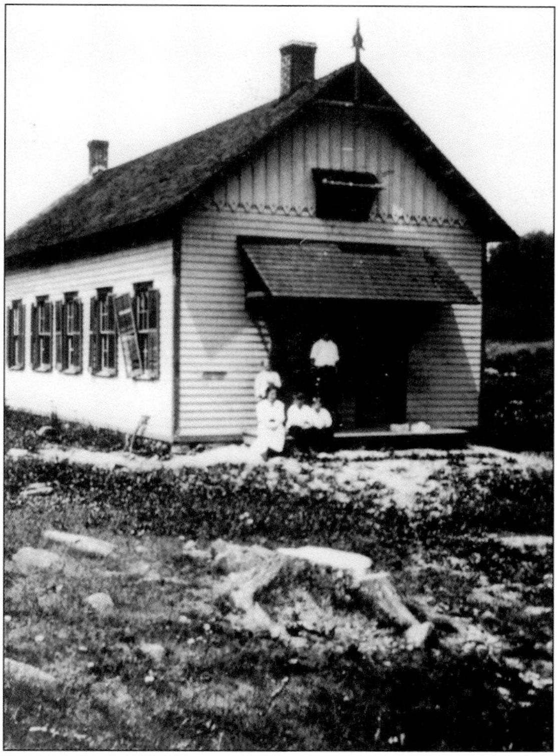

Third Coman Hill School, 1921. A private home today at 636 Bedford Road, Armonk, this school was built in 1915 using materials donated by Gen. Samuel McRoberts. From left to right are teacher Cecelia McDonough, William Cregier, Tom Kirby, unidentified, Frank Horton, Fred Kirby, Clinton Ferris, Elliot Cregier, Edith Horton, Helen Ferris, Marie Worden, Elwin Horton, Marion McCabe, Marguerite Cregier, unidentified, Frances Myder, Harry Wilson, Nathan Ferris, Richard Schnoor, and Alfred Sniffin.

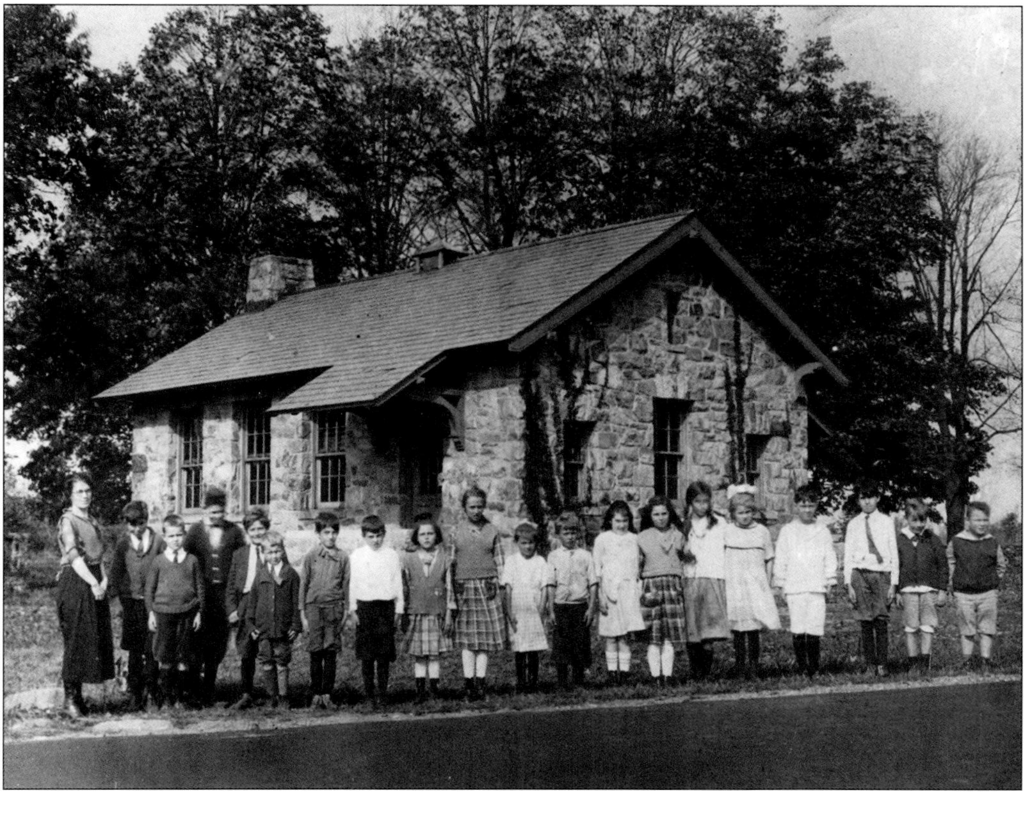

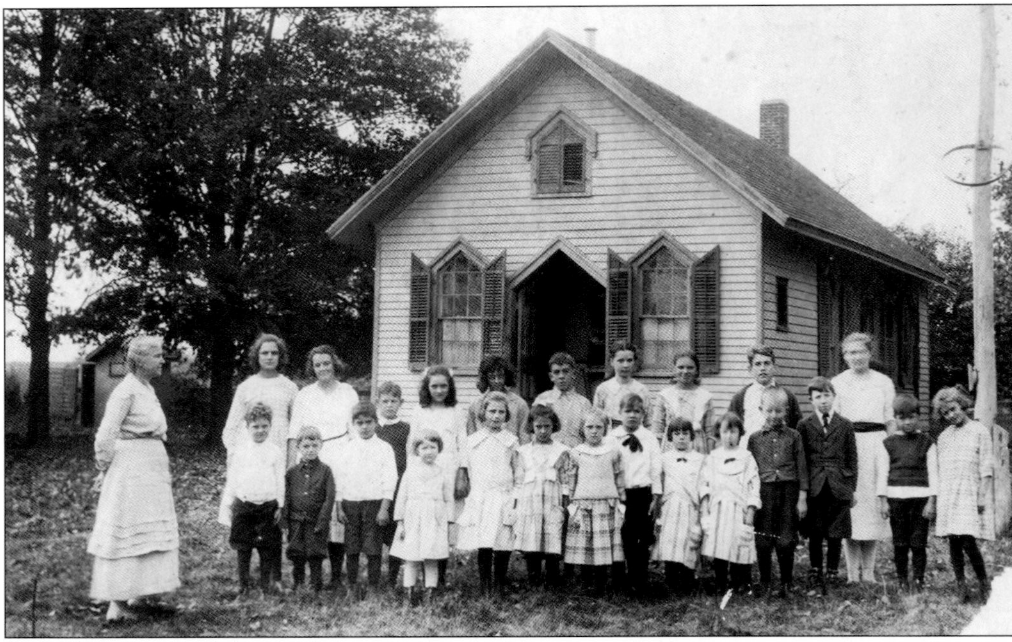

COX AVENUE/WEBSTER SCHOOL, 1920. This school stood at today's 23 Cox Avenue, Armonk. From left to right are (first row) teacher Lillian Webster, Edgar Huestis, Thomas Maryscuk, Anthony Krouch, Marguerite Hopkins, Ethel Bates, Rose Krouch, Julia Maryscuk, Bertram Simmons, Rose Jones, Annie Jones, Amos Remsen, James D. Hopkins, Arthur Mahoney, and Frances Mahoney; (second row) Marge Bennett, Margaret Deal, George Abrams, Kate Donnelley, Theresa Lorent, Wallace Remsen, Rose Donnelley, Mary Maryscuk, Stanley Waterbury, and Annie Wesley.

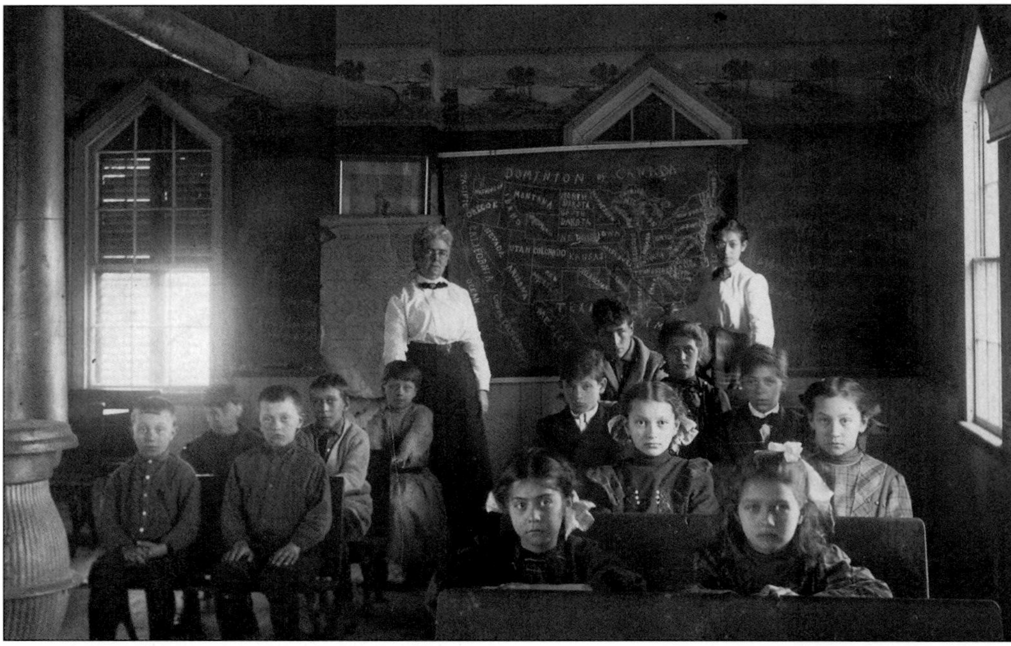

INTERIOR VIEW COX AVENUE/WEBSTER SCHOOL. Children pictured include Tony, Charles, Mary, and Clara Stoorza; Ed, Ann, and Rose Wesley; Grace and Mabel Farrington; and Albert and Harry Donnelly. The teacher is Lillian Webster.

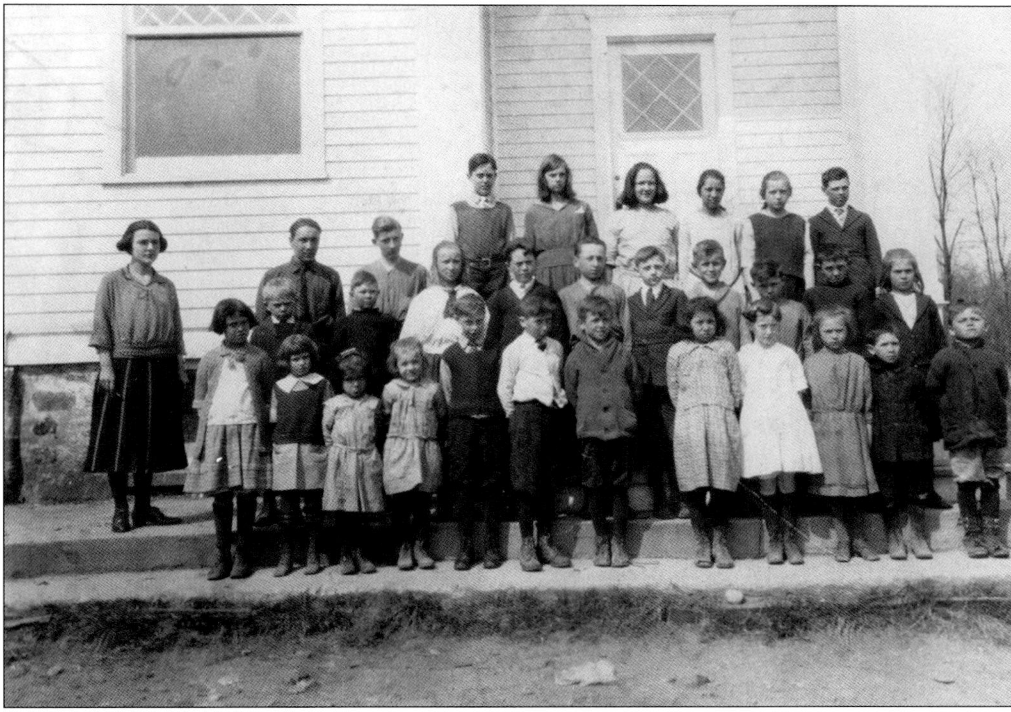

Middle Patent School, 1923. This school stood at today's Gina Lane and Round Hill Road, Bedford. From left to right are (first row) Mildred Contoit, Carol Emery, two unidentified, George Kaiser, unidentified, Victor Mead, Lena Ritacco, Grace Waterbury, Mary Zygmont, Angelo Ritacco, and unidentified; (second row) teacher Miss Waite, unidentified, Lyndon Waterman, Annie Zygmont, James O'Brien, Raymond Zygmont, unidentified, Gilbert Mead, Mike Zygmont, Ray Waterman, and Mary Cheriott; (third row) unidentified, Leo Mazarak, Joe Hegeman, Flora Robbins, Flora Merlow, Carmela Ritacco, Ruth Mead, and George Robbins.

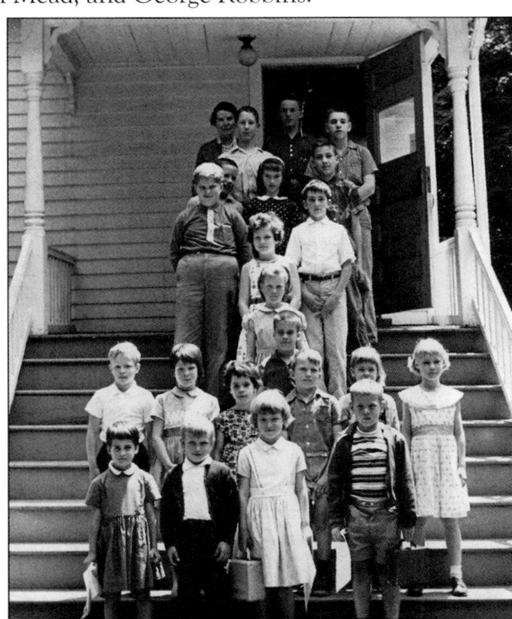

East Middle Patent School, c. 1960. From left to right are (first row) kindergartners Debbie Longcope, Eddie Sullivan, Sonja Johnson, and David Alexander; (second row) first-graders Jimmy Sullivan, Baille Sause, Francesca Rossi, Andrew Gleason, Debbie Hewitt, and Anita Trembone; (third row) second-grader Jeffrey Longcope; (fourth row) third-grader Barbara Sause; (fifth row) fourth-grader Debbie Sullivan; (sixth row) fifth-graders David Bugli and Curt Gleason; (seventh row) sixth-graders Paul Mead, Donna Gleason, and Eddie Johnson; (eighth row) seventh-graders Stephen Walton and Robert Gibb; (ninth row) teacher Geraldine Lanfair and eighth-grader Mark Gleason.

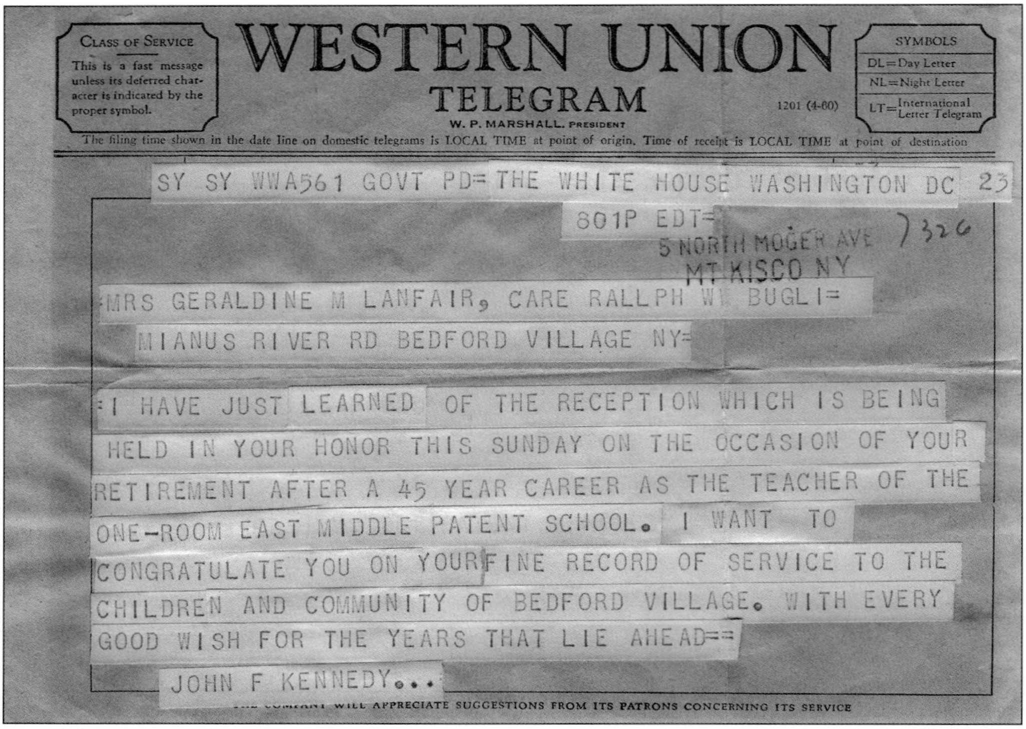

CLASS OF SERVICE
This is a fast message unless its deferred character is indicated by the proper symbol.

WESTERN UNION
TELEGRAM
W. P. MARSHALL, PRESIDENT

1201 (4-60)

SYMBOLS
DL=Day Letter
NL=Night Letter
LT=International Letter Telegram

The filing time shown in the date line on domestic telegrams is LOCAL TIME at point of origin. Time of receipt is LOCAL TIME at point of destination

SY SY WWA561 GOVT PD=THE WHITE HOUSE WASHINGTON DC 23
801P EDT=

5 NORTH MOGER AVE 7326
MT KISCO NY

MRS GERALDINE M LANFAIR, CARE RALLPH W BUGLI=
MIANUS RIVER RD BEDFORD VILLAGE NY=

=I HAVE JUST LEARNED OF THE RECEPTION WHICH IS BEING HELD IN YOUR HONOR THIS SUNDAY ON THE OCCASION OF YOUR RETIREMENT AFTER A 45 YEAR CAREER AS THE TEACHER OF THE ONE-ROOM EAST MIDDLE PATENT SCHOOL. I WANT TO CONGRATULATE YOU ON YOUR FINE RECORD OF SERVICE TO THE CHILDREN AND COMMUNITY OF BEDFORD VILLAGE. WITH EVERY GOOD WISH FOR THE YEARS THAT LIE AHEAD==

JOHN F KENNEDY...

WILL APPRECIATE SUGGESTIONS FROM ITS PATRONS CONCERNING ITS SERVICE

TELEGRAM FROM PRES. JOHN F. KENNEDY TO GERALDINE LANFAIR, 1961. Geraldine McCoy came to North Castle in 1916 at age 18 and soon married local mail carrier Lawrence Lanfair. She taught at East Middle Patent School for 45 years. President Kennedy sent this telegram congratulating her on her retirement.

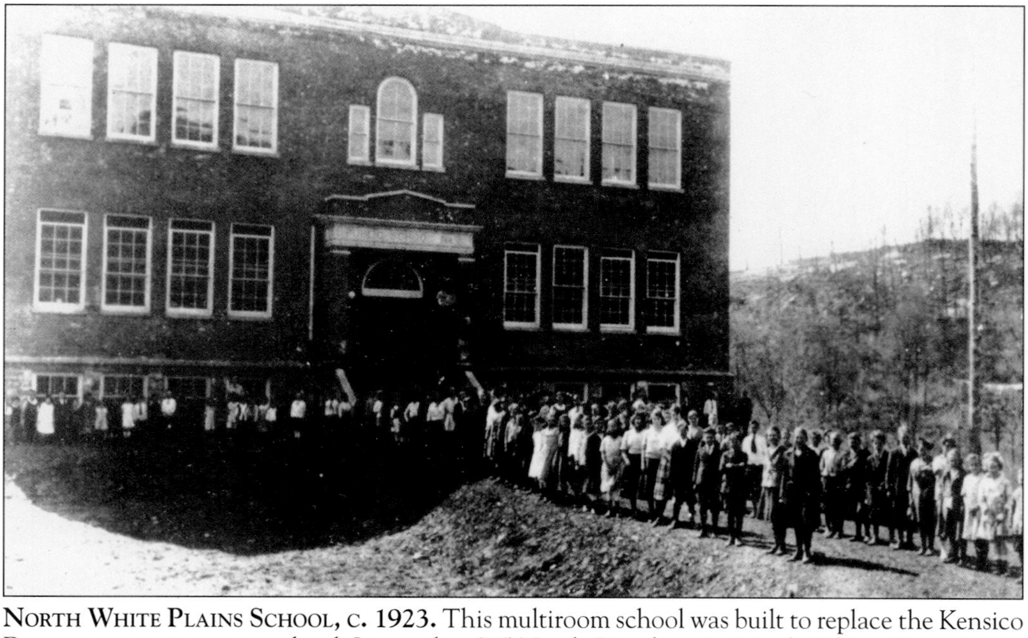

NORTH WHITE PLAINS SCHOOL, C. 1923. This multiroom school was built to replace the Kensico Dam construction camp school. Located at 845 North Broadway in North White Plains, it has been remodeled into an office building.

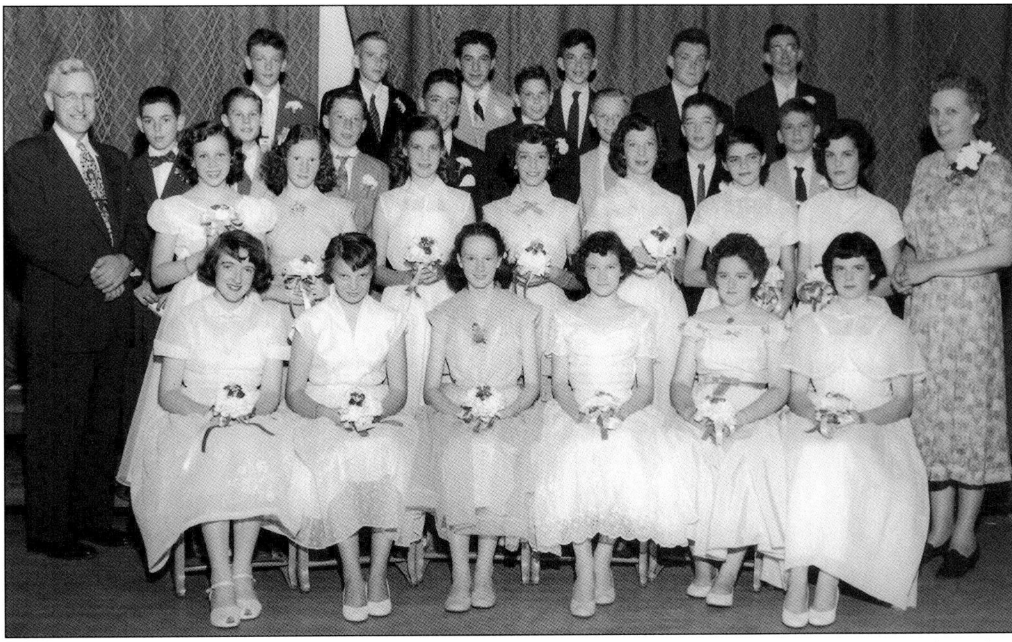

WHIPPOORWILL SCHOOL, ARMONK, 1952. From left to right are (first row) Janet Adams, unidentified, Edith Ringwood, Susan Jaeger, Pat Remsen, and Paige Gordon; (second row) Principal Harold Crittenden, Sandy Schnoor, Barbara Ringwood, Betsy Pyle, Leona Guidali, Jennifer Grant, Molly Frank, Hope Finch, and teacher Lula Whipple; (third row) William Taylor, Kenneth Berry, Jack Korner, Vincent Scarpa, Steven Bernie, Lonny Petersen, Robert Burbank, and Thomas Torlish; (fourth row) Robert Finch, J.P. Curry, Herman Munoz, Richard Dennison, Peter Smith, and Harold Davies.

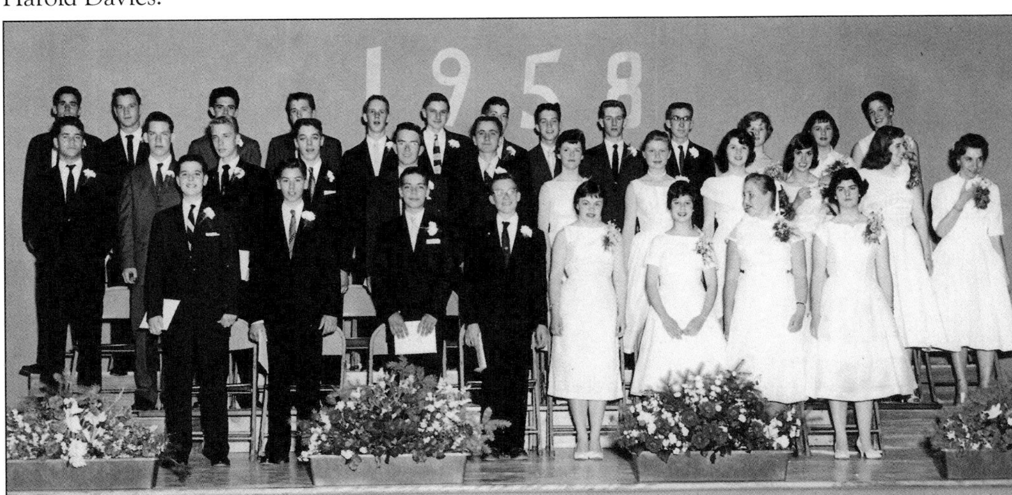

HAROLD C. CRITTENDEN SCHOOL, 1958 GRADUATING CLASS. From left to right are (first row) Bobby Caruso, Skipper Mahoney, John Zanine, Craig Horner, Susan Lape, Judy Rosenbery, Gail Jones, and Gay Badia; (second row) Kenny Vermettee, Mickey Ross, Ron Schwalbe, Jack Dilger, Eddie Rasche, Fred Coupe, Carolyn Puff, Kay Winkler, Bonnie Urso, Daffy Rheiniger, Mary Ellen Cole, and Violet Kuhn; (third row) Anthony Ingani, Richard Weir, Harry Mattison, Jim Carter, Ray Alger, Paul Reiffus, John Morris, Steve Jaeger, Bob Egdell, Bob Kotch, Penny Moorehead, Emmy Erda, and Ceci Winston.

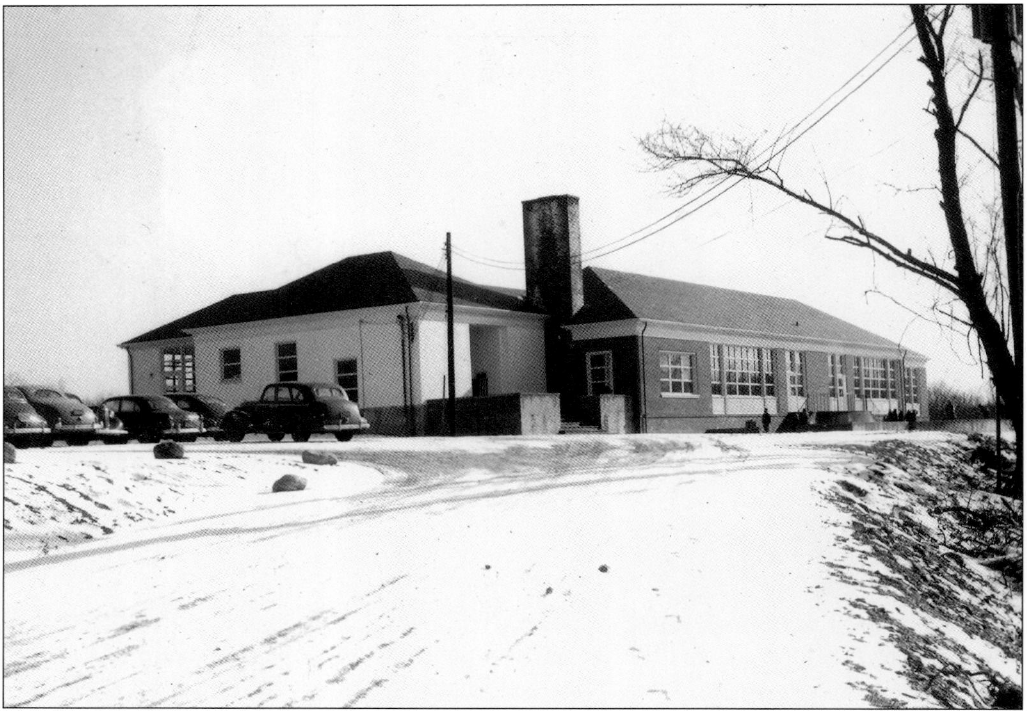

Wampus Elementary School, Opened in January 1951. The community voted a bond issue for $18,000 for property and $287,000 for a new building to provide a school with six classrooms and an all-purpose room on a 25-acre tract of land at the south end of Wampus Avenue, Armonk.

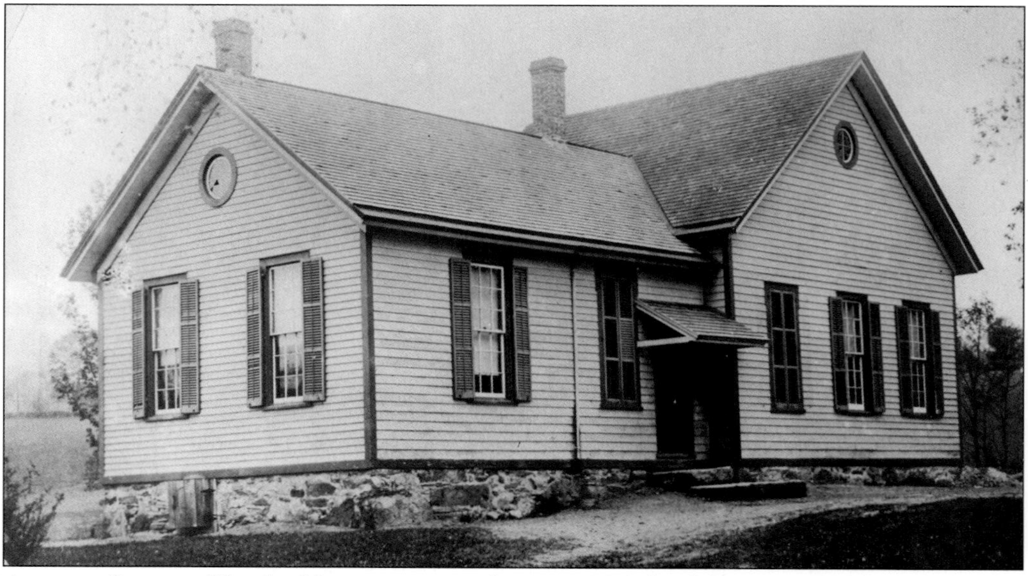

Armonk School. This building is a private home at 28 School Street, Armonk, today and is almost opposite the north end of present Wampus Avenue. It was a two-room school that was one of three small districts consolidated into one in 1923. Dorothy Poole Jones and Lula Aldous West taught here.

Nine

SERVICE TO COMMUNITY AND COUNTRY

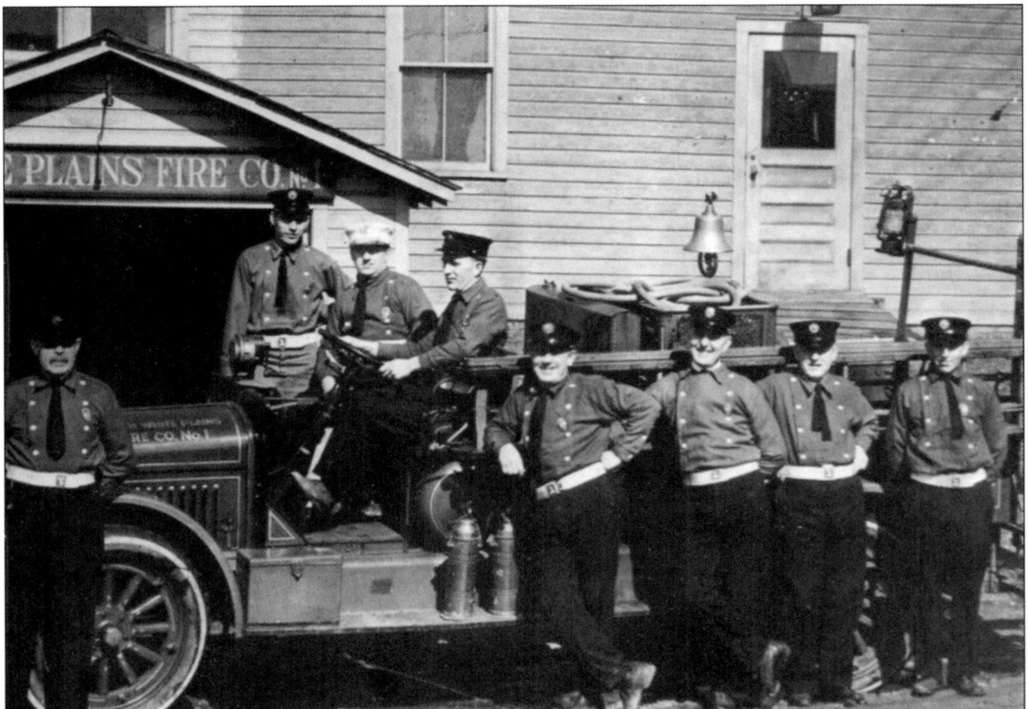

NORTH WHITE PLAINS FIRE DEPARTMENT, C. 1920. From left to right are George Butler, Harold Cook, Ernest Winker, Albert Cook, Robert Adams, Frank Ruland, Robert Nightingale, Al Losee, and Victor Bodman. Also pictured is the department's first motorized apparatus, a Brockway chemical hose wagon that was purchased used. The original wooden fire house is in the background.

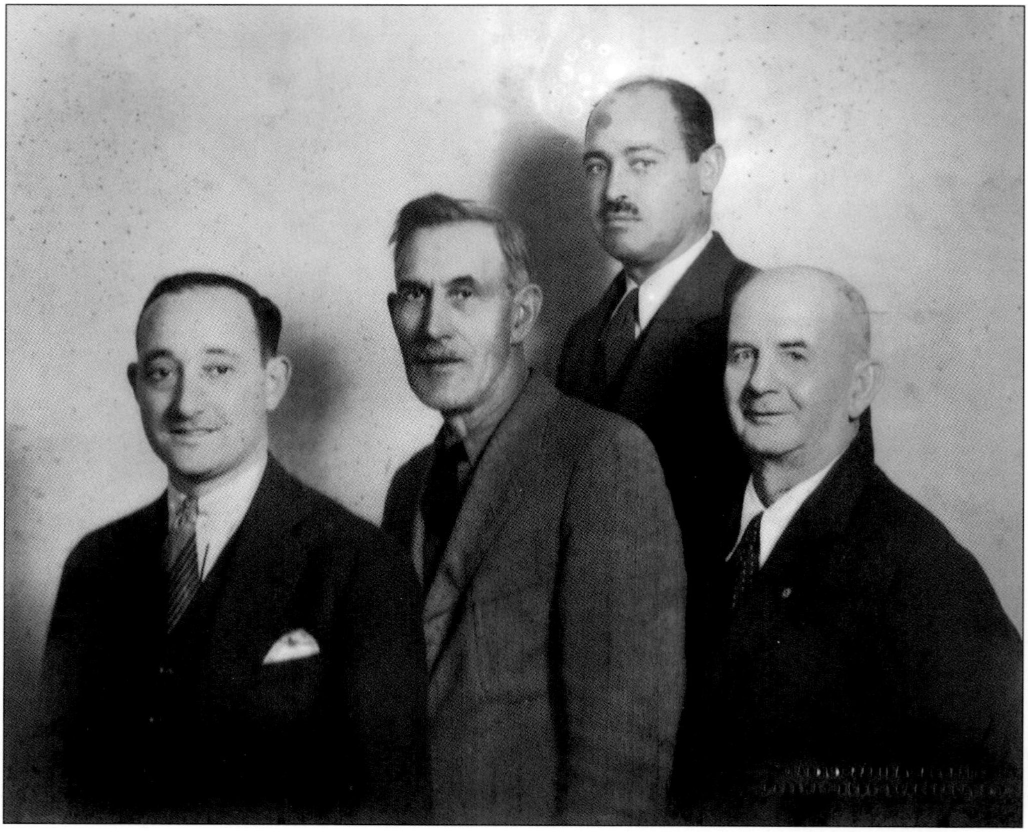

Fire Commissioners, Armonk Fire Department, 1930s. From left to right are Walter Wohlfeil, William Grover, George P. Schmaling, and James Young.

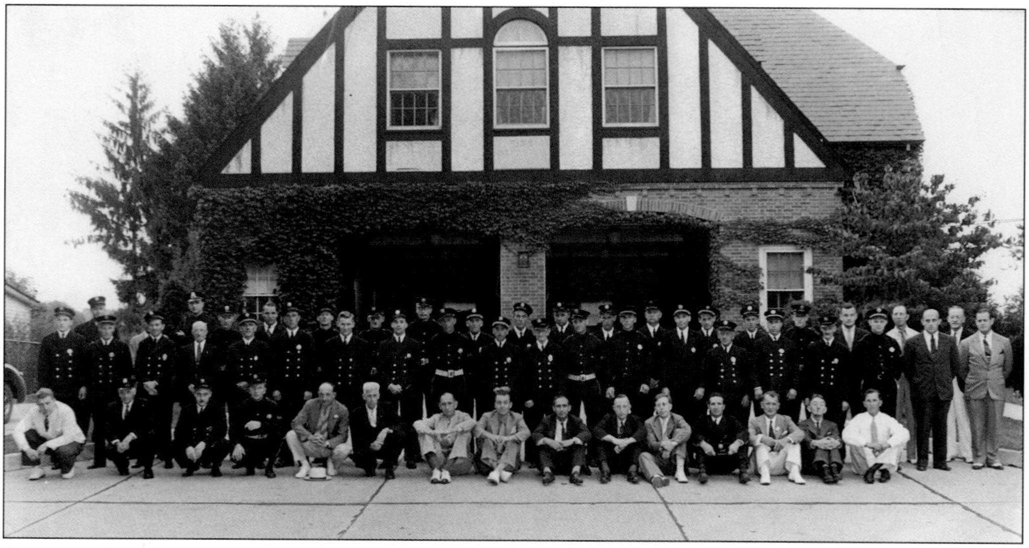

Armonk Fire Department, 1930s. A very large group from the small Armonk hamlet volunteered as firemen. The building on today's Maple Avenue was completed in 1932. It is the Goldie and John C. Hergenhan Recreation Center today, named in honor of longtime North Castle police chief John C. Hergenhan and his wife, Goldie (Wago).

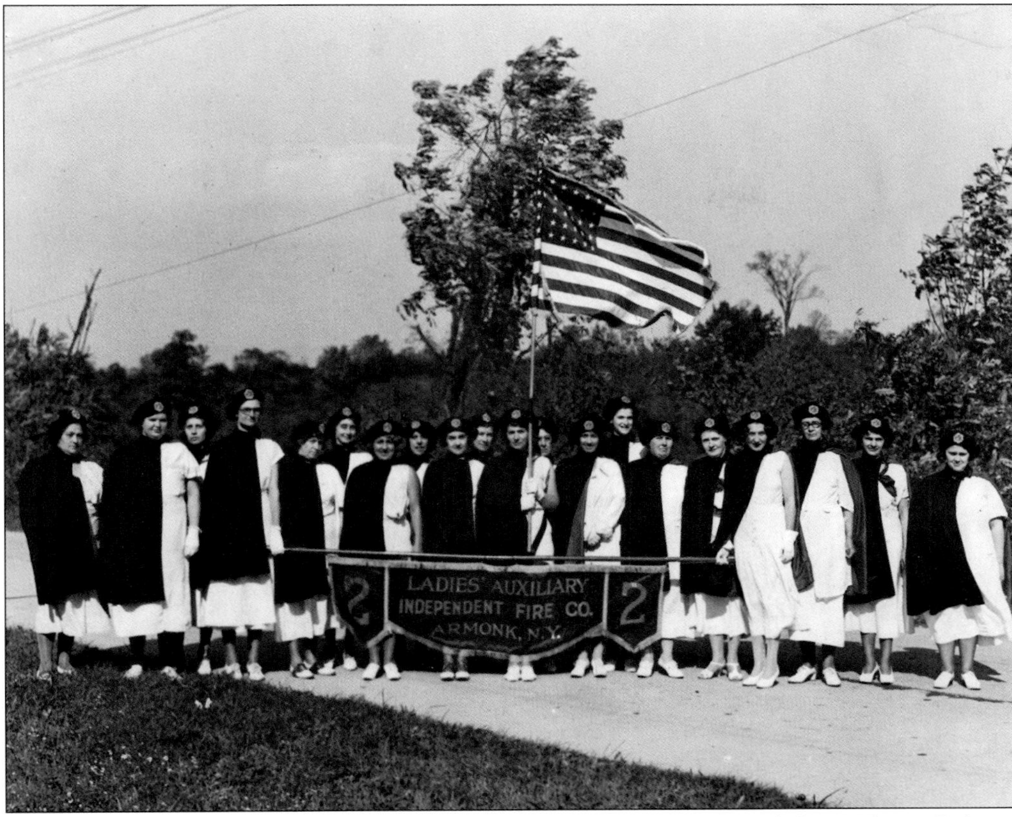

LADIES AUXILIARY, INDEPENDENT FIRE COMPANY, ARMONK, 1940s. From left to right are Rebecca Calabrese, Stella Simmons See, Alma Aruilio, Marge Bennett Dennison, Kathryn Hopkins, Viola Taylor, Wardetta Love, Mrs. Valentine, Frieda Abrams, Alice Farrington, Mrs. Clifford Payton Carpenter, Dora Abrams, Emma Tompkins, Hazel Torlish Mignotte, Peggy Wago, Ruby Lewis, Goldie Wago Hergenhan, Emma Quimby, Mathilda Ferris, and Marian Lovelett See.

BANKSVILLE INDEPENDENT FIRE COMPANY, 1949. The first fire truck the company purchased was an old second-hand 1926 American LaFrance at a cost of $318. The first fire call was at the Henker farm, where a bolt of lightning struck the barn. The company emblem is a reminder of that first fire: a fire helmet with a bolt of lightning emblazoned across it. The building in the background is Banksville's first firehouse.

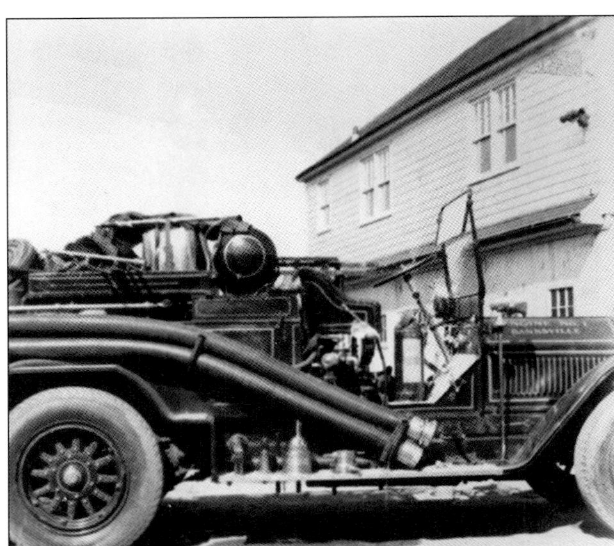

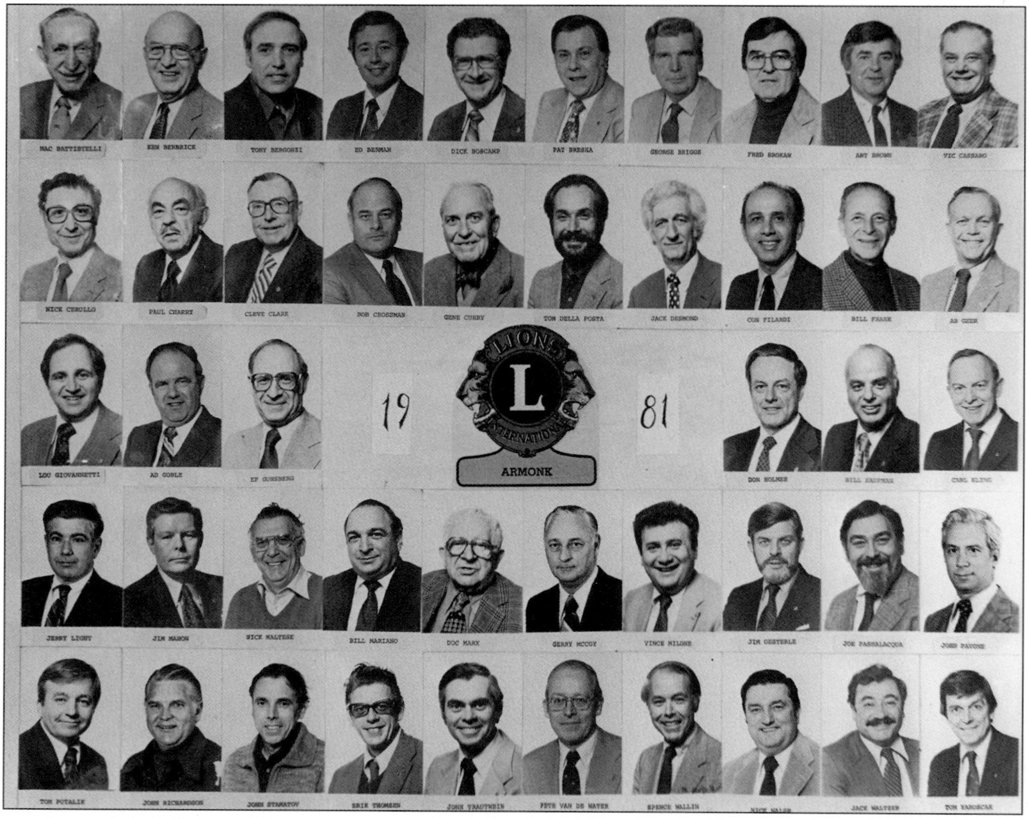

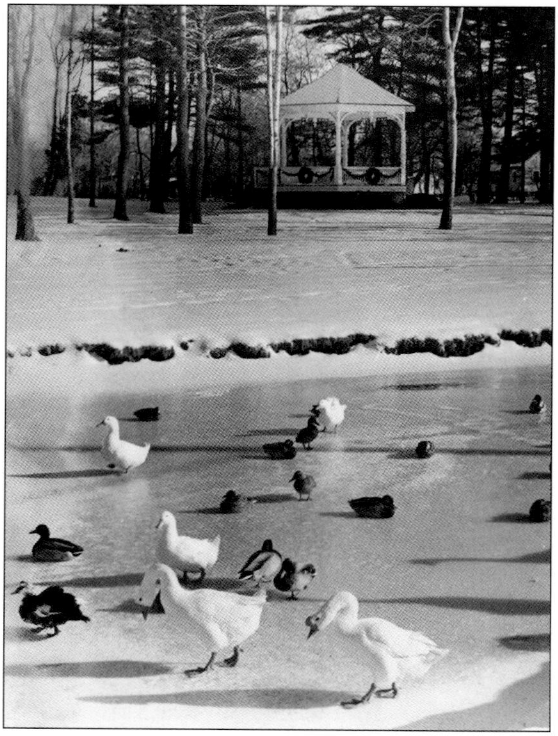

ARMONK LIONS, 1981. From left to right are (top row) Mac Battistelli, Ken Berbrick, Tony Bergonzi, Ed Berman, Dick Boscamp, Pat Bresha, George Briggs, Fred Brokaw, Art Brown, and Vic Cassaro; (second row) Nick Cerullo, Paul Charry, Cleve Clark, Bob Crossman, Gene Curry, Tom Della Posta, Jack Desmond, Con Filardi, Bill Frank, and Ab Geer; (third row) Lou Giovannetti, Ad Goble, Ep Gunsberg, Don Holmes, Bill Kaufman, and Carl Kling; (fourth row) Jerry Light, Jim Mahon, Nick Maltese, Bill Mariano, Doc Marx, Gerry McCoy, Vince Milone, Jim Oesterle, Joe Passalacqua, and John Pavone; (bottom row) Tom Putalik, John Richardson, John Stamatov, Erik Thomsen, John Trautwein, Peter Van de Water, Spence Wallin, Nick Walsh, Jack Waltber, and Tom Yaroscak.

GAZEBO AT WAMPUS BROOK PARK, ARMONK. The gazebo, used for public events, is one of the many community donations from the Armonk Lions.

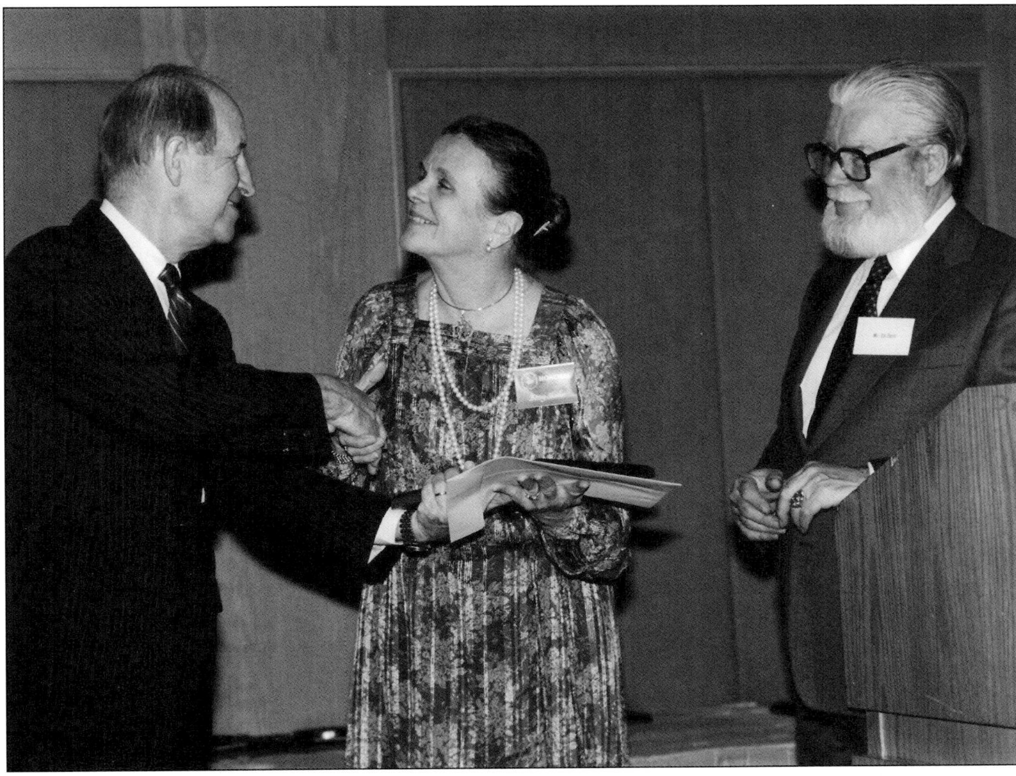

1984 Gulf Oil Conservation Award Given to North Castle's Betsy Sluder. From left to right are James E. Lee, chairman and chief executive officer of Gulf Oil Corporation; Betsy Sluder; and Ed Zern, director of conservation awards for Gulf. Betsy was recognized for her efforts to recycle waste, acquire green space, protect watersheds, and develop parks. She served as chair of the North Castle conservation board for many years.

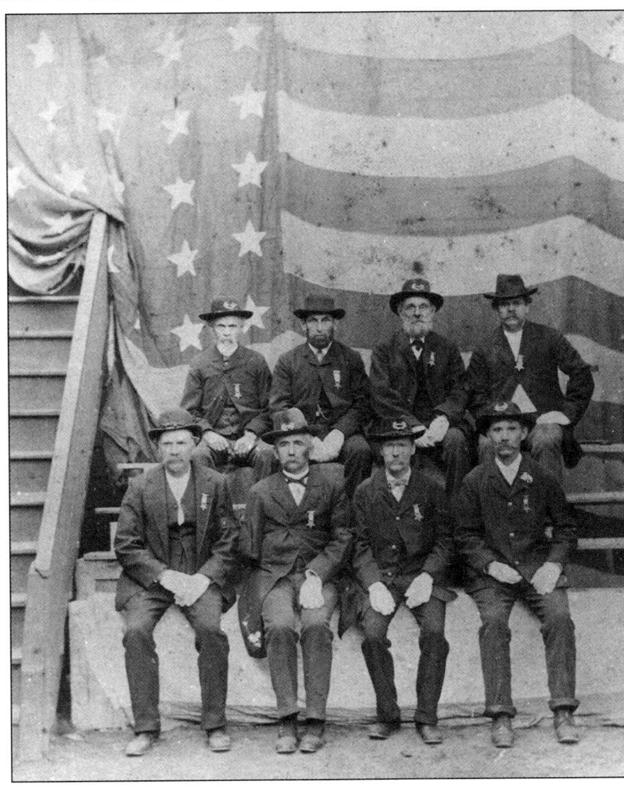

Grand Army of the Republic, 1890. Pictured are some of North Castle's Civil War veterans. From left to right are (first row) Willet Ackerman, Thomas J. Ackerman, William Mathers, and William B. Williams; (second row) John Palmer, Samuel W. Palmer, Charles Raymond, and Samuel Tucker. Other North Castle veterans were not present.

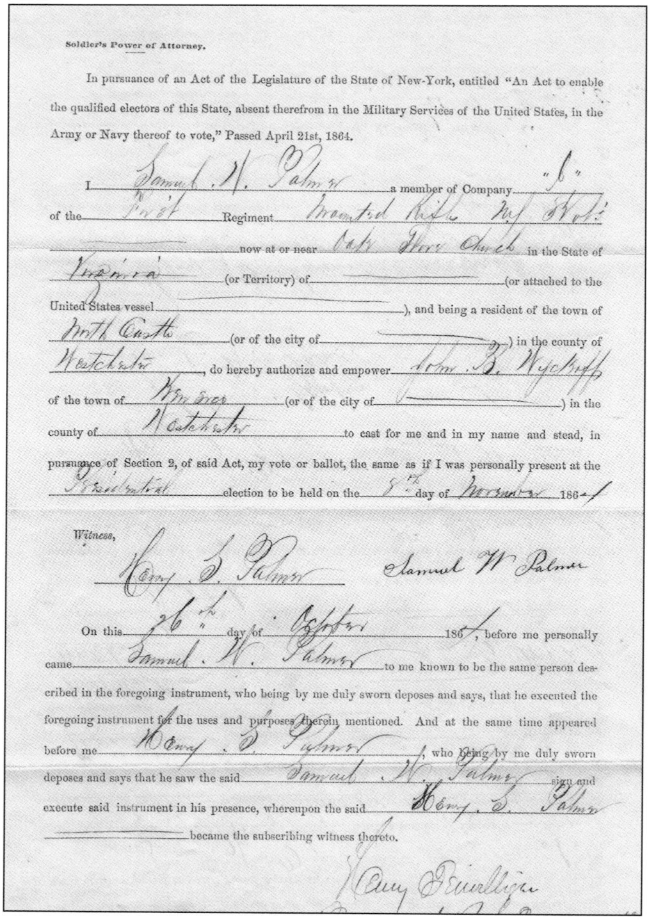

Soldier's Power of Attorney.

In pursuance of an Act of the Legislature of the State of New-York, entitled "An Act to enable the qualified electors of this State, absent therefrom in the Military Services of the United States, in the Army or Navy thereof to vote," Passed April 21st, 1864.

I Samuel W. Palmer a member of Company "I" of the First Regiment Mounted Rifle NY Vols now at or near Oak Grove Church in the State of Virginia (or Territory) of (or attached to the United States vessel), and being a resident of the town of North Castle (or of the city of) in the county of Westchester, do hereby authorize and empower John B. Wyckoff of the town of Kensico (or of the city of) in the county of Westchester to cast for me and in my name and stead, in pursuance of Section 2, of said Act, my vote or ballot, the same as if I was personally present at the Presidential election to be held on the 8th day of November 1864

Witness,

Henry S. Palmer Samuel W Palmer

On this 26th day of October 1864, before me personally came Samuel W. Palmer to me known to be the same person described in the foregoing instrument, who being by me duly sworn deposes and says, that he executed the foregoing instrument for the uses and purposes therein mentioned. And at the same time appeared before me Henry S. Palmer, who being by me duly sworn deposes and says that he saw the said Samuel W. Palmer sign and execute said instrument in his presence, whereupon the said Henry S. Palmer became the subscribing witness thereto.

Henry [illegible]

SAMUEL W. PALMER, POWER OF ATTORNEY, OCTOBER 26, 1864. Samuel Palmer gave John B. Wyckoff of Kensico the power to cast his vote in the November 8, 1864, election. Lincoln was running for reelection against George McClellan. Palmer was a member of Company I, 1st Regiment Mounted Rifles, New York Volunteers. He was at the Oak Grove Church in Virginia when he signed. It is unknown who he voted for.

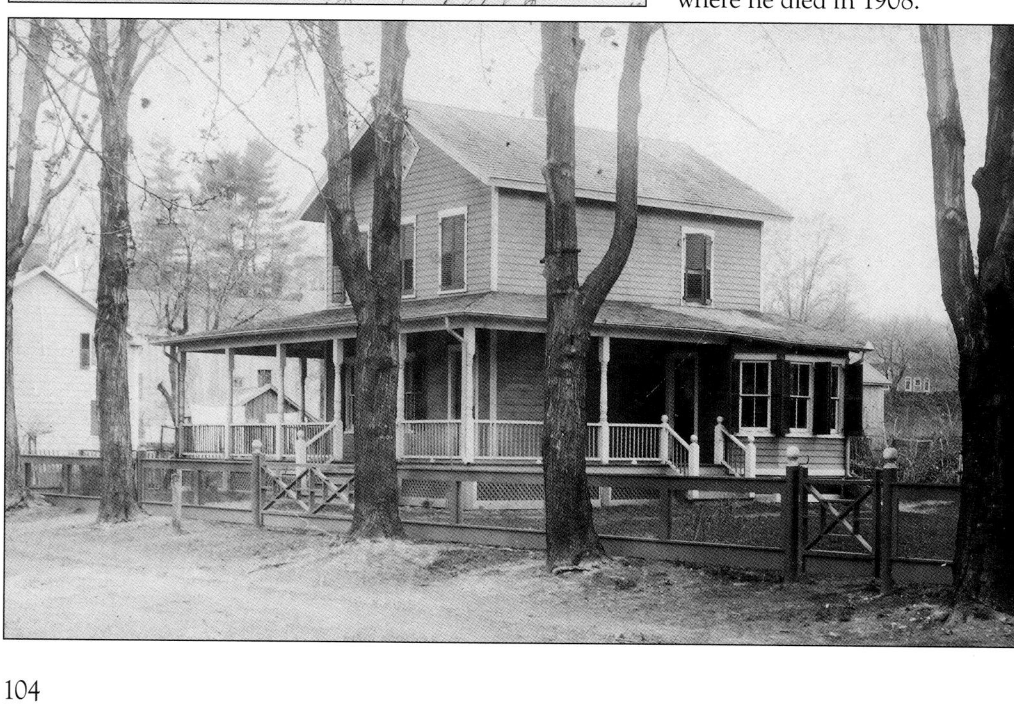

THOMAS JEFFERSON ACKERMAN HOUSE. Thomas Jefferson Ackerman, born in 1838, was a son of Hyatt and Mary Ann Slagle Ackerman. On October 19, 1864, he lost an arm in combat at the Battle of Cedar Creek in Gen. Philip Sheridan's Shenandoah Campaign. He survived, came home, and farmed another 44 years on today's Maple Avenue, Armonk, where he died in 1908.

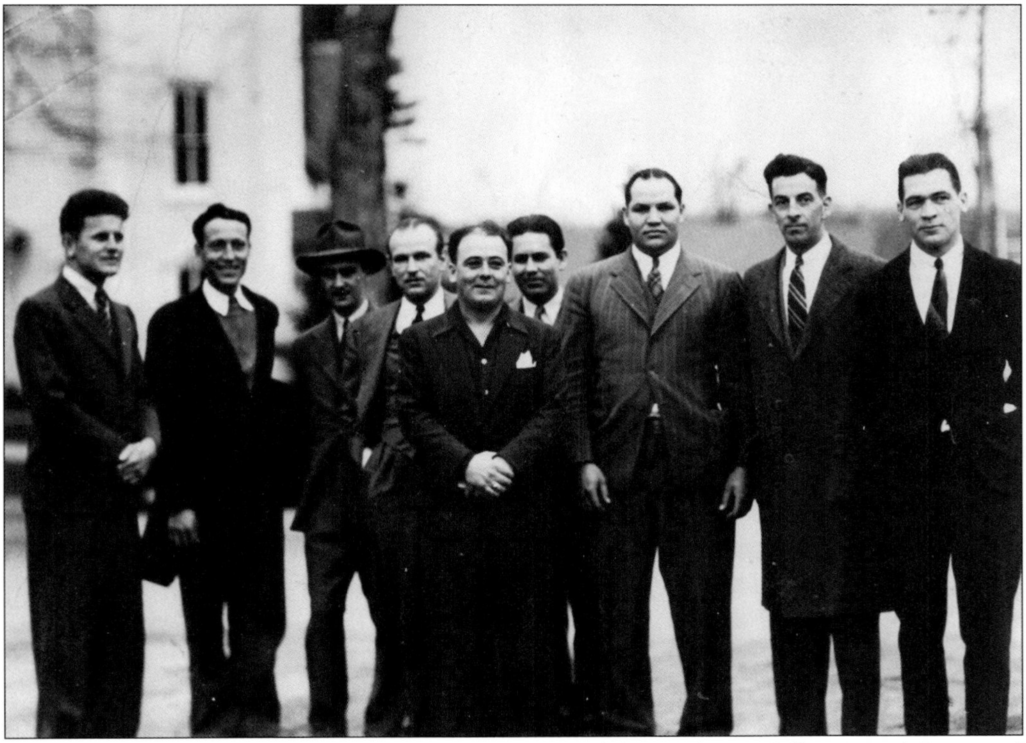

Departing for World War II, Armonk, 1942. From left to right are Gilbert Mead, Raymond Thibodeau, Edward Ferris, Thomas Bouchoux, George J. Smith, Victor Nation, Bertram "Pete" Simmons, Orrin Husted, and Edward Wedge. Others departing North Castle were not present for the photograph.

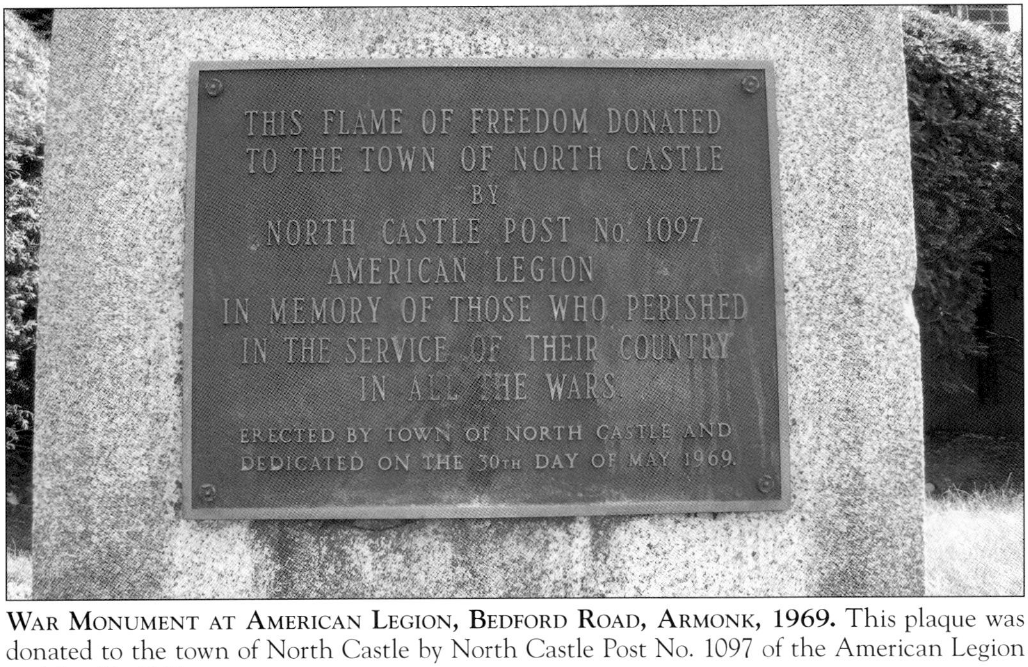

War Monument at American Legion, Bedford Road, Armonk, 1969. This plaque was donated to the town of North Castle by North Castle Post No. 1097 of the American Legion on May 30, 1969.

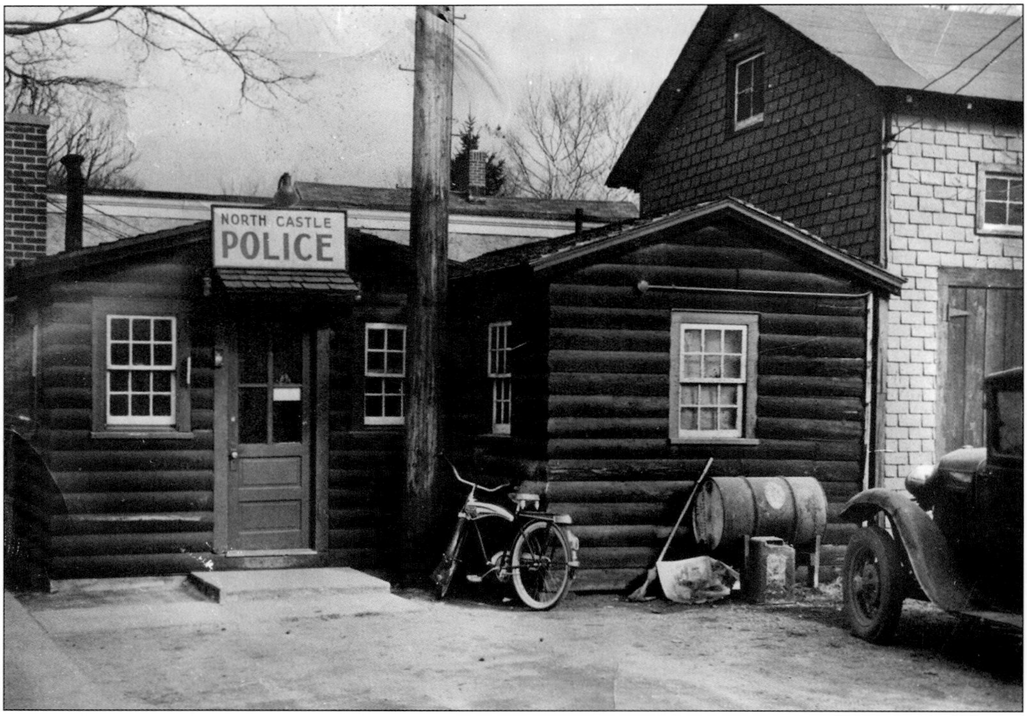

Police Booth, North Castle's First Police Headquarters. Some say the police booth was built around a telephone booth. The booth faced south and was at approximately today's 400 Main Street, Armonk. According to Joyce Hergenhan, Chief John Hergenhan's daughter, her dad and friends built the booth, which served as headquarters until 1954.

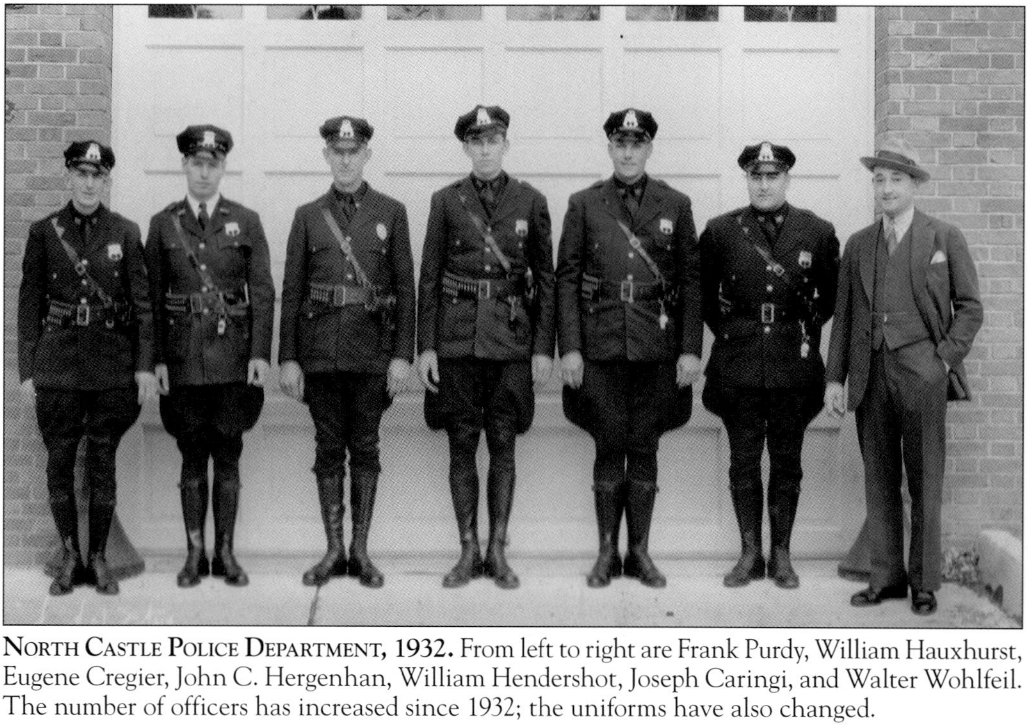

North Castle Police Department, 1932. From left to right are Frank Purdy, William Hauxhurst, Eugene Cregier, John C. Hergenhan, William Hendershot, Joseph Caringi, and Walter Wohlfeil. The number of officers has increased since 1932; the uniforms have also changed.

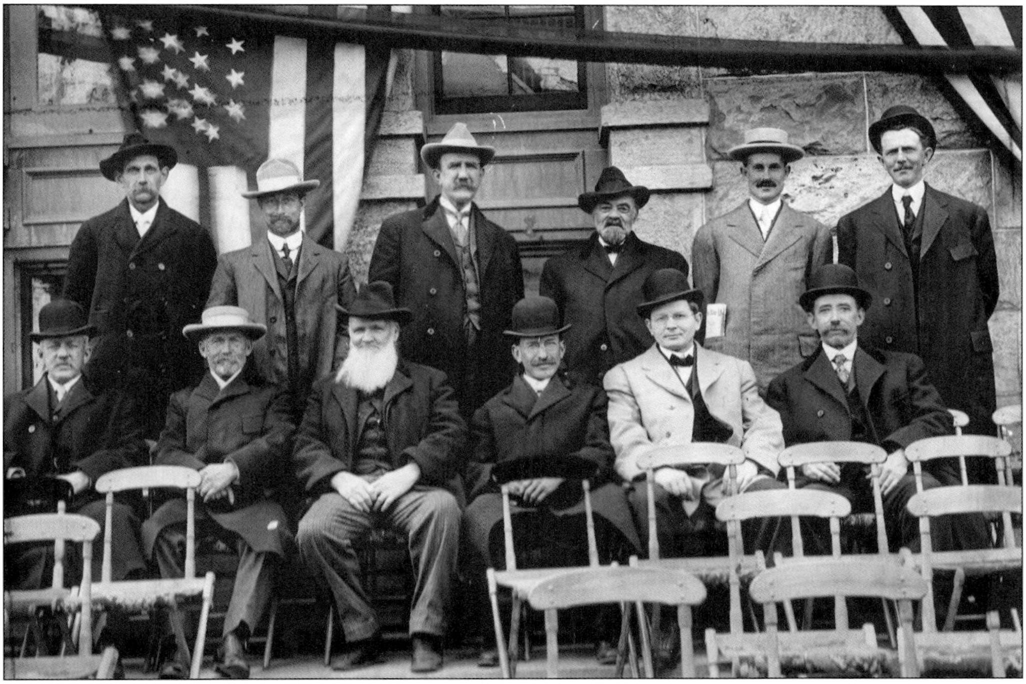

North Castle Town Officials, 1906. This photograph was taken at the 1906 laying of the cornerstone of the supreme court wing of the county courthouse in White Plains. From left to right are (seated) W.K. Haviland, Thomas P. Brundage, Edward Riley, Albert H. Waterbury, Albert Virsen, and guest Daniel Ryan; (standing) Charles H. Ferris, T. William Brundage, A. Smith Hopkins, Dr. Ralph B. Griswold, Horace G. Arnold, and Charles M. Sherwood.

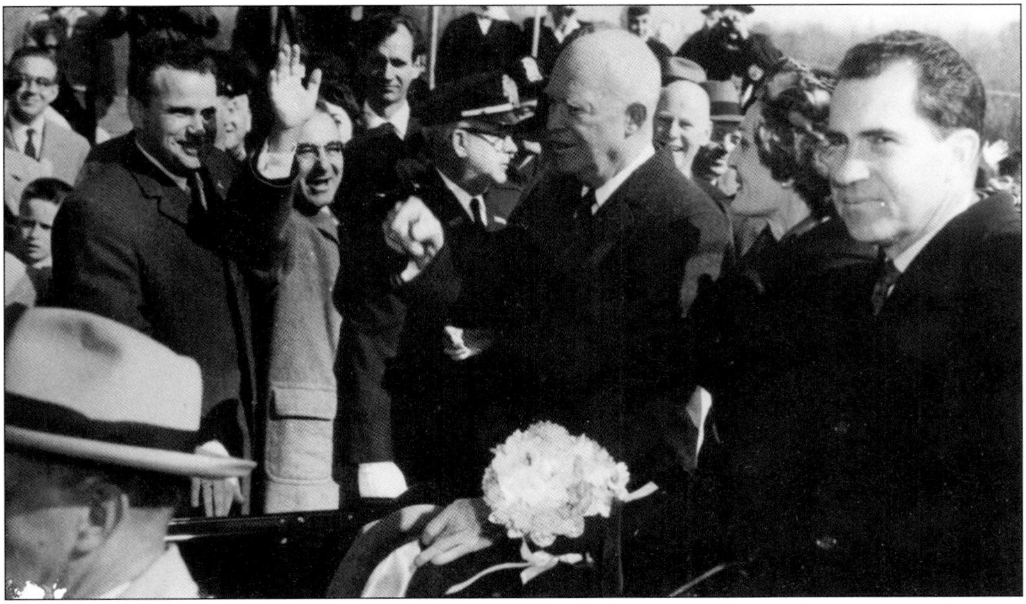

Campaign Visit, 1960. North Castle supervisor John A. Lombardi (left) welcomed Pres. Dwight D. Eisenhower, Pat Nixon, and Vice Pres. Richard Nixon to North Castle. Eisenhower was subject to the 22nd Amendment; Nixon won more states than Kennedy but narrowly lost the popular vote and the election. Two sitting US senators became president and vice president.

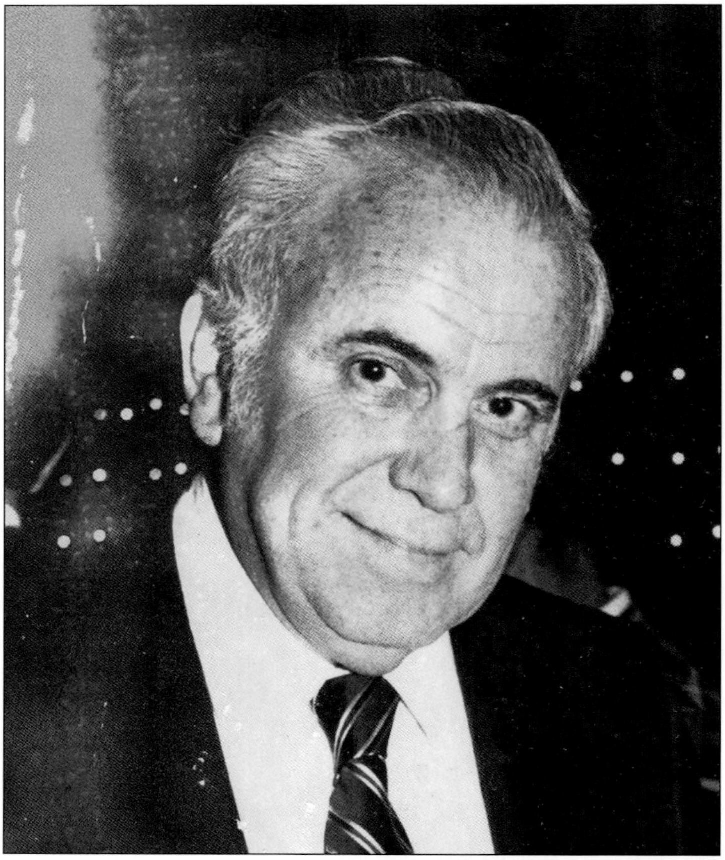

John A. (Jack) Lombardi (1924–2008). Elected supervisor in 1961, Jack served in that role in North Castle for 44 years. He was one of the longest-serving supervisors in Westchester County. During his tenure, North Castle grew to become a respected and prosperous place to live and work due to his competence and leadership.

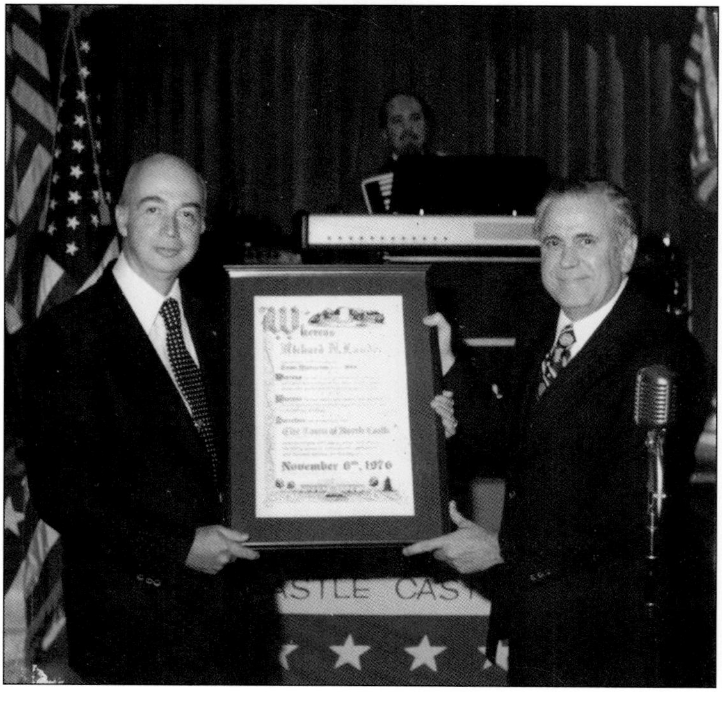

Richard (Dick) N. Lander Receiving a Proclamation, November 6, 1976. Supervisor John A. Lombardi (right) is shown presenting a proclamation to Lander honoring his accomplishments. Lander was a commissioner of jurors for Westchester County, a North Castle councilman, and the first town historian.

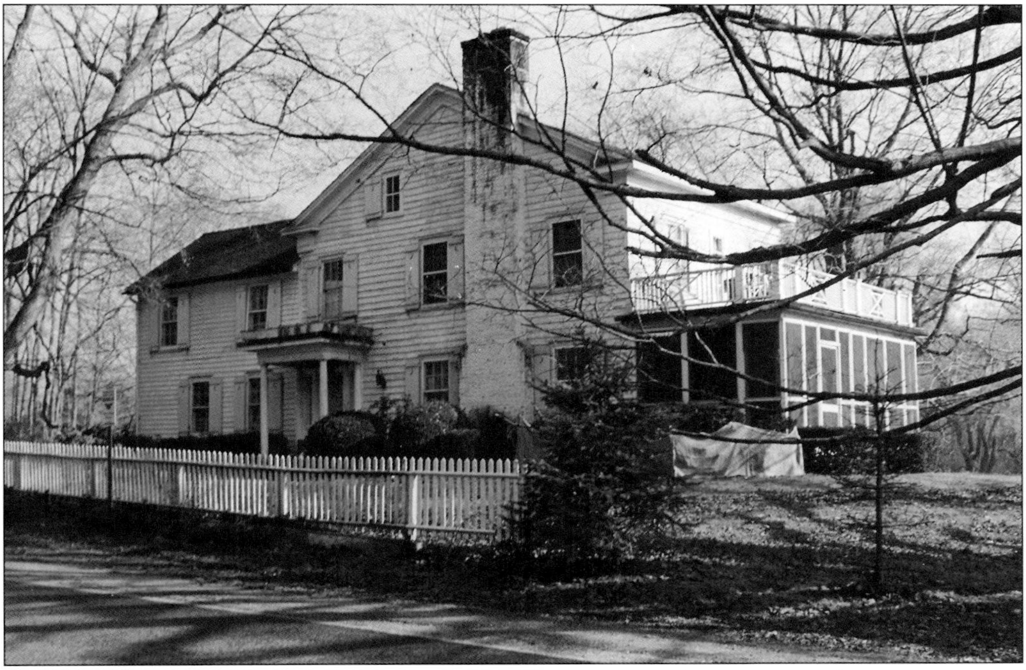

Dr. David Dayton House, Town Supervisor, 1771–1777. Dayton served as supervisor of North Castle in 1776. He was elected to the First Provincial Congress of the State of New York, serving from May 22 to November 4, 1775. His property, at today's 148 North Greenwich Road, Armonk, remained in the Dayton family until the 1880s. The house was heavily damaged by fire in 1984 and subsequently torn down.

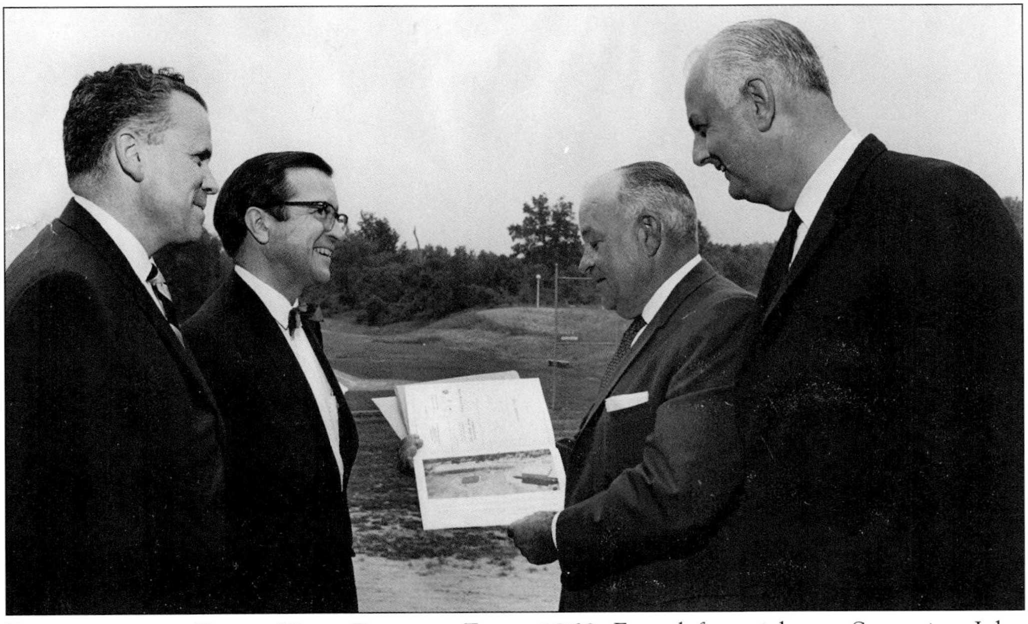

Dedicating the Byram Hills Baseball Field, 1968. From left to right are Supervisor John Lombardi; Guy Papale, board of education president; Ruben Chase, event chair; and Bill Milvaney, Dads' Club president. The Dads' Club held fundraising events, including dances and spaghetti suppers, to support the project.

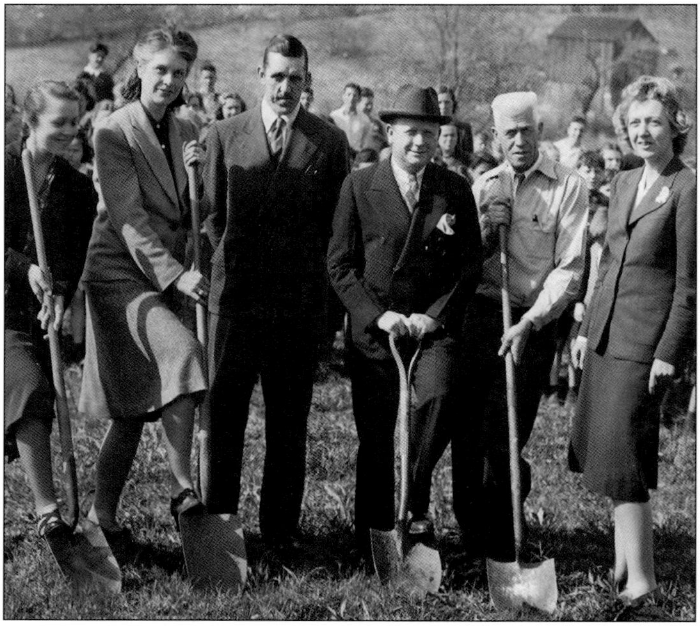

Ground-Breaking Ceremonies for New North Castle Free Library, April 28, 1941. From left to right are Emily Stephens, former head librarian; Esther Hall, chair, executive committee and building campaign; Henry Moger, architect associated with Lawrence Loeb, who designed the building without charge; Courtney C. Brown, president of the library's board of trustees; Clarence Abrams, contractor; and Mae Smith, head librarian. Two hundred Armonk school children witnessed the ceremonies.

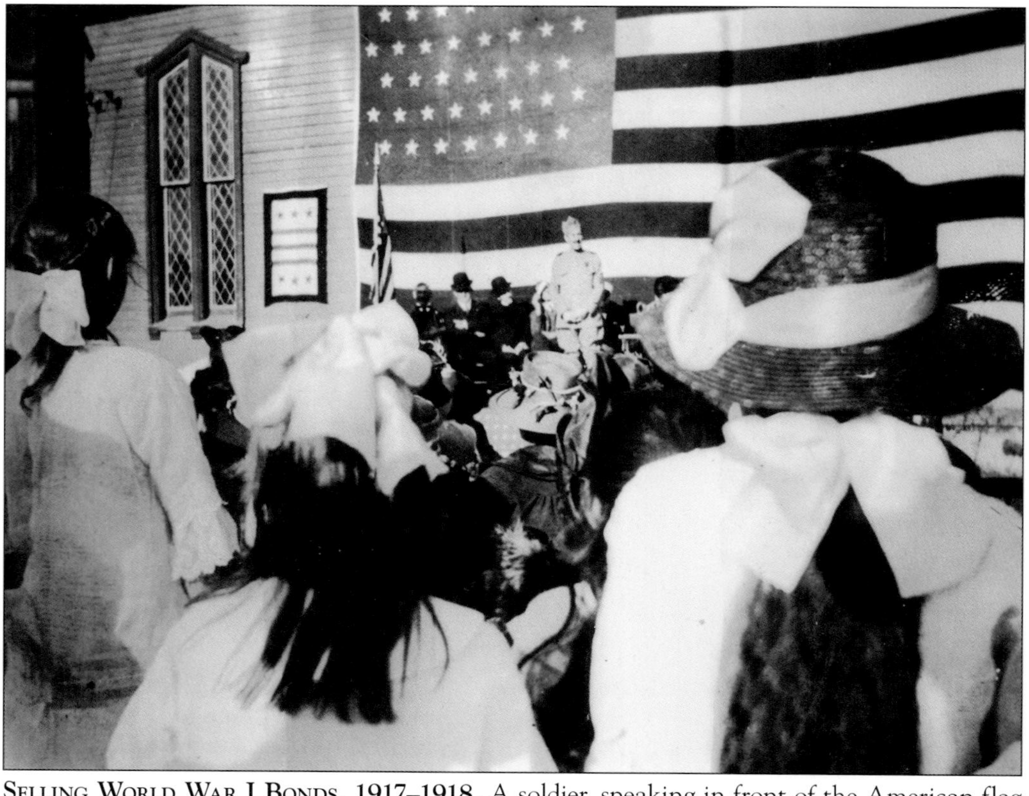

Selling World War I Bonds, 1917–1918. A soldier, speaking in front of the American flag mounted on the Armonk Methodist Church building (today's 3 Bedford Road, Armonk), is selling bonds to finance the war. There were multiple issues of bonds. The government defaulted on the fourth Liberty Bond but substantially repaid all the others by the end of the 1920s.

Ten

OF INTEREST

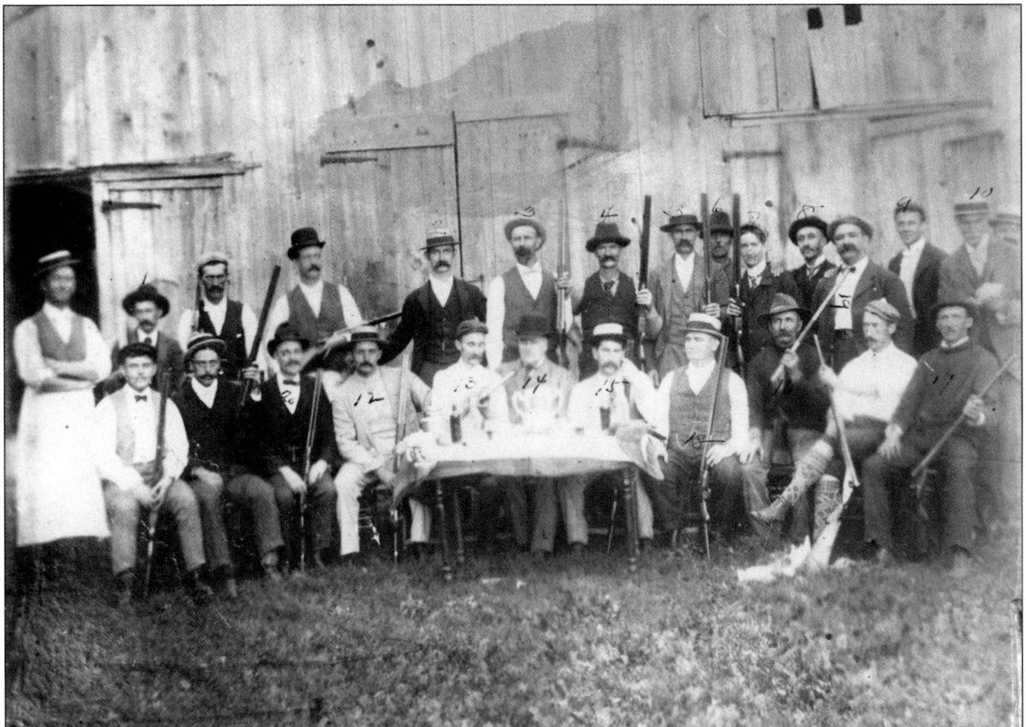

GUN CLUB AT JACOB LOUIS LONG'S BARN, ARMONK, 1900. From left to right are (first row) Floy Coles, Whitmond Sniffin, Melvin Horton, Robert Quinby, William F. MacDonald, Mr. Walton, Joseph S. Carpenter, James S. Young, Ezekiel Flewellin, George Wood, and Charles Barnard; (second row) unidentified waiter, Edwin F. Acker, George Mulner, Lewis Platt, Thomas Taylor, John Read, Gerald Howett, Gilbert Flewellin, Danny See, William Howett, William H. Acker, Fred Boemer, Harry Wayne, Col. Samuel Roe, and unidentified. The barn sat near the southern property line of today's Harold C. Crittenden Middle School at 10 MacDonald Avenue, Armonk.

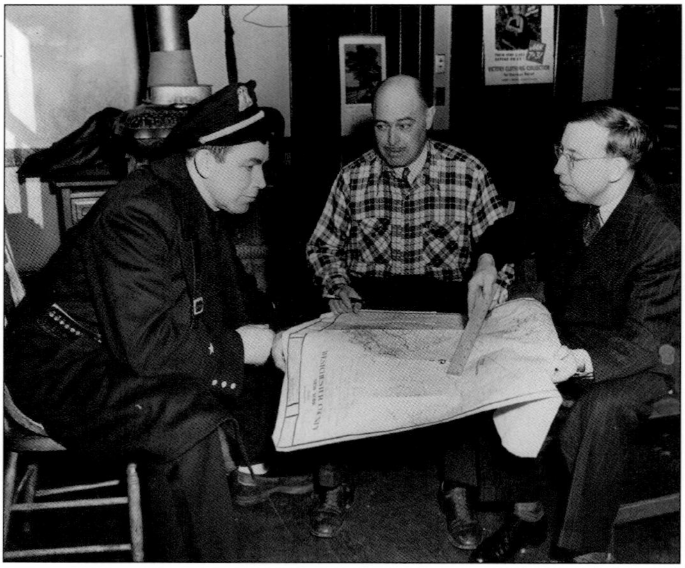

United Nations Wanted Banksville for World Headquarters, 1946. From left to right are Chief John Hergenhan, Tax Receiver George P. Schmaling, and Supervisor James Hopkins. The UN wanted 42 square miles—more than half of it in North Castle—and tax exemptions. Local newspaper headlines screamed "WE DON'T LIKE IT!" and "TOWN UP IN ARMS!" John D. Rockefeller Jr. donated several million dollars. The UN picked New York City instead for its headquarters.

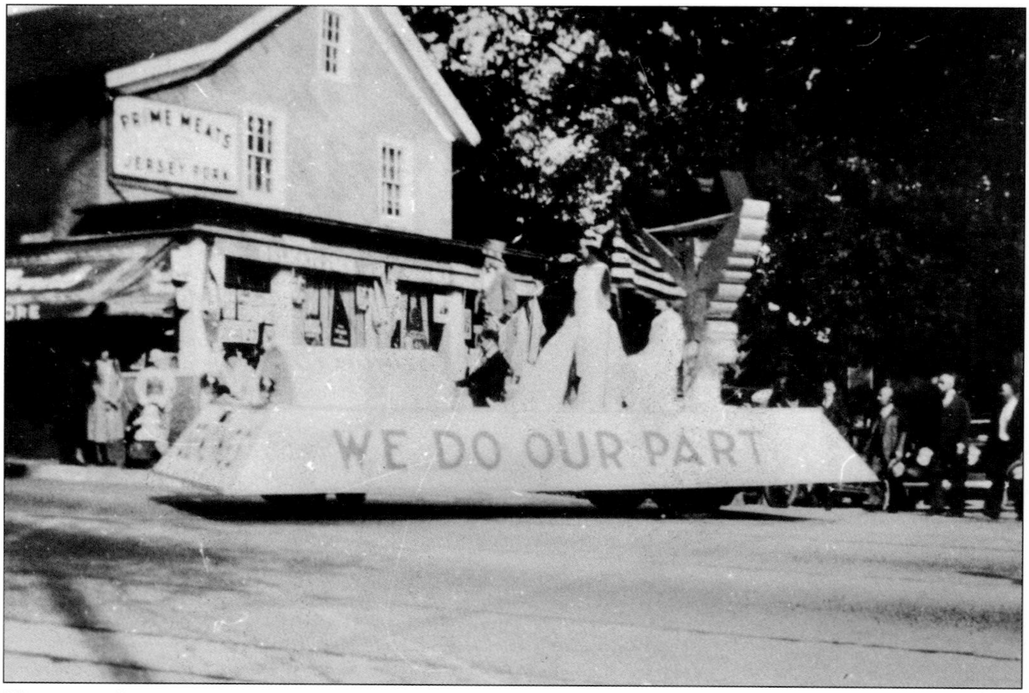

National Industrial Recovery Act Parade, 1933. Attempting to stimulate economic recovery, the US Congress passed the National Industrial Recovery Act in 1933. Shown is a float in North Castle's parade at the corner of today's Main Street and Maple Avenue, Armonk. Although businessmen cheered at first, by 1934 they were hissing. The US Supreme Court declared the Act unconstitutional in 1935.

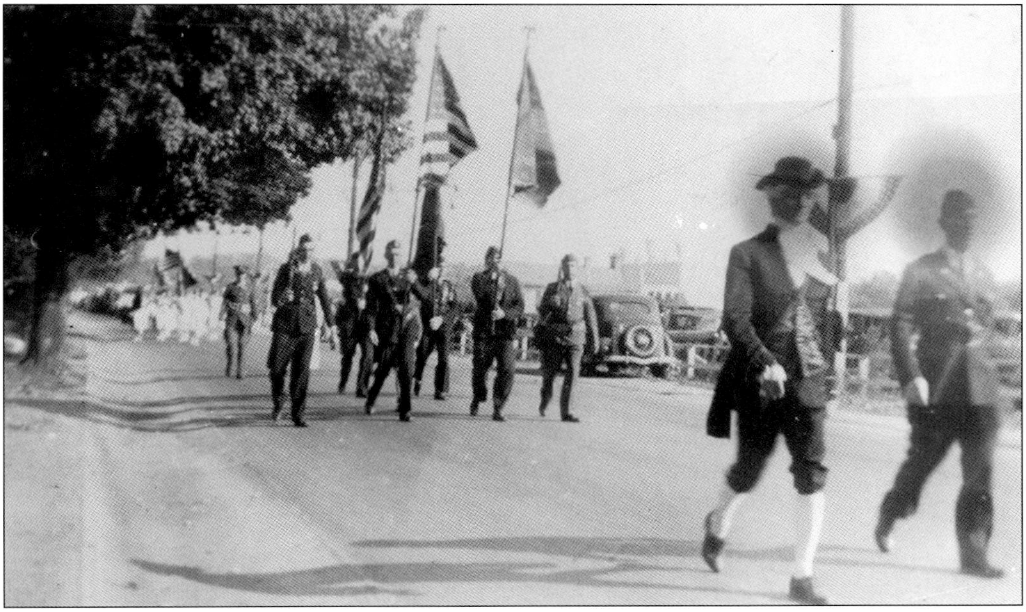

CELEBRATING 200 YEARS, NORTH CASTLE'S 1936 PARADE. The first recorded town meeting minutes are dated "April ye 6th 1736." Two hundred years later, the town residents staged a grand parade in honor of the residents of 1736. Activities were spread over three days, including a historic pageant, a costume ball, homecoming church services, inspection of Colonial homes, and fireworks.

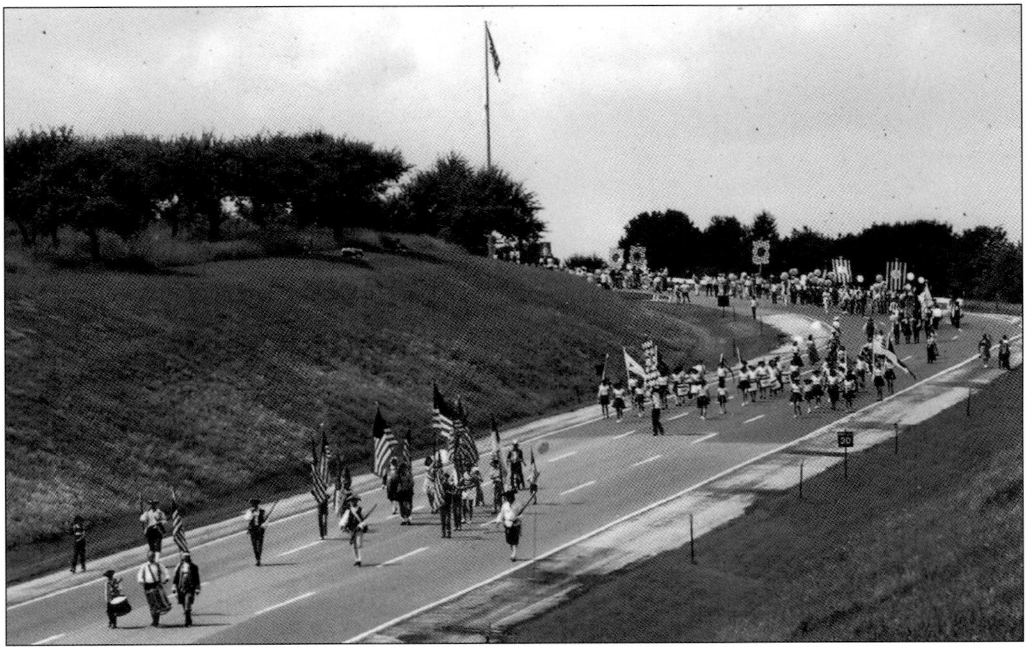

NATIONAL BICENTENNIAL PARADE LINING UP, 1976. Led by R. Eugene Curry and Charlotte Devers, co-chairs of the bicentennial celebrations, and Charles Elson, vice chairman, North Castle celebrated America's bicentennial with grandeur. The spectacular Fourth of July parade included 40 organizations with impressive quilted banners. The parade started from atop IBM hill and marched down today's Main Street, Armonk.

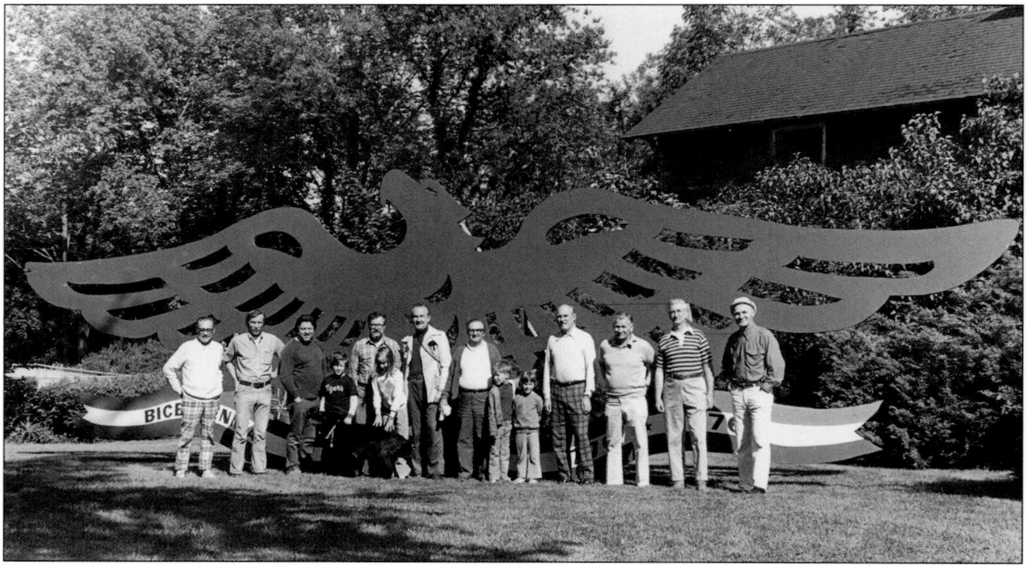

Constructing the First Bicentennial Eagle, 1976. From left to right are David Stech, Rolf Lunde, Orestes Mihaly, John Mihaly, Guy Papale, Amy and Alfy Frank, Arthur Soka, Norman Egdell, Ted Frank, Diana Frank, Anthony Ellrodt, John Schnoor, Jack Desmond, and Seymour Gage. Arthur Soka designed the 40-foot eagle with wings spread. John Schnoor led the construction team.

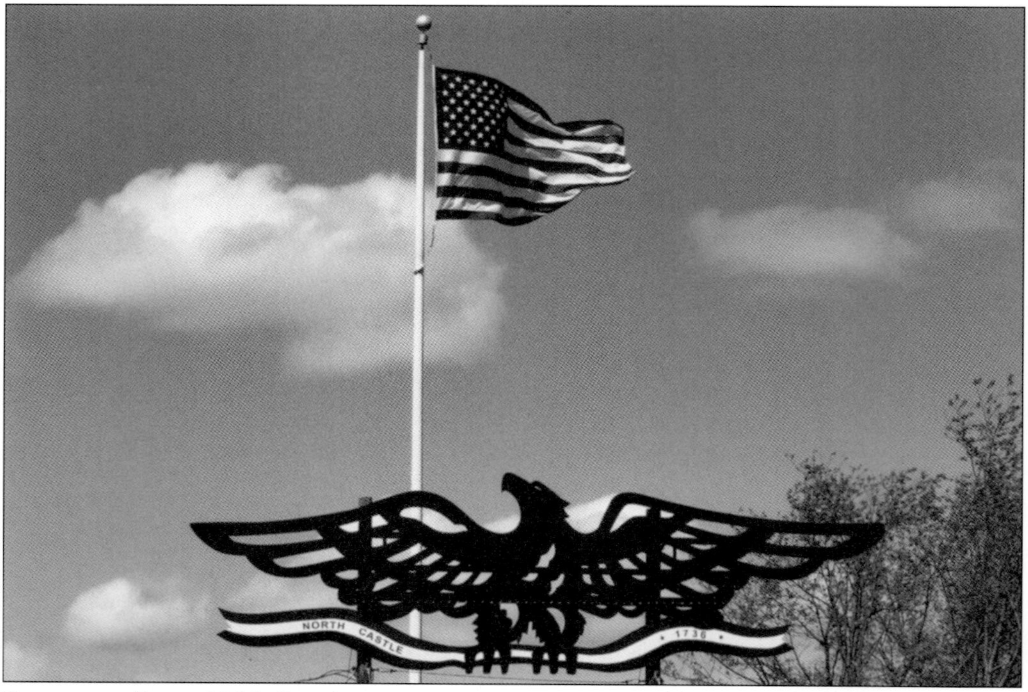

Eagle and Flag, 2016. Proud monuments to patriotism and heritage, the flag of the United States and the North Castle eagle fly at the intersection of today's New York State Routes 128 and 22 in Armonk. First made of plywood by members of North Castle American Legion Post No. 1097 and others, the replacement is a metal eagle donated by the owners of the Bristal Assisted Living Facility in Armonk. (Courtesy of Stephen Tomback.)

Best Dressed, R. Eugene (Gene) and Margery Curry, 1976 Bicentennial. Co-chair Gene Curry and his wife, Margery, won the award at the 1976 bicentennial costume ball. Gene Curry was a member of the town board from 1934 until 1941 and an incorporator of the historical society. His enthusiastic support included the Lions, St. Stephen's Episcopal Church, Banksville Community House, and the library. Today's Gene Curry Drive is named in his honor.

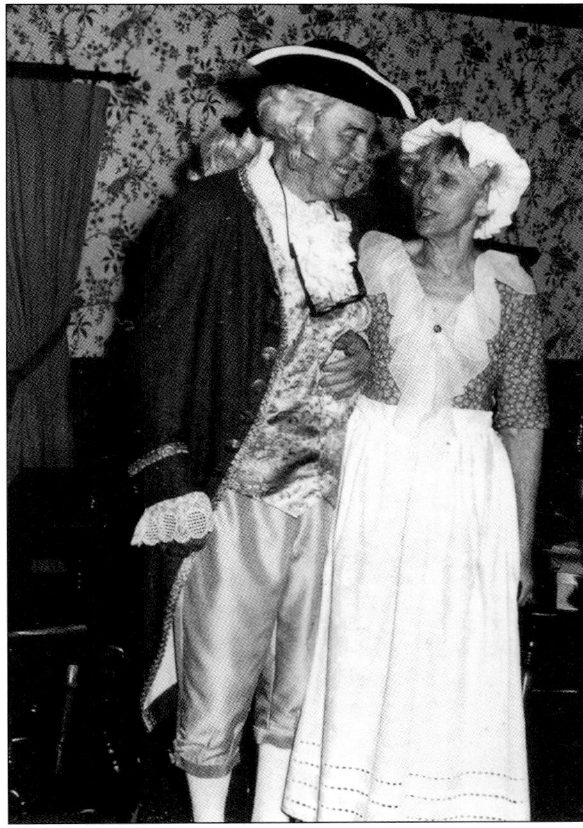

Armonk Village Residents, c. 1885. From left to right are Martha Taylor (married Henry Taylor, no relation), unidentified, Albert Cox, unidentified, Jane E. Acker and unidentified baby, Annie Smith (married Edwin F. Acker), Martha Ackerman (married Coleman Clark), and unidentified. This photograph was taken in a beautiful meadow facing east at the site of today's Armonk Post Office at 403 Main Street.

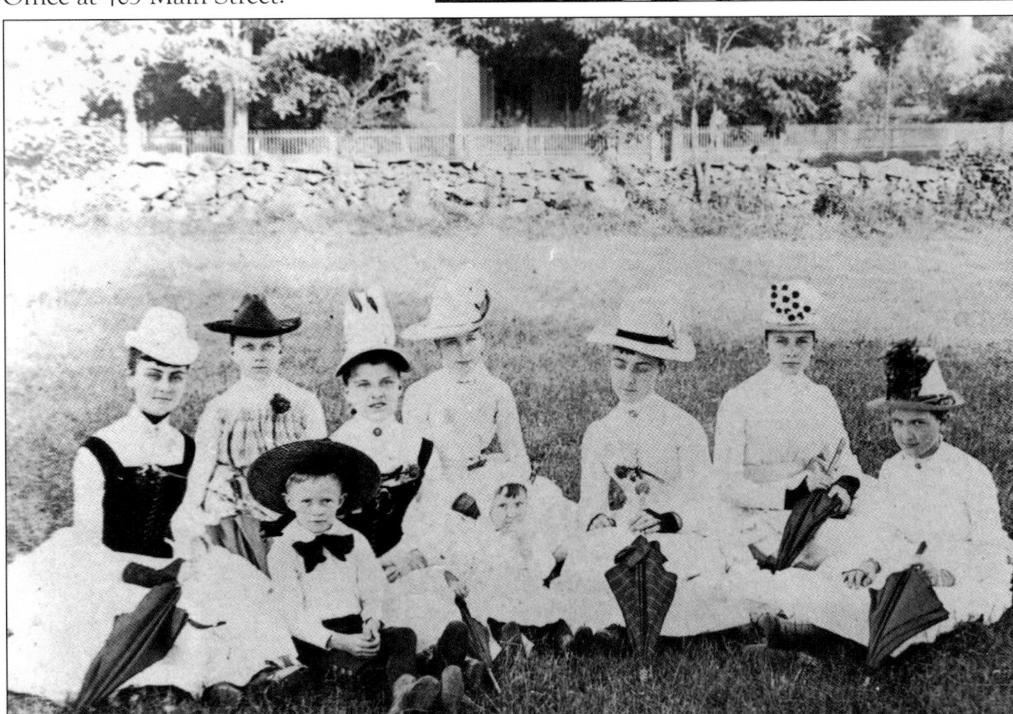

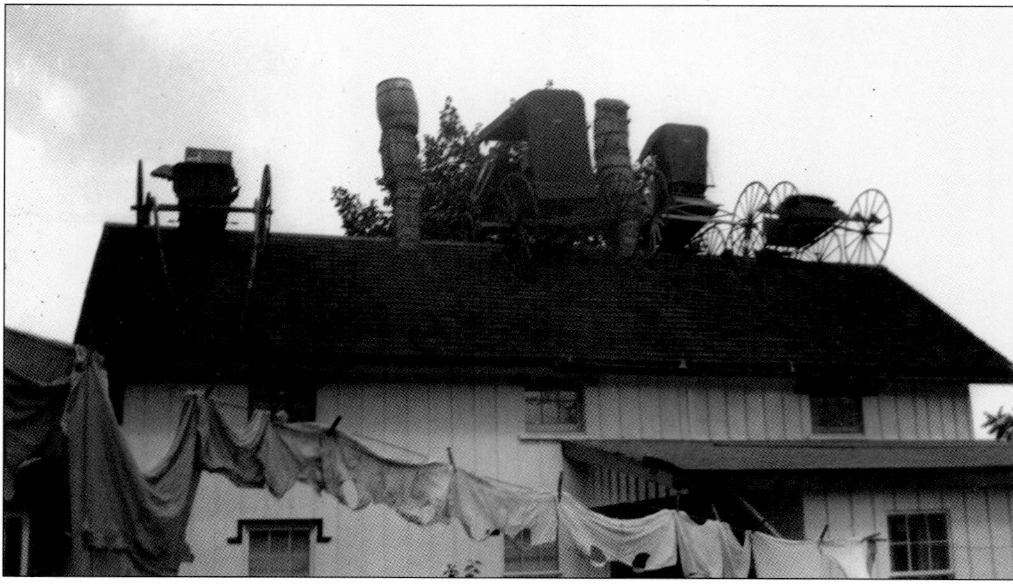

Skimatin in Banksville Style, 1920s. Also known as skimmerton, skimmelton, and shivaree, pictured is Banksville's presentation of the Colonial custom of treating a newly married couple to a noisy wedding night reception, including pranks with barrels and carriages on the roof and laundry on the line, jeers, and noisy clatter.

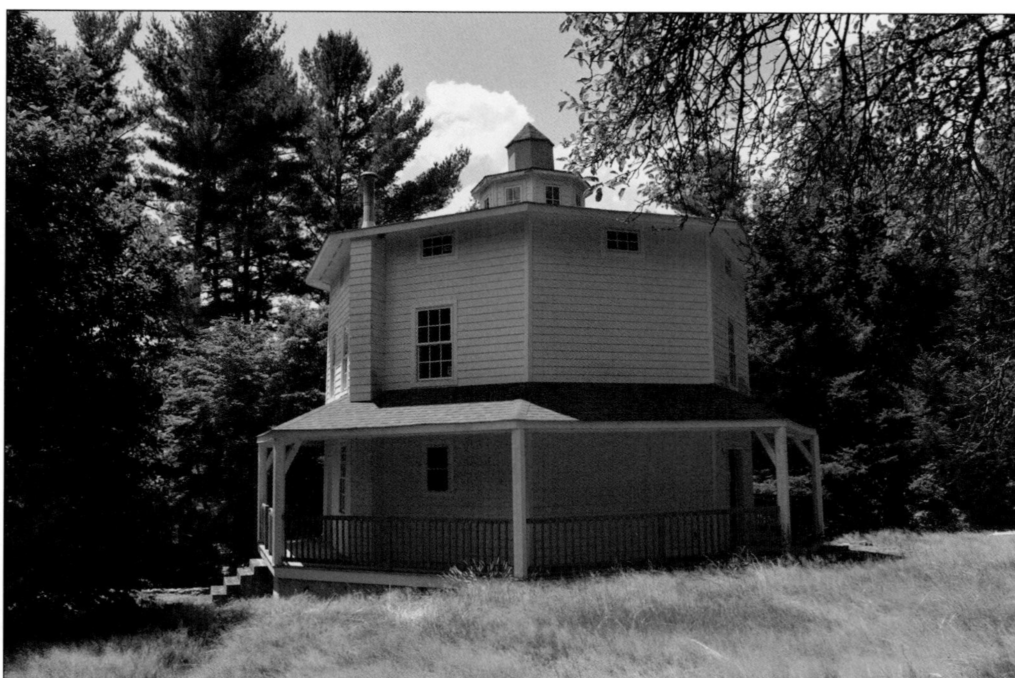

Round House, Banksville, Built before 1859. Sometimes called the Octagon House, Dr. Ralph Griswold bought it in 1859 from Harvey Palmer for $800. Griswold sold to Lizzie Crispo, who sold to the Middle Patent Church, which used the building as a parsonage. It is on today's Round House Road near Jackson Road, Banksville. (Courtesy of Stephen Tomback.)

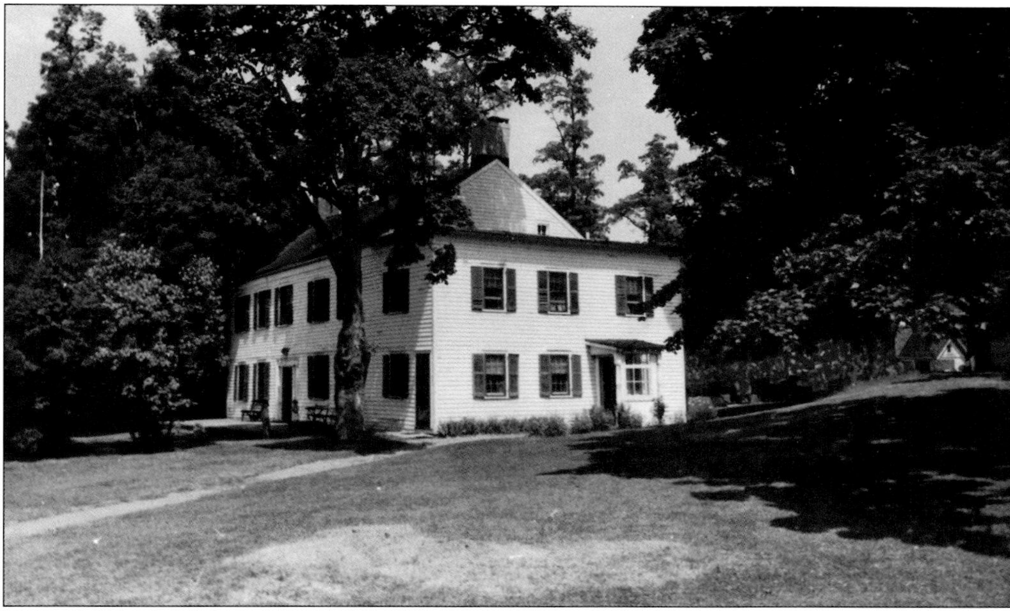

Cornell-Birdsall House, Late 1700s. The first recorded owner of this house was Willett Cornell. The Birdsalls, Joseph and later his son Benjamin, owned it until the late 1880s. IBM moved, renovated, and donated it to North Castle in the mid-1960s. Today it houses some of the town government offices.

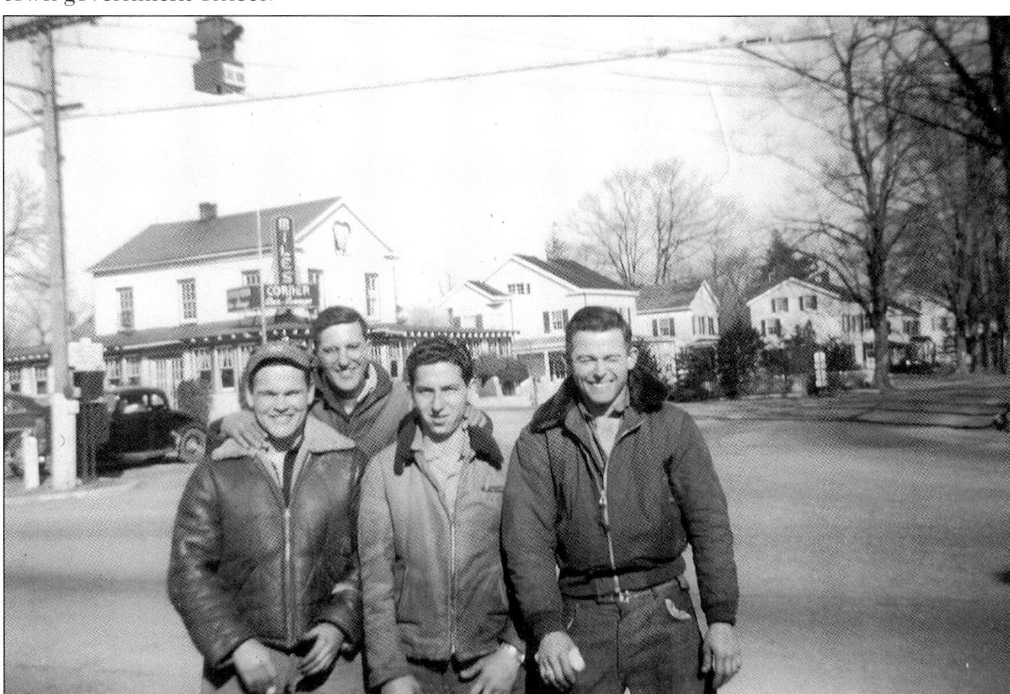

Four Friends, Armonk's Miles Corner, 1947. From left to right are Billy Kraft, Moon Fatagoni, Larry Munoz, and Kenny Abrams. Previously this corner was also known as Church, Raven's, and Kromer's Corner. Houses in today's Bedford Road Historic District can be seen in the background.

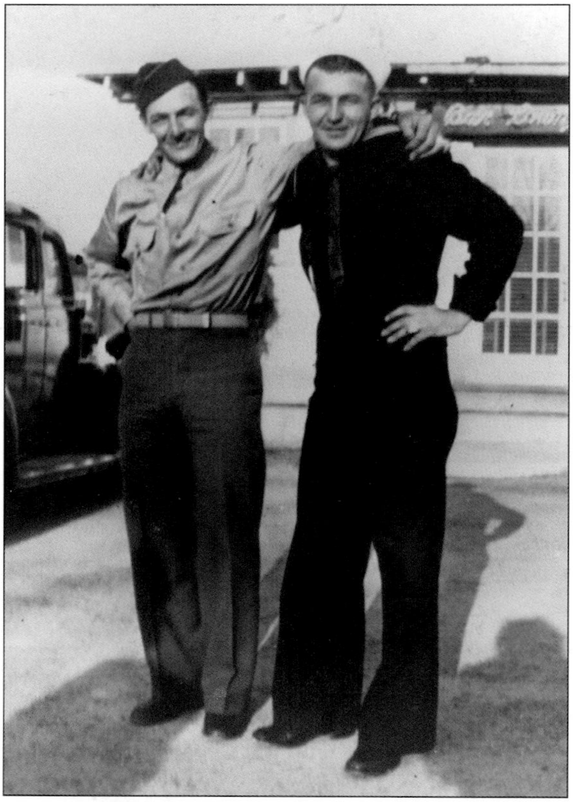

TWO ARMONK BROTHERS—ONE ARMY, ONE NAVY—DURING WORLD WAR II. Joseph (left) and Charles were sons of Elizabeth and Joseph Wago and brothers of Goldie Wago Hergenhan. Joseph and his wife, Peggy, were the parents of today's town board member Barbara DiGiacinto. Charlie and his wife, Mildred, were the parents of two daughters, Linda Herbst and Charlene Decker. Later, Mildred served as North Castle's tax receiver for 41 years.

IBM CORPORATION HEADQUARTERS, SOUTH GARDEN, ARMONK, 1964. A new world headquarters building was dedicated in 1997. In 1977, Robert W. Hubner, IBM senior vice president, presented an $85,000 contribution to the North Castle Historical Society. The gift had been pledged contingent upon the society's ability to raise the balance of the funds needed to purchase Smith's Tavern.

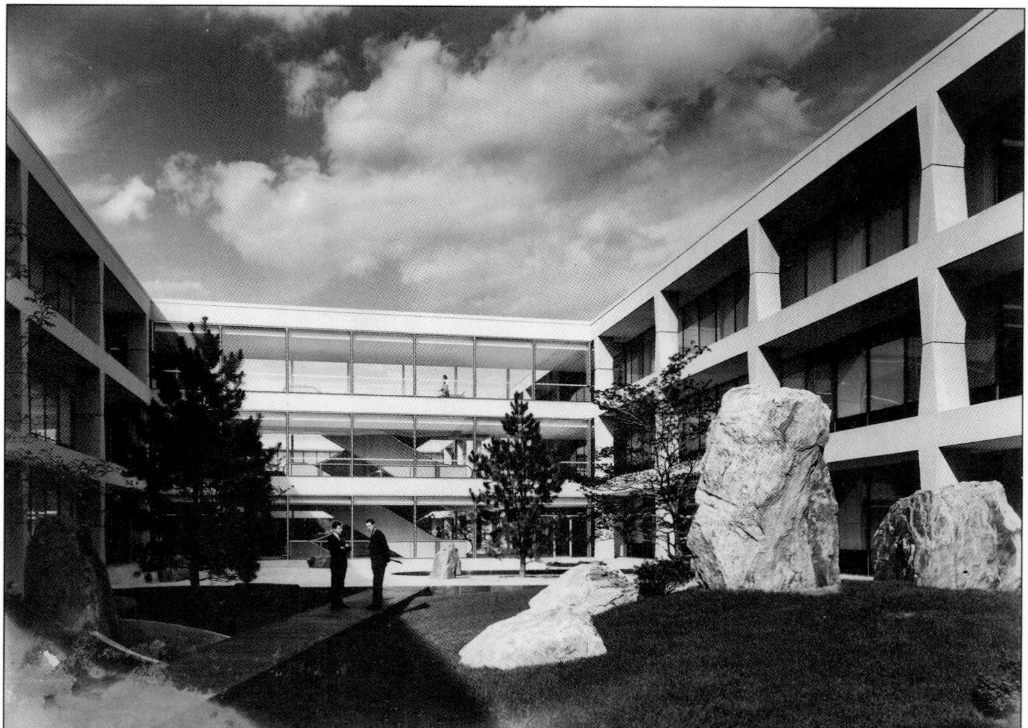

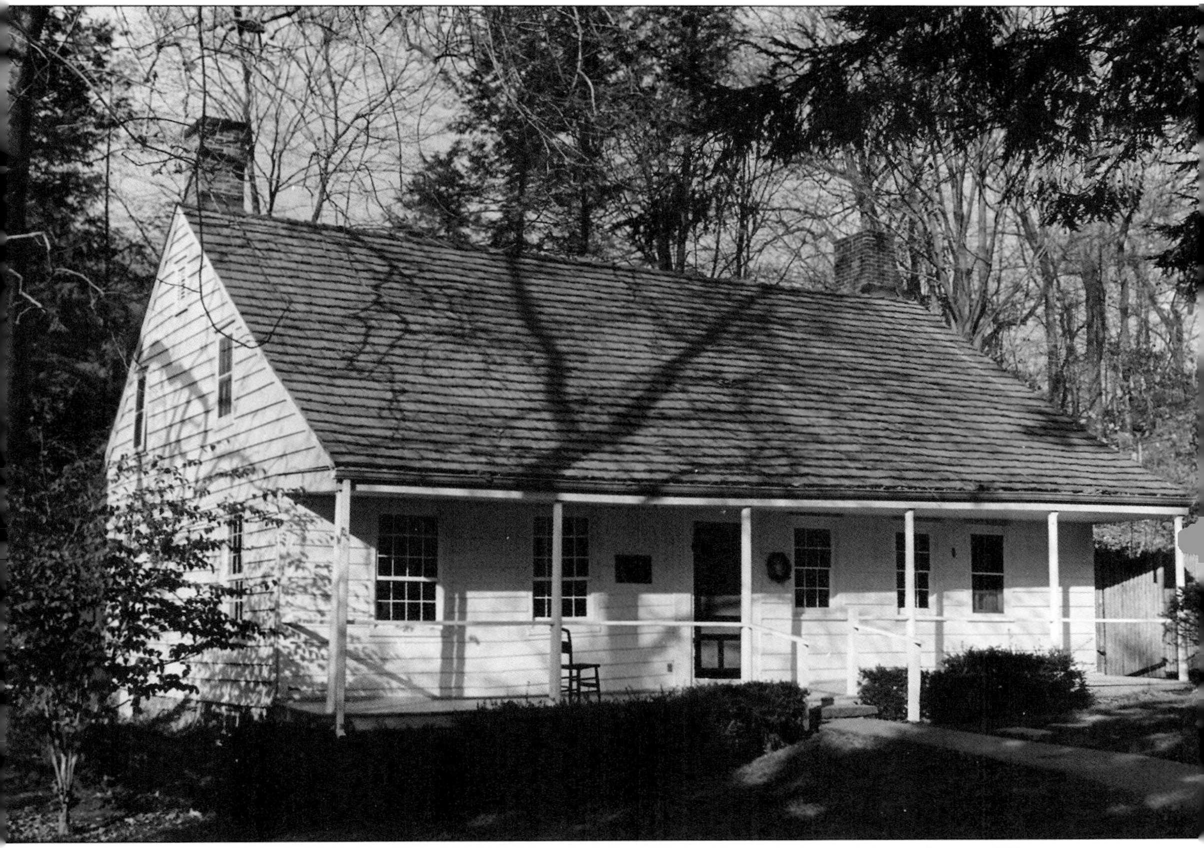

Elijah and Ann Fisher Miller House, Washington's Headquarters, Today's 140 Virginia Road, North White Plains. Great decisions concerning the future of our country were made by Revolutionary War generals who lived and headquartered in this farmhouse. Elijah Miller and two of his sons, John and Elijah, died while in the Continental Army in 1776—Elijah in late August and both boys three days before Christmas. Ann carried on, kept the farm, and raised their five remaining children: Sarah, James, Martha, Abraham, and Zipporah. She nursed wounded soldiers and hosted the first White Plains Methodist services here. Listed in the National and New York Registers of Historic Places and the Westchester County Inventory of Historic Places, this house is a North Castle Local Landmark. Westchester County bought it in 1917.

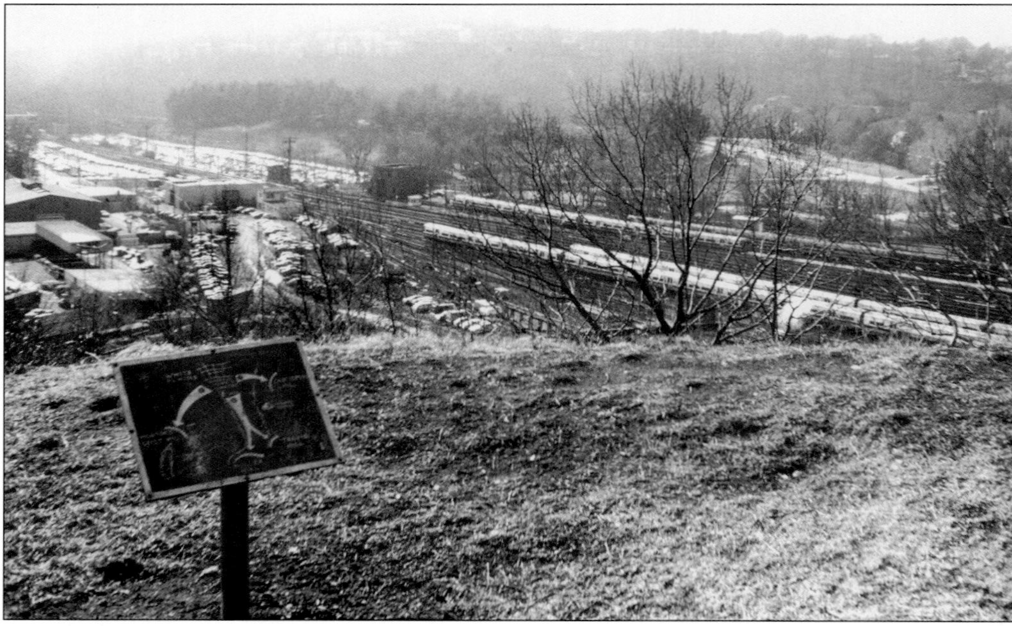

Miller Hill Park, Today's McDougal Drive, North White Plains. Imagine the commanding view during the Revolutionary War, without railroad tracks and development. After losing Chatterton's Hill, Patriot fighters continued retreating northward. The last shots of the 1776 battle at White Plains were fired from atop Miller Hill. British forces turned back towards New York City. Miller Hill is the only Revolutionary War battle site in Westchester County surviving in its natural setting.

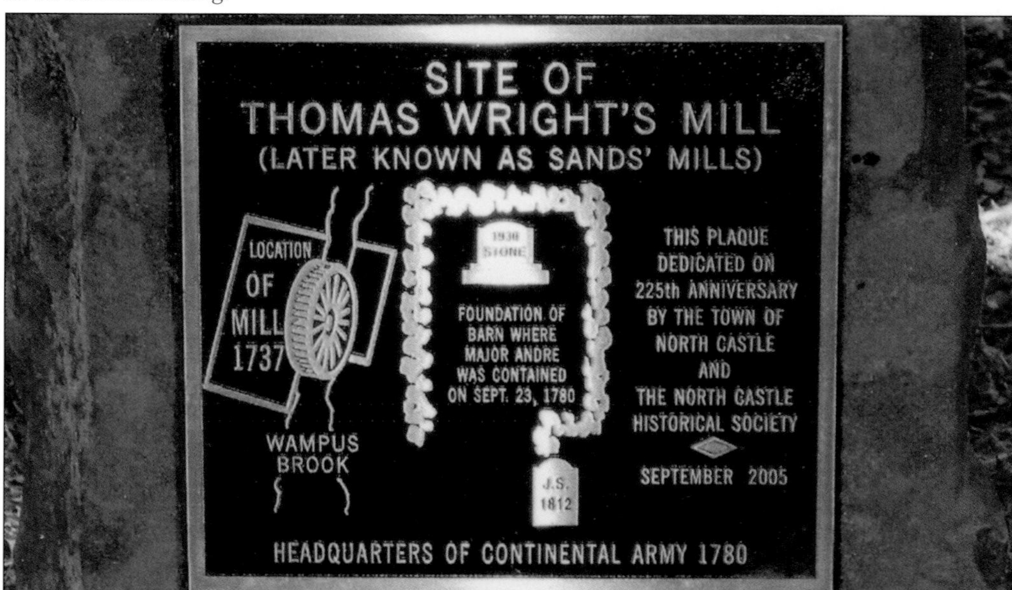

Plaque Commemorating the 1780 Containment of British Spy Maj. John Andre, Armonk. Taking information from traitor Benedict Arnold at West Point to the British commanders in New York City, Andre was stopped by Patriots in Tarrytown and held overnight in a barn at Thomas Wright's Mill, headquarters of the local Patriot forces. Designed by then town historian Doris Finch Watson, this plaque was dedicated on the 225th anniversary of the event.

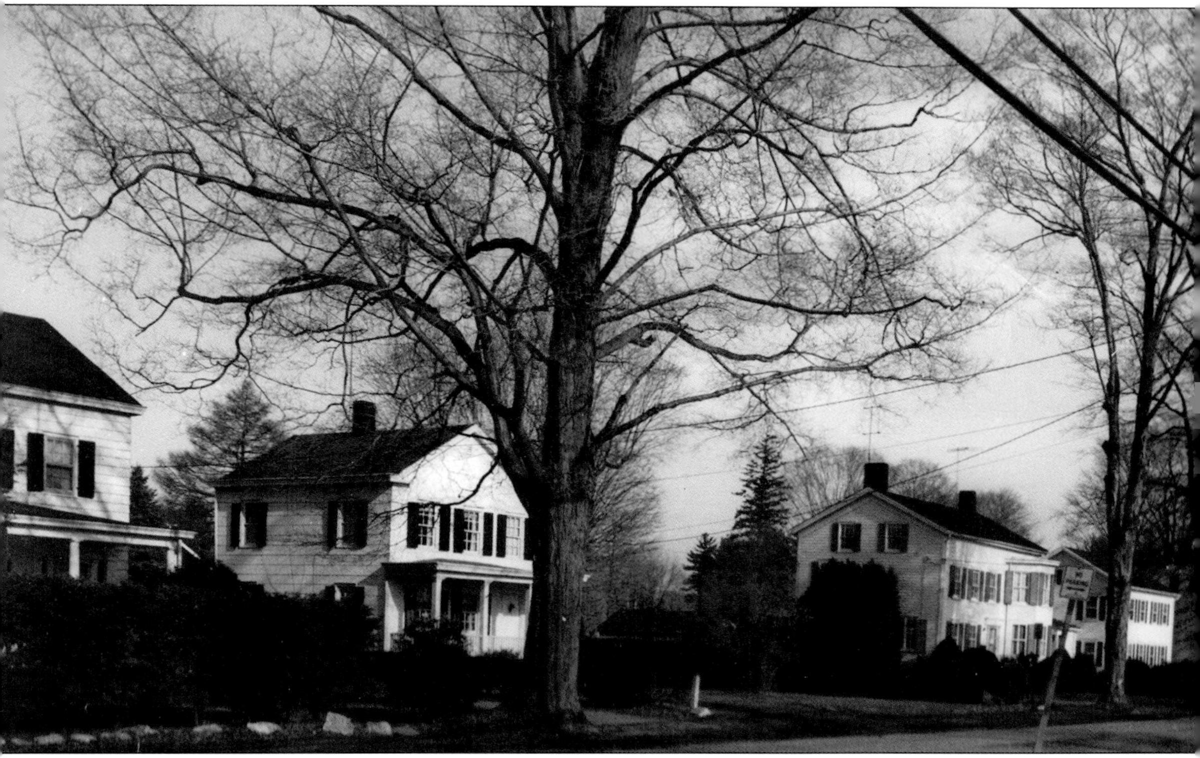

Bedford Road Historic District, Armonk, 1972. Listed in the National Register of Historic Places and part of Landmarks Preservation District No. 1, the district reflects the unique aspects of Armonk's origins and development. It consists of St. Stephen's Church and Cemetery and six houses primarily representing the 1850s. It is on Bedford Road between today's Main Street and Maple Avenue.

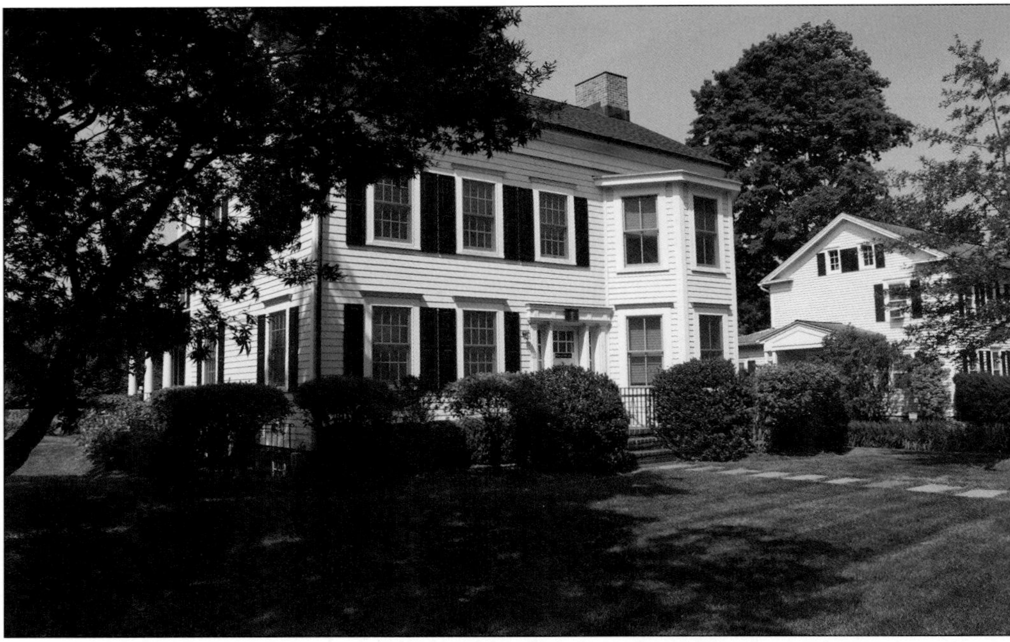

24 Bedford Road, Armonk, a Bedford Road Historic District House. This house dates to about 1850. It is a two-story house built in the Greek Revival style with a bay window addition about 1880. The house had fallen into major disrepair but was saved and restored by Michael Fareri. (Courtesy of Stephen Tomback.)

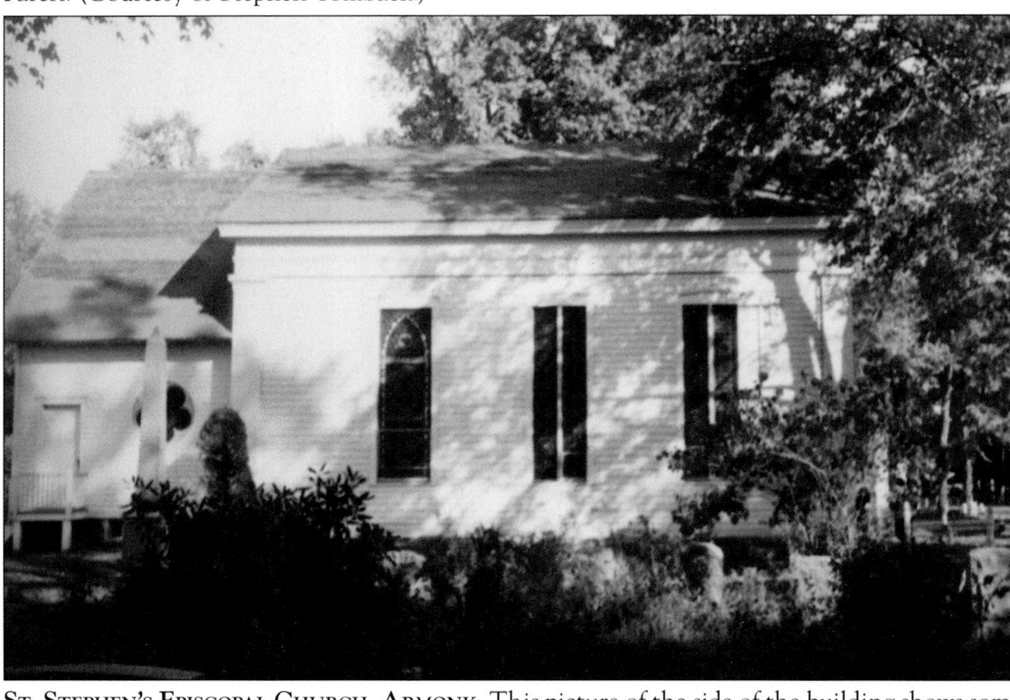

St. Stephen's Episcopal Church, Armonk. This picture of the side of the building shows some of the gravestones. There are approximately 450 gravesites in the cemetery. The square between present-day Main Street, Bedford Road, and Maple Avenue was subdivided by church officials about 1850 and building lots were offered for sale.

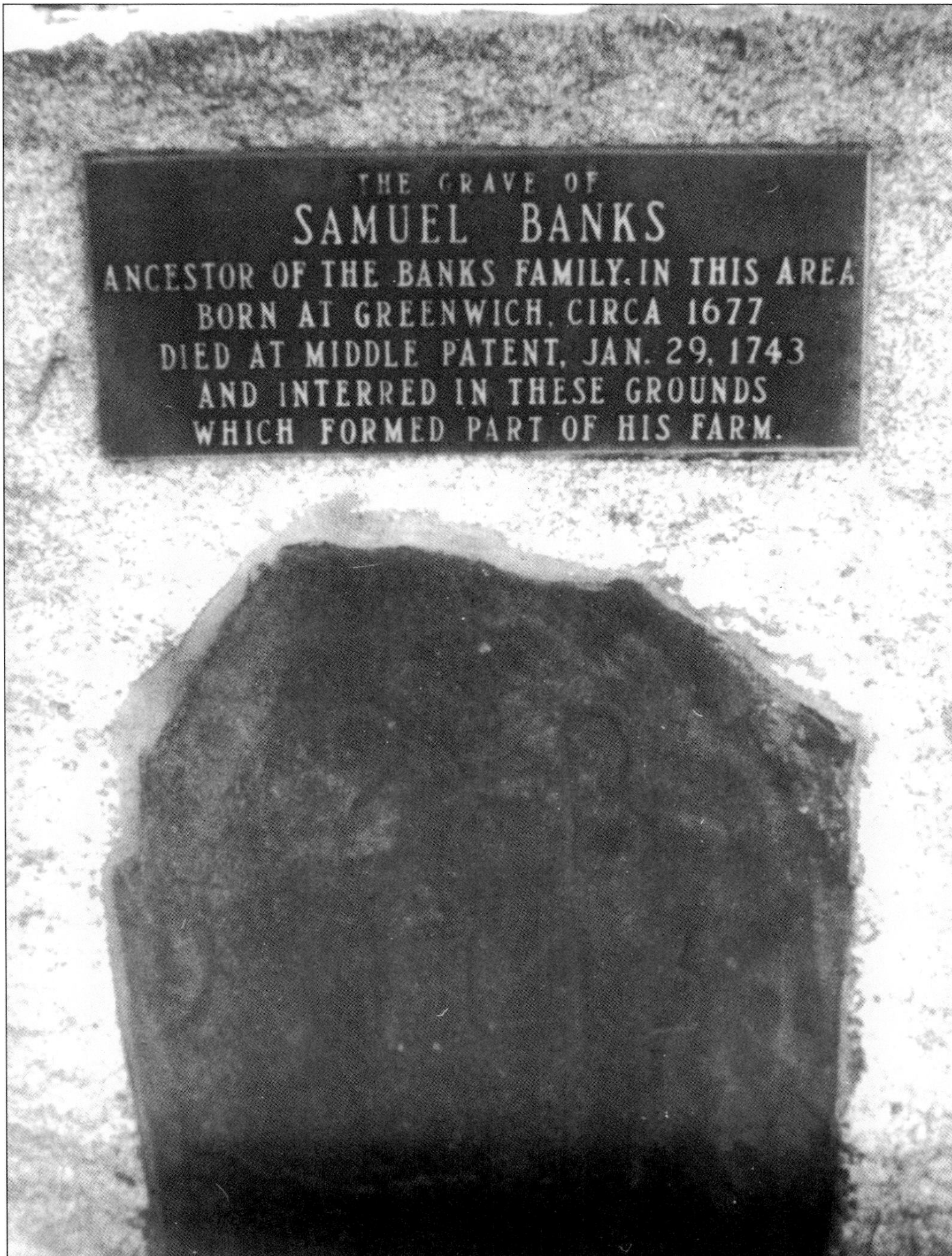

MIDDLE PATENT RURAL CEMETERY, 1743 STONE OF SAMUEL BANKS. The oldest known gravestone in North Castle is that of Samuel Banks, with the backwards *S* on his stone. The plaque reads, "The grave of Samuel Banks—ancestor of the Banks Family in this area. Born at Greenwich circa 1677. Died at Middle Patent, Jan. 29, 1743 and interred in these grounds which formed part of his farm."

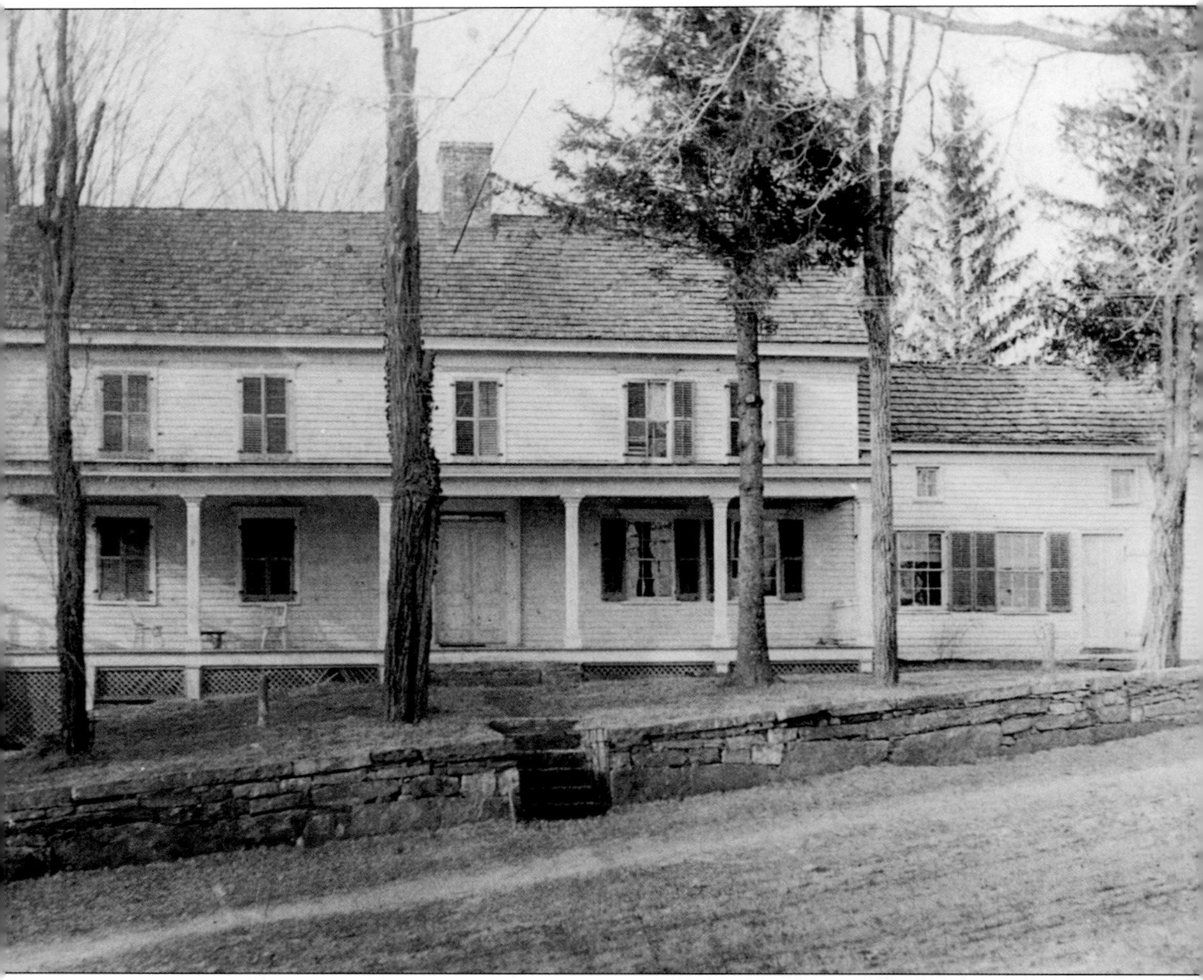

Smith's Tavern, 1898. Capt. John Smith purchased this pre–Revolutionary War tavern in 1797. For generations it served as an early stagecoach stop, tavern, post office, town hall, and center of community life. At today's 440 Bedford Road, Armonk, it is the headquarters of the North Castle Historical Society, where the educational complex includes the tavern, Brundage Blacksmith Shop, one-room East Middle Patent School, 1798 Quaker Meeting House, and an outdoor privy.

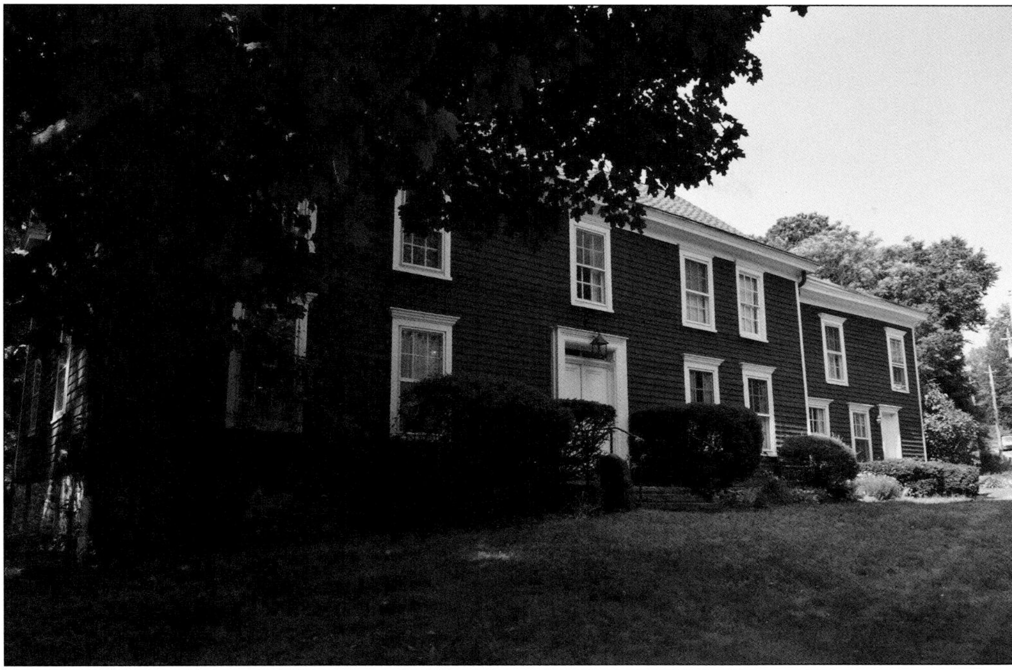

Historic Smith's Tavern, 440 Bedford Road, Armonk. If this building could talk, what history would it teach? The right portion predates the American Revolution, and the building is listed in the National Register of Historic Places. The North Castle Historical Society headquarters are located here. (Courtesy of Stephen Tomback.)

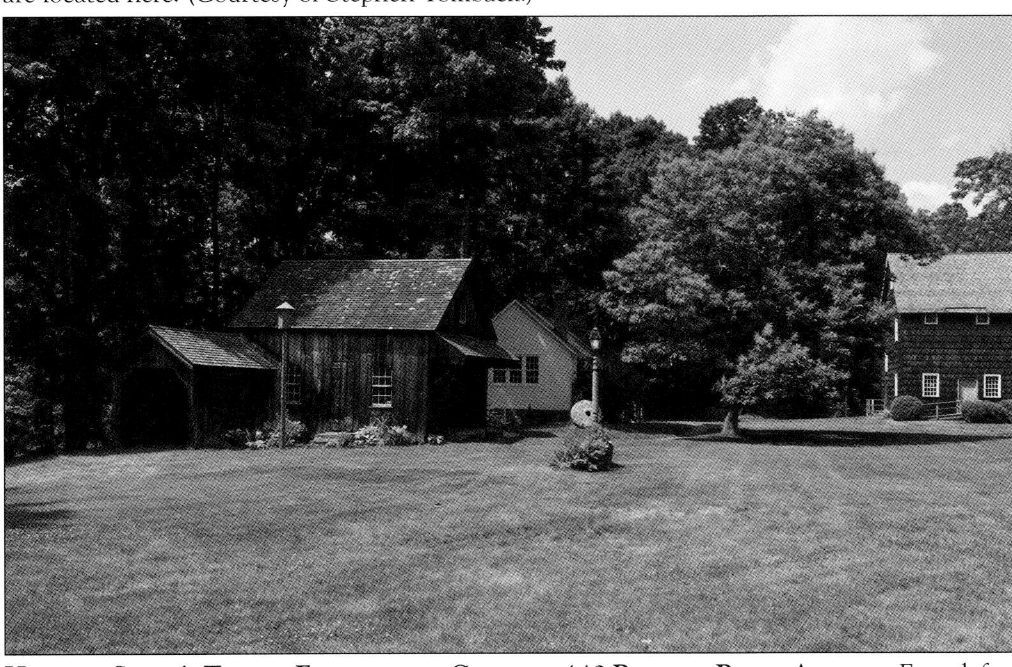

Historic Smith's Tavern Educational Complex, 440 Bedford Road, Armonk. From left to right are the Brundage Blacksmith Shop, East Middle Patent One Room Schoolhouse, and 1798 Quaker Meeting House. These ancient buildings were moved to today's 440 Bedford Road, Armonk, where the North Castle Historical Society protects them. (Courtesy of Stephen Tomback.)

Bibliography

The City of New York Department of Environmental Protection. "History of Kensico Dam." www.nyc.gov/html/dep/html/watershed_protection/kensico_history.shtml.

Close, Everett Reynolds Jr. *The Four Daughters of William Emmet Smith and Amanda Jane Banks (Smith) and Their Progeny—1875–1975*. Riverside, RI: privately printed, 1975.

Historical North Castle newspapers. Digitized by the North Castle Historical Society and the North Castle Public Library. www.northcastlelibrary.org.

Lander, Richard N., and Barbara S. Massi. *North Castle Historical Records 1791–1848*. Vol II. North Castle, NY: Town of North Castle, 1986.

Lee, Frances Cook, and Richard N. Lander. *North Castle/New Castle Historical Records 1736–1791*. Vol. I. New Castle, NY: Towns of North Castle and New Castle, 1975.

North Castle Historical Society. *North Castle History*. Annual publication since 1974.

Sandford, Harry, and Michael J. Kern. *American Revolutionary History in North Castle*. Armonk, NY: The North Castle Bicentennial Committee, North Castle Historical Society, and Town of North Castle, 1976.

Index

A comprehensive index for this book is available at the North Castle Historical Society's website: www.northcastlehistoricalsociety.org.

Discover Thousands of Local History Books Featuring Millions of Vintage Images

Arcadia Publishing, the leading local history publisher in the United States, is committed to making history accessible and meaningful through publishing books that celebrate and preserve the heritage of America's people and places.

Find more books like this at
www.arcadiapublishing.com

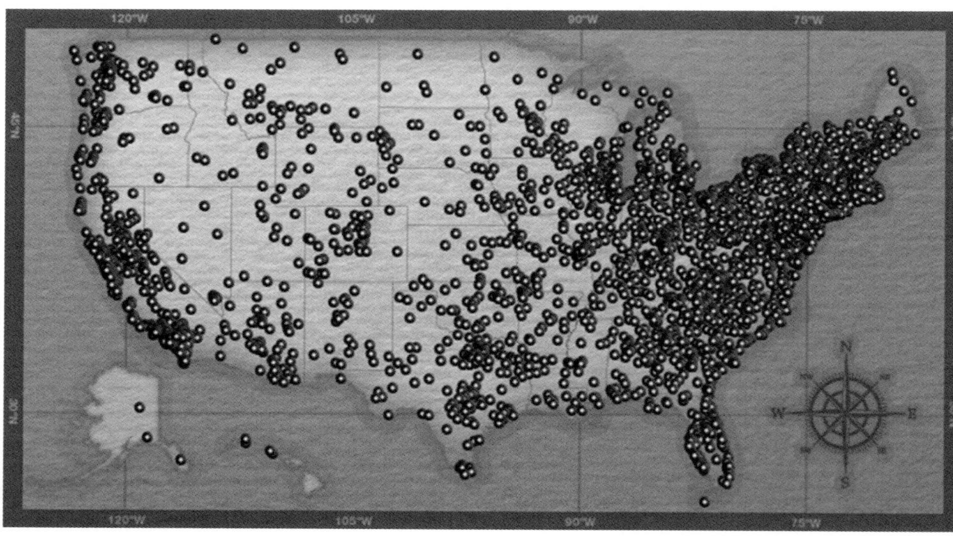

Search for your hometown history, your old stomping grounds, and even your favorite sports team.

Consistent with our mission to preserve history on a local level, this book was printed in South Carolina on American-made paper and manufactured entirely in the United States. Products carrying the accredited Forest Stewardship Council (FSC) label are printed on 100 percent FSC-certified paper.

MADE IN THE USA